The
Politics
of
African
Nationalism

THE
POLITICS
OF
AFRICAN
NATIONALISM

CHALLENGE TO AMERICAN POLICY

George W. Shepherd, Jr.

FREDERICK A. PRAEGER
Publisher • New York

BOOKS THAT MATTER

First published in the United States of America in 1962 by
Frederick A. Praeger, Inc., Publisher
64 University Place, New York 3, N.Y.

Library of Congress Catalog Card Number: 62-13737

THE POLITICS OF AFRICAN NATIONALISM
is published in two editions:

A Praeger Paperback (PPS-66)
A clothbound edition

Manufactured in the United States of America

Preface

This book is an attempt to present an over-all view of the patterns and problems in the development of African nationalism. I have written it especially for those thoughtful readers who may have become dissatisfied with the numerous quick-tour surveys and superficial, sensationalized accounts of African nationalism that have been pouring from American presses recently. My analysis is based on several years of living and traveling in Africa and ten years of research, discussion, and teaching. Nevertheless, what I have written is only introductory. Some of the major principles and trends have yet to be thoroughly substantiated. As the explorer penetrates deeper into Africa, he realizes how much more there is to know.

Yet, despite incomplete knowledge, we must act. In a world that cries out for leadership, inaction is in itself an endorsement of the status quo. Therefore, I have probed the basis of policy and offered suggestions for alternative actions that I hope will provoke both thought and controversy.

Ideas are never the exclusive result of one's own thought processes. I wish to acknowledge my debt to the African nationalists of Uganda and Kenya—men like Ignatius Musazi and Jomo Kenyatta, who first presented me with the opportunity to observe and even participate in the development of nationalist ideas—and to Julius Nyerere of Tanganyika, with whom I have had many discussions concerning his own nationalist philosophy. The lives and thoughts of these men served as my introduction to Africa. In the American Committee on Africa, with George Hauser, Donald Harrington, Hugh Smythe, Peter Weiss, Elizabeth Landis, and numerous others, I have had the pleasure and stimulation of participating in the exciting attempt to awaken the American consciousness to the significance of the new Africa.

Through the pages of our publication *Africa Today* (begun in 1953), we have sought to capture some of the inner meaning and challenge of African nationalism. We have often differed, but I owe more to our sometimes heated editorial discussions and to the many channels of information opened to me by this group than to any other single source. In no sense, however, does this book speak for these people; nor should they be held accountable for any mistakes or errors of judgment I may have made.

I also wish to acknowledge the inspiration and encouragement I have received from men who have gone much further and achieved far more than I in the field of African studies. The methodology I have employed has been influenced by political scientists like James Coleman, David Apter, and Thomas Hodgkin, who have looked at Africa in terms of the political-cultural process of change as seen in men, parties, movements, and ideas rather than in terms of the transient legal structures. Vernon McKay and Robert Good, both pioneers in the field of African International Relations, have read parts of the manuscript and made valuable suggestions. Melville Herskovits has read sections, and his comments regarding American policy have been most helpful. However, I do not wish to imply an endorsement of my ideas by these scholars, who would doubtlessly differ with me at many points.

I should also like to thank Josef Korbel of the Social Science Foundation at the University of Denver and H. Field Haviland of the Brookings Institution for enabling me to undertake summer research in Washington, D.C., on aspects of American policy toward Africa.

I have employed a substantial amount of the growing literature on African affairs and have attempted to give credit wherever possible. My function, in many cases, has been that of interpreter and transmitter of the findings of others. Without the help and encouragement of the friends, colleagues, and scholars I have mentioned and numerous other unsung heroes of the growing American scholarship on Africa, this book could never have been completed. Nor could it have been completed without the editing, typing, and critical assistance of my wife, Shirley. The generous editorial advice of Arnold Dolin, my editor at Praeger, and of

Shirley Zimmerman helped to give the book more focus, perception, and readability.

Finally, I hope the reader will remember the perils of interpreting a continent in transition, where revolutions occur overnight. My effective research reaches only to mid-1961; but the test of my analysis will be how it stands up against the constantly changing African scene. I first went to study and live in Africa ten years ago because I considered the aspirations of the peoples of Africa for self-rule to be the most important development in the postwar period. I still see the fulfillment of the African nationalist revolution as the major challenge of the second half of the twentieth century, as Africans seek recognition of their equality with all peoples in race and culture. We may not approve of all they do, but we cannot afford either to stand in the way of this achievement or to be bystanders. I have written this book because I believe that, given the correct information on the nature of African nationalism, Americans will help Africa to move forward.

G.W.S.

Denver
February, 1962

Contents

To my wife, SHIRLEY

who has given much to Africa

God bless Africa.
Bless its leaders.
Let wisdom, unity, and peace
Be the shield of Africa and its people.

—Bantu National Anthem

We in Tanganyika do not believe that mankind has yet discovered ultimate truth—in any field. We do not wish to act as if we did have such a belief. We wish to contribute to man's development if we can, but we do not claim to have a solution; our only claim is that we intend to grope forward in the dark toward a goal so distant that even the real understanding of it is beyond us—toward, in other words, the best that man can become.

This means that the people who anxiously watch to see whether we will become "Communists" or "Western democrats" will both be disconcerted. We do not have to be either. We shall grope forward, and it may be that we shall create a new synthesis of individual liberty and the needs of man in society; freedom for each individual to develop the spark of divinity within himself at the same time as he contributes benefits from his membership in the community.

—Julius Nyerere

Address on the opening of Kivukoni College, Dar es Salaam, July 29, 1961

The
Politics
of
African
Nationalism

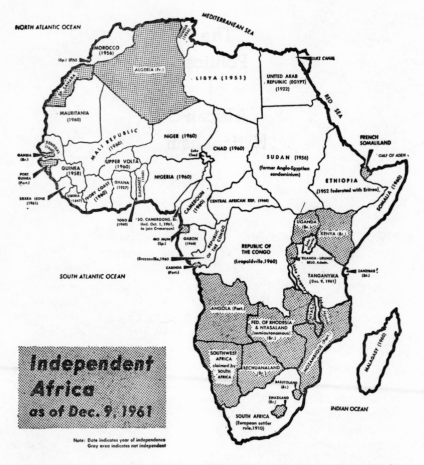

Independent Africa as of Dec. 9, 1961

Note: Date indicates year of independence
Gray area indicates not independent

Reprinted, by permission of the Foreign Policy Association, from *Headline Series* No. 149, *Aid to Africa: New Test for U.S. Policy*, p. 5.

Introduction:

The Political-Cultural
Conflict in African Nationalism

Africa is a continent of contrast, conflict, challenge, and change.
This is what is so immensely fascinating and important about the
developments in the human drama of this great emergent continent now moving into the center of the world stage.

African cultures offer the most vivid contrasts. Much that has
been written about Africa's sudden leap from Stone Age to Space
Age is a gross distortion. Many parts of Africa were ahead of
Europe in learning and culture during Europe's Dark Ages. The
Yoruba, Bakango, Baganda, and Amhara, not to mention many
North African peoples, have rich cultures and long histories
rivaling those of most European nations. Yet, at the same time,
such tribes as the Bushmen of South Africa carry on life much
as they did before the dawn of history. The modern and the traditional dwell together in vivid contrast, giving rise to much conflict in changing Africa. Thus, the sight of a nomadic herdsman
watching his flock of goats as they graze beside a new jet airfield
at Entebbe, on the shores of Lake Victoria, symbolizes the two
worlds of superstition and science, separated by centuries of
progress, yet geographically united in the Africa of today.

Nature, too, offers great extremes in Africa. In few other places
is it possible to be shut off from the sky by the intertwined
branches of lush, tropical trees, minutes after you have crossed
a rocky, barren land which can support human life only on the
lowest level.

3

Very few parts of the world can match the ebullient enthusiasm of the peoples of the new West African states as they take over the responsibility for government from the colonial powers that have dominated their trade and political life for two centuries or more. Yet, farther to the south, on the same continent, African nationalists and the Afrikaner nationalists in the Republic of South Africa are moving slowly and inevitably toward a final, tragic showdown. Like the protagonists in Greek tragedy, they see their doom but are helpless to prevent it.

The greatest challenge of Africa arises from the new force of African nationalism, which today, with Samsonlike power, shakes the pillars of the traditional structure. Out of the ruins is emerging a new African giant determined to break the bonds of ignorance and servility and to become master of his own environment and destiny. He is the "new African personality," as President Nkrumah of Ghana describes him.

Some people in the Western world are frightened of this African giant, perhaps expecting that he will seek revenge for all the cruelty and abasement he has suffered; others see in this new force another hopeful step in the expansion of man's freedom. Which it will be depends upon the new relationship now being hammered out between the "new African personality" and the pillars of the old order, the Western nations.

All over the world, the nineteenth-century system of Western domination of technologically weaker peoples has crumbled. Asians and Africans have acquired the technological skills and political patterns of their former masters and have proclaimed their right to equality. By joining the United Nations, they have asserted their claim to full membership in the world community. This is the most important political phenomenon of our age. To find a method of peaceful adjustment to the new Africa is the basic challenge before the West.

Africa is where it will be decided whether there is a basis for a continuing, cooperative relationship between the Western and the non-Western world. If such a friendship cannot be achieved in Africa, it can scarcely be accomplished elsewhere.

Economically, politically, and culturally, Africa has been more closely related to the West than has any other part of the non-Western world. There are more than 35 million Christians in Africa. English and French are the languages of trade and education. Most African leaders have been educated in mission schools and in Western universities, and some 6 million Europeans regard Africa as their home. Moreover, Africa is vital to the survival of the Western productive system.

Trade and investment in Africa have skyrocketed since World War II. Capital investments are running at the rate of $4–$5 billion annually; gross production has been rising 5 per cent per year. Africa produces a large supply of uranium, one-sixth of the world's lead, and one-third of its manganese; mineral production has increased 300 per cent in the last decade. She has rich veins of copper and iron ore, and large deposits of oil. Her potential hydroelectric power is the greatest in the world.

Because of the vastness of the continent and the variety of historical background, African nationalism takes many forms and poses many enigmas, making it very difficult to generalize. There are three basic racial areas in Africa: Arab North Africa, black West and Central Africa, and multiracial East, Central, and South Africa. These are by no means distinct divisions, and there are many confusing subdivisions. Arab culture penetrates deeply into West and East sub-Sahara Africa, and some 30 million Moslems constitute half the population of French-speaking West Africa. Black Africa contains hundreds of tribal and language differences, cutting across national boundaries.

The resurgent tribalism of the Ashanti, the fanaticism of the Mau Mau in Kenya, the blind bigotry of the Afrikaners in South Africa, the supranationalism of Nkrumah's pan-Africanism, and the self-sacrificing determination of the *fellaga* of Algeria to win independence at any price are all manifestations of the varied faces of African nationalism. No two groups seek the same kind of state, and few possess a clear concept of democracy. For some Africans, nationalism means the recovery of the greatness of past empires; for others, it means the building of a powerful, economically viable, modern state; for still others, it means the creation of a "federal united states" of Negro Africa.

The Content of Nationalism

Is there a definition of nationalism that can encompass these widely divergent phenomena? Many social scientists believe there is. James Coleman has produced this valuable brief definition of nationalism in Africa:

> Broadly, a consciousness of belonging to a nation (existent or in the realm of aspiration) or a nationality, and a desire, as manifest in sentiment and activity, to secure or maintain its welfare, prosperity, and to maximize its political autonomy. The reference group for "nationalism" can be a de facto nation or nationality, or a territorially defined group in which certain members believe and advocate that it ought, or is destined, to become a nation.[1]

Nationalism in Africa, as Professor Coleman so well perceives, cannot be delineated by a common language, culture, or even boundary. It is a "consciousness of belonging" to a common group in being or in creation. This view of nationalism as a psychological phenomenon was described in 1882 by Ernest Renan in his famous Sorbonne lecture "Qu'est-ce qu'une nation?" as a sense of "having accomplished great things in common in the past and the wish to accomplish them in the future." In Africa, remembrance of the greatness of past kingdoms has accompanied the modern surge toward the establishment of new states. Modern Ghana took its name from the ancient kingdom of Ghana, although it is located considerably to the west of the site of the historic kingdom and covers a much smaller territory. The memory of the great accomplishments of the past strengthens the sense of common destiny shared by today's Ghanaian citizens.

The idea of freedom is integral to African nationalism. "Freedom! Freedom!" was the chant of the Gold Coast nationalists that I heard ringing through the streets of Accra during my first visit there, in 1953. By capturing political power, they hoped to create conditions of greater freedom under their leader, Kwame Nkrumah.

It has been said that freedom is like a beautiful woman with many lovers, each possessing a different idea of her beauty. In their quest for freedom, African nationalists have been influenced by five major concepts of freedom: independence, political freedom and unity, social rights, racial equality, and national dignity and independence.

Independence is viewed by the African nationalist not as a privilege, not as something to be either earned or bestowed upon him, but as a natural right of self-determination possessed by all members of the human race. This is what Jomo Kenyatta meant when he said to me, in Kenya, in 1952, "The European colonial powers robbed us of our birthright." The mind of the African nationalist is not cluttered with complicated formulas equating readiness for self-rule with education and economic advance. "Self-government now" was the slogan of the Convention Peoples Party (CPP) in the Gold Coast by which it rallied mass support.

The African nationalist struggles to recapture his heritage. He feels that the greatness of his own past makes it unnecessary for him to acquire all the characteristics of Western culture before he may rule himself.

Political freedom and unity are important elements of freedom in African nationalism, especially among the educated elite. The masses of peasants and illiterate laborers have little understanding of representative democracy or civil liberties. In the struggle against colonial rule, African leaders employed the arguments of Western democratic revolutions and often quoted the American Bill of Rights and the United Nations' Universal Declaration of Human Rights, which specifies that "Everyone has the right to freedom of thought, conscience, and religion." The African nationalists also took as models the political parties and many constitutional forms of Western democracies. Despite certain difficulties in applying these concepts under African conditions, their influence has been strong and continues to be so, in many parts of Africa. I have found that many African nationalists—among them Nkrumah, Mboya, Nyerere, and Bourguiba—are genuinely devoted to these ideas. Yet each is confronted with the immense difficulty of maintaining national unity within tribal diversity. The disunifying pressures of tribal groups destroy the authority of the new governments. Thus, the new leaders are compelled to limit political freedom by the overriding need to centralize authority. The limits placed on democratic practices have not always been justified, in my opinion. But then, the practice of democracy in our own society has been far from perfect. And as we shall see later, the basic conditions required for true democratic practice have yet to be established in Africa.

Social rights are an integral part of the African nationalist's concept of freedom. Most of Africa's new leaders consider themselves democratic socialists. "Of course I am a socialist," declared Kwame Nkrumah, in an interview I had with him shortly after he took power. African leaders have committed their parties to various programs for welfare and economic planning. In their view, the state is responsible for providing a rising standard of living and combating sickness, poverty, and ignorance. In an underdeveloped state, they argue, there is not time to allow the natural forces of production and social adjustment to work. The state must step in and provide the development plans, the capital, and the technical skill without which rapid progress would be impossible.

Racial equality is another key concept of freedom in African nationalism. All Asia and Africa have reacted vigorously against what Gandhi called "the white man's incurable pride." The achievement of nationhood is one way in which African nationalists assert their equality with the white race. Nothing arouses greater emotional opposition than racialism, as in the *apartheid* doctrine of South Africa and other forms of white supremacy maintained by dwindling European powers.

Article One of the Universal Declaration of Human Rights states: "All human beings are born free and equal in dignity and rights. They are endowed with reason and conscience and should act towards one another in a spirit of brotherhood." This statement is especially meaningful to South African nationalists, who daily see this truth denied. Professor Z. K. Matthews, a past President of the African National Congress, in a letter written from South Africa when he and ninety-five others were on trial for their lives in the Treason Trials, said: "We have not changed our political beliefs and have no intention of doing so. We still believe that all men were created equal, and no amount of intimidation will make us believe otherwise."

National dignity and independence are extremely important to all the new African states, which are especially eager to participate in world affairs as duly recognized and respected independent nations. In joining the United Nations, they fulfill this aspiration symbolically. By entering negotiations with countries from which they were previously cut off, they gain a further sense of self-determination. However, their continuing dependence upon the Western world for trade and technological development is a source of much irritation and political unrest. Indeed, many Africans believe that the Western powers maintain a neocolonial control over them that prevents their realizing true independence.

One means by which African states seek to overcome this dependence is pan-African unity. Another is the establishment of trade and aid relationships with the Communist bloc. Out of this drive for full independence emerges the demand of African leaders, from Nasser to Houphouet-Boigny, for "nonalignment and neutrality." The desire to eliminate all vestiges of the umbilical tie to former colonial powers, though often expressed in anti-Western terms, is actually but one phase of the search for identity and the "African personality."

The Pattern of Change

Although virtually all political movements in Africa reflect these basic ideas of freedom through nationalism, there is great variation of emphasis on both ends and means. These differences of perspective, and hence of strategy, are highly confusing to the outside observer, who at first glance is likely to believe that African nationalists are involved in a hopeless tangle of conflicting and poorly defined goals without any core of political philosophy. But closer study will reveal that there are three major types of African nationalism, determined by local political and cultural conditions. All of these types fit into a single pattern of development, with few exceptions, moving from one stage to the next. Once this pattern is understood, much which might have seemed confusing takes on new significance, and it is possible to perceive a great deal more about the possible and probable direction of political development in many parts of Africa.

This progression is impelled by a challenge-and-response conflict among cultures and classes. Such seasoned observers as
Arnold Toynbee and Barbara Ward have outlined the stages
of resistance, assimilation, and reaffirmation in the non-Western
world, following the impact of Western culture and technology.
The traditional mode of life in non-Western culture is challenged to its very core by Western science and values. Initially
it resists the innovations. But the second stage, of assimilation,
soon begins, partly as a result of conquest and partly in response
to the challenge of new possibilities. Barbara Ward has described
this change as she observed it in Asia:

As a result of incoming Western influence, the belief has arisen
that something can be done about these evils, that the appalling
fatalities, the grinding, unbelievable poverty of the Asian world
can be countered, that countries can expand and their economies
grow. It is the change from fatalism to hope, from resignation
to expectation, and this is perhaps the biggest revolution that a
country can make.[2]

The same psychology is under way in Africa. Dramatic evidence
is found in the universal-education systems being developed by
all the new states and the increasing application of scientific
agricultural methods. To be sure, most people of the "dark continent" continue the mode of life of their ancestors; but, like
rising flood waters, Western influence is seeping through all the
cracks of the traditional structure.

The third phase of reaction to Western influence has evolved
more recently. So far it is apparent only in certain parts of the
non-Western world and therefore has not yet been clearly identified by most observers. In this phase, the political-cultural conflict produces a reaffirmation of the non-Western people's identity. This stage has many of the earmarks of a renaissance which
seeks to combine the greatness of the past with the new power
of modernism. In Africa, this can best be described as "ultra-
Africanism." It is a form of nationalism that refuses to look upon
Africa's past as a shameful, barbaric episode, as much Western
thought has depicted it. Instead, it seeks to glorify African history
and culture as being great in itself, and second to none. Moreover,

it criticizes Western democracy and advocates a new, African democracy. It attempts to assert full cultural and economic independence, as well as political independence, from the West, vigorously denouncing dependence on any bloc outside Africa as compromising the emergence of African culture.

Three major types of nationalism have resulted from this political-cultural conflict: Traditionalism, which seeks to retain primary historic values and political institutions against the modernizing influences of the West; Westernization, which has assimilated Western ideas and institutions; and ultra-Africanism, which reacts against Westernization and asserts neotraditional African cultural and new African political concepts.

Class-Culture Conflict

A class-culture conflict is a major characteristic of the progression from one stage to the next in African nationalism. Traditional society in Africa has been ruled for centuries by chiefs or kings, whose source of power has been the customs and institutions of tribalism. These tribal systems have survived only as long as their values held firm against outside pressures. Thus, resistance to change has been a major characteristic, and in some cases this traditionalism has effectively resisted Western modernization.

In certain traditional cultures, kings and chiefs have been actually strengthened by the challenge to their authority. In Morocco and Ethiopia, the authority of traditional rulers has grown despite modernization in the lower social strata. In many instances, tribal chieftains, fearing the loss of their power and privilege to the new, Westernized classes, have sided with colonial powers against the Westernized nationalists, in order to slow down modernization and national unification. But in most of Africa, tribalism was weakened by the colonial system, which reduced and sometimes even eliminated the power of the traditional rulers.

Into this vacuum of power and values came the new, Westernized leaders, who had been educated in Western schools and had developed independent sources of income by imitating Western economic practices. They became a new middle class, and from their ranks emerged the heralds of the new age in Africa. Well educated and often, by African standards, wealthy, these African nationalists generally were content to wage a moderate struggle for political power. Their antagonists were both the traditional rulers and the colonial powers. In their eagerness to assimilate the new values of the West, many of them became more English or more French than their colonial rulers. Some of them regarded their past as savage—as the missionaries and colonial officials had taught them. Christianity, education, democracy, and a cash economy were the virtues with which they hoped to build the new Africa. Joseph Danquah in the Gold Coast, and Lamine Guèye in Senegal were among the first to form African nationalist movements. Some of them were successful, after a protracted struggle with the colonial powers. Thus, Tunisia, Liberia, Nigeria, and Tanganyika became moderate, highly Westernized centers of influence. But most of Africa did not achieve independence until the third phase of development, ultra-Africanism, had begun, plunging the continent into a new and more profound series of conflicts.

Although similar in many ways to Westernized nationalism, ultra-Africanism has a class base and an ideological orientation of its own. The failure to distinguish it from Westernized nationalism accounts for much of the inadequacy of many recent interpretations of African nationalism. Rupert Emerson grasped the essence of this culture conflict in Africa, in his study of the larger process of political change in the non-Western world, *From Empire to Nation:*

> If the first reaction of the peoples on whom the West imposed itself was generally a xenophobic defense of the existing order, the next phase was likely to be a swing in the direction of an uncritical self-humiliation and acceptance of alien superiority. The third phase in the fashion of the Hegelian dialectic was a nationalist synthesis in which there was an assertion or reassertion of a community with pride in itself and in its past but still looking, at least as far as its leaders were concerned, in the direction of Westernization and modernization.[3]

Ultra-Africanism is primarily a reaction against Westernization, and it therefore appeals to those groups that have not received full status and political power in the Westernized phase. Trade unions, the military, the lower middle class, and the peasants constitute the base of power and are often the source of leadership. With the exception of a few intellectuals, most ultra-Africanists have not been educated abroad. Their orientation is primarily African rather than European. Impatient to build independent African economies and democracies, they attack the moderate pace of Westernized nationalists and advocate rigid controls to speed up development. They may have cooperated with the Westernized nationalists in the early phases of the revolution, but they now spurn them as "collaborationists" and "neocolonialists."

The casual observer is likely to conclude that the more militant ultra-Africanists are Communists because they use much Marxist terminology and some Communist techniques. But the ultra-Africanists are wary of new types of imperialism and conscious of Soviet ambitions. Once in power, they generally ban the Communist Party but eagerly accept offers of assistance from the Communist bloc. It is conceivable that, if the ultra-Africanist nationalists fail to create stability, unity, and progress, Communism may be able to recruit sufficient converts to threaten a takeover, but this is not an immediate possibility. It is thus a mistake at this stage to associate ultra-Africanism with Communism. What we should fear above all else is the failure of Africa's nationalists to build their own political-cultural alternative to both the West and the East.

It is the major thesis of this study that the existing African governments and the power struggle among African political movements can best be analyzed in terms of a dominant culture conflict and a secondary class conflict. Of course, numerous variations and subgroups exist within each of the three major groups—traditionalist, Westernized nationalist, and ultra-Africanist. These will be discussed in due course.

Ultra-Africanism is spreading throughout the African continent. Today, Guinea, and, to a lesser degree, Ghana, are the two principal exponents of ultra-Africanism in sub-Sahara Africa.

In North Africa, Cairo subscribes to a pan-Islamic form that allies itself with the sub-Sahara states. "We, too, are African," claims President Nasser of the U.A.R.; and sub-Sahara ultra-Africanists cooperate with the Moroccans, Algerians, and Egyptians in the Casablanca Group.

All over Africa, the intellectuals and the youth movements are echoing the slogans of Accra, Conakry, and Cairo. They are forming mass-based political groups and parties to bring to power more militant African leaders who seek to restore the glories of past empires and to achieve the abundant life within a generation. This struggle for full cultural and economic independence generates much anti-Western sentiment, so that help from non-Western sources—primarily Eastern Europe—is eagerly grasped. Despite the anti-Western sloganeering and pro-Communist expressions, the new African leaders radiate a deep sense of African destiny. They believe they are building a new world that is peculiarly their own—an African civilization.

Can the Western world adjust rapidly enough to this phase of African nationalism? Again, basic Western interests are affected, democratic values are challenged, and totalitarian forces appear to have a vantage point. Is it possible for the West to have enough confidence in ultra-Africanism not to oppose but to support its leaders in building a new Africa?

The Challenge to the West

The task of building stronger trade, cultural, and educational ties between continents drifting apart in seas of sweeping change poses an enormous challenge. In the past, American policy toward Africa has been confused and lacking in any clear principles or direction. Above all, it has been Europe-oriented and unaware of the major forces shaping the African revolution. Thus, in most cases, the United States has supported the colonial powers against the rising tide of nationalism and, more recently, the Westernized nationalists against the ultra-Africanists. Exaggerated fears of Communism and naïve notions of democratic possibilities have made American policy exceedingly narrow and inflexible. Although the Kennedy Administration has made substantial improvements (Africa has been designated one of the "new frontiers"), many attitudes remain from the past.

The growth of authoritarian patterns of government anywhere in the world frightens Americans. We have been brought up to believe that a free society is best for all men. The new African states, even most of the Westernized ones, are not democracies in the Western sense. Free play of ideas and unrestricted peaceful opposition to the party in power are rare in Africa. Even Westernized nationalists like Julius Nyerere of Tanganyika justify the necessity of a one-party system. They maintain that preservation of national unity plus the traditional use of the principle of unanimity in tribal practices indicate a different kind of political system for Africa. Although we may disagree with their way of doing things, it would be a form of paternalism to attempt to impose our predilections on Africa. The time is fast approaching when the United States will find it necessary to accept the plural nature of the world's social forms. There are many kinds of authoritarian rule, just as there are numerous forms of democracy. Authoritarian regimes are not static, they are capable of moving toward greater freedom. To make snap judgments concerning those in Africa who are "for" and those "against" our system would be a fatal error.

A basic proposition of this study of African political patterns is that democracy requires certain minimal conditions in order to function. Without these conditions, which we shall call the "threshold of democracy," this particular form of society cannot be achieved. Such conditions—consisting of sufficient education systems, economic growth, political experience, plural centers of power, and machinery for peaceful exertion of power—can be developed even in an ultra-Africanist country (and sometimes more rapidly there). The greatest possibility for a more constructive U.S. policy toward Africa lies in patiently and persistently seeking ways of promoting these conditions of a free democratic society. The extent to which America has perceived this possibility and acted upon it is the subject of the second part of this study.

Since African nationalism falls naturally into the three major areas of the traditional, the Western, and the ultra-Africanist, its manifestations will be considered in that order. A fourth category, white-racialist nationalism, is the expression of certain dominant immigrant European minorities and is quite distinct from African nationalism and in direct conflict with it.

No attempt is made here to cover all of Africa. Particular African states have been analyzed because they offer typical examples of the patterns of government and trends in nationalist development. Of course, each state differs from the others in some ways, but there are broad, basic similarities of great importance.

ONE

Patterns
of
African
Nationalism

1.

Vanishing Patterns of Traditional Nationalism

Some observers believe that tradition, not change, is the dominant characteristic of modern Africa. They point out that as much as 90 per cent of the population today have a pattern of life substantially unchanged by the impact of Westernization. Over much of Africa, the family system, kinship patterns, methods of deriving a living, and even forms of local government have remained intact for centuries. The peasant is still illiterate, and most still worship the tribal gods of their ancestors.

However, the elite in any society exert the greatest influence, and Westernization has swept through the top strata of African society like a forest fire. Very few African states have a traditional system of government or economic life. Traditionalism is much more to be found on the local or regional level, where it continues to have an important influence. In some states, traditionalists are the major opposition to new national governments—for instance, the Ashanti of Ghana and the Baganda of Uganda. Traditionalism attempts to preserve the precolonial, indigenous methods of organizing and transferring political power, usually a system of chieftainship or kingship. Because these institutions are interwoven with other institutions and values such as land tenure and religion, the struggle to preserve the authority of a traditional ruler becomes, in the eyes of his followers, a struggle to preserve a revered way of life from destruction by an encroaching, alien (Western) ideology.

19

Probably no new African state fails to find its attempts to organize the people into a united national effort resisted by tribal traditionalism. The younger nationalist leaders react to such obstructionism by forming the one-party national fronts so characteristic of the new African states.

The fate of the Belgian Congo is a warning to all African governments not to underestimate the power of traditionalism. Although it is losing its sway over African minds as Westernization trickles down from the upper social strata, nonetheless an incident can still arouse the traditionalist feelings of a tribal people and overnight destroy the progress of decades. This happened among the Baganda of Uganda when their Kabaka (king) was exiled in 1953. The Baganda rallied to the support of what had been a fading monarchy, creating a strong anti-unification bloc in Uganda.

Paradoxically, there is also a progressive potential in traditionalism. Under certain conditions, it can provide a base for ultra-Africanism. Appeals to familiar, African modes of life can arouse an illiterate peasant population to a national consciousness more easily than appeals to modern Western concepts. Most Africans have not been Westernized, and they may never be, if the ultra-Africanists continue to gain power by building mass-based political parties and evoking latent traditionalism.

There are two major traditionalist governments in Africa: Morocco and Ethiopia. Both are ancient theocracies, but Morocco is a progressive, rapidly modernizing monarchy, while Ethiopia is a regressive monarchy that, although it has adopted certain Western forms in the middle strata of society, rejects any real revision at the top. Morocco and Ethiopia represent the two major currents in the fast-receding tide of traditionalist nationalism. The first moves progressively, but not without difficulty, toward Westernization and perhaps ultra-Africanism; the second is held in a rigid mold that may ultimately be shattered.

Morocco's Modern Monarchy

Morocco has been well described by a recent prime minister as "a modern country inhabited by people living mainly in the

The ruler of Morocco is the chief religious authority to his followers, who trace his lineage directly back to the founder of Islam. Not all Moroccan sultans have been thought to possess the mystical quality *baraka*, best translated as "saintliness," but Mohammed V was believed to have it, and this heightened the fervor of his subjects. In a chance, informal encounter with him in Morocco in 1956, I was impressed by his quiet self-possession and air of mystical attractiveness.

King Hassan II does not possess this quality. Trained in Paris as a lawyer, he is more Westernized than his father. Forced to abandon certain leanings to the life of a playboy when he became commander in chief of the armed forces, he soon got deeply involved in palace politics. As Crown Prince, he allied himself with reactionary traditionalists and against the neo-Istiqlal and other radical democratic parties. Intimidation of the "left" by the police and the army roused considerable opposition to the Prince. In 1960, he played a leading role in ousting the left-wing government of Premier Abdallah Ibrahim, a leader of the neo-Istiqlal. King Mohammed assumed the title of Premier and made his son Deputy Premier, openly bringing the monarchy into the center of the political turmoil.

Political Parties

A confused and sometimes bloody struggle has developed among the rival political groups that hope to succeed or to share power with the monarchy. The Istiqlal Party, which led the nationalist resistance against the French, subsequently splintered into two major factions—the Istiqlal and the neo-Istiqlal—and, in the passionate Arab tradition of politics, they are now at each other's throats. The disputes in this exceedingly complex political struggle are mainly class and cultural in nature. The old Istiqlal, led by the mystical Allal el-Fassi, is more traditionalist and conservative, and it appeals largely to the middle class and the traditional craftsmen of the towns and villages. The neo-Istiqlal (National Union of Popular Forces) movement has many of the earmarks of ultra-Africanism. Its leaders are Ben Barka, former Secretary General of the Istiqlal, and Mahjub Ben Seddik, trade-

Middle Ages." As yet, only the coastal regions have l
pact of Western ideas and technology, and most of l
live according to ancient Islamic custom.

Morocco is ruled by a theocratic monarch who, alt.
possesses virtually absolute power, is greatly influenced
ern democratic practices. King Mohammed V, who rule(
the first five years after his country gained independen
France in 1956, was a modern and a beloved monarch. He
to achieve the transition from the ancient rule of the Sult
modern constitutional monarchy. Toward this end, he cl
his title from "sultan" to "king" and began a gradual tran,
royal authority to representative constitutional instrur,
Mohammed V died in 1961 and was succeeded by his son, M
Hassan. King Hassan II is a more controversial ruler, but h,
proclaimed a fundamental code under which Morocco will
tinue to move toward constitutional monarchy.

This process of democratization has proved to be far m
difficult than anticipated by the nationalist leaders of the revo
tion against France. The great palace and the mosque in t
center of Rabat are still the seats of religious and tempoi
authority. In the view of informed observers, the king's authori,
under Mohammed V grew, rather than diminished, despite th
creation of political parties and representative instruments.[1]

The Monarchy

The unusual popularity of the monarchy is the result of the
leading role played by Mohammed V in the struggle for independence. The mild-mannered king became a martyr when the
French sent him into exile in 1953 for refusing to cooperate with
their rule. This was the first time since the French acquisition
of the Moroccan Protectorate in 1912 that a Moroccan ruler had
dared to oppose France openly and support Moroccan nationalism. Throughout the strife-torn country, Mohammed V became
a symbol of resistance. Many people even claimed to see his pro-
file on the moon, and called it a sign from Allah that the King
would return.[2] After his triumphant return from exile, this
intense devotion reached a new zenith, which continued until
his death.

union leader of the Union of Moroccan Workers (UMT), who are leftist, secular, and appeal to the proletariat and the discontented peasantry. Far-left and even Communist-influenced intellectuals have a minor role in this movement. The neo-Istiqlal leaders are younger than those of the old Istiqlal and are impatient for rapid social reform. They favor stricter neutrality in foreign policy and less dependence upon the West.[3]

In the spring of 1960, the nation-wide elections of representatives to the local communes developed into a major contest between the old Istiqlal and the neo-Istiqlal. The Istiqlal showed great strength in the countryside and towns, and the neo-Istiqlal demonstrated unexpected support in the coastal cities. The Istiqlal won the largest number of local council seats and claimed to be Morocco's governing party. However, no election of a national government is likely to be held until there is greater political stability and cooperation between parties, although King Mohammed had set 1962 as the year for devolving his legislative authority upon a national assembly. Some observers saw in the 1960 communal elections "the prelude to an important new phase of Moroccan political development, the transition from an absolute to a constitutional monarchy."[4]

When the French restored sovereignty to Morocco in 1956, they turned it over to the King, who from that moment possessed absolute, decree-making power. Shortly thereafter, the King created a Cabinet and a National Consultative Assembly. The latter was superseded, under the Royal Charter of 1958, by a National Deliberative Assembly, in which a wide cross-section of labor, agricultural, business, and political groups was represented. But the King appointed its members, and it could only advise. Nevertheless, in 1961, the King proclaimed his intention of achieving a true democracy "that will draw upon the spirit of Islamic teachings, the revolution of our country, and the progressive participation of our people in the conduct of our country's affairs."

A first step toward decentralizing the government was taken with the creation of representative local government (communes). About 85 per cent of the eligible voters were registered. Accomplishing this was especially difficult in the more primitive regions of Morocco, because tribal traditionalists resisted the innovation.

Berber tribesmen in the Atlas Mountains are a stronghold of opposition to the king, whose rule they have never completely accepted.[5]

Economic Progress

Morocco is potentially one of the wealthiest regions of North Africa. Its coastal plain is endowed with a climate and rainfall pattern like that of California. In agriculture, the production of grains and wines is already extensive. Of mineral resources, iron ore and phosphates are being exploited. Inadequately charted deposits exist in the interior, especially in the Mauritania and Sahara regions. It is believed that oil may be found in sizable quantities in Mauritania, to the south.

Before independence, most of the modern sector of the economy was dominated by France and French citizens, who numbered 350,000 at their peak. They controlled nearly all banking, industry, and mechanized farming. Since independence, the French have been shunted into a precarious and undefined status. Some of their land has been expropriated, and they have lost the special privileges and subsidies they enjoyed under French rule. Their control of finance and industry has also been weakened. About one third of them have left, taking considerable capital with them. Those who remain are cowed and no longer provide aggressive leadership. The responsibility for economic development has fallen to the Moroccan Government. But unfortunately for all concerned, the French, during their forty-four years of governing Morocco, did little to train Moroccans for self-government. Very few Moroccans were given administrative responsibility in the protectorate government; even postal clerks were French. Nor was the educational system geared to producing political or administrative leaders.

Since the departure of the French, the inexperienced Moroccan Government has shown a determination to come to grips with the task of economic development. Under the direction of Abderranim Bouabid, once Minister of National Economy and later a neo-Istiqlal leader, a planning council drafted a two-year development plan for 1958–59; despite insufficient capital and too few technicians, it was completed successfully, and a new five-year plan was launched. These programs have made remarkable progress.

A spectacular advance has been achieved in education. Although Moroccan children, prior to independence, outnumbered French children thirty to one, the French spent twice as much on the education of French children in Morocco as on Moroccans. After national sovereignty was gained, primary education for Moroccans soared; between 1953 and 1957, the number of Moroccan schoolchildren rose from 180,719 to 481,000. However, this rapid expansion of education has run into problems at the higher levels, where facilities are inadequate and standards have fallen deplorably. Several thousand well trained French schoolteachers have remained, but many newly employed Moslem teachers have proved to be not only inexperienced but also inadequately trained. A disastrous attempt was made to introduce Arabic as the language of instruction in several subjects, in an effort to break the French grip on education, but the experiment was abandoned when it was found that the children could not learn science and mathematics as easily in Arabic as in French.[6]

Approximately 17 per cent of Morocco's budget is spent on education. The training of a technically skilled and educated elite has been undertaken with the establishment of the University of Rabat and several other institutions of higher learning. During the years of the Protectorate, the French built nothing for education at the higher level.

Morocco's economic planning has two objectives: To improve the standard of living, and to break the country's dependence upon the French economy.[7] Moroccan nationalists point out that 60 per cent of their export and 50 per cent of their import trade is with France. Because their country belongs to the franc zone and many of their financial institutions and industries are still controlled by the French, Moroccans feel they are not masters in their own house, even though the protectorate has ended.

They are caught in a basic dilemma. The Moroccan Government has nationalized some French-owned land, as well as banks and certain industries. This not only has precipitated the departure of many French settlers but has cut to a trickle the flow of capital from France. To achieve rapid economic growth, Morocco desperately needs substantial outside help. But France has great influence on the Western sources of aid and will not tolerate assistance to Morocco to the damage of French interests there.

Under the five-year plan, Morocco is attempting to develop several new industries, such as steel in the north. "Operation Plow," the effort to modernize agriculture; is mechanizing in part an ancient system based on the donkey and the camel. A cooperative system utilizing tractor stations is expected to raise the peasant standard of living by 20 to 25 per cent. Currently, 875,000 acres are covered by this program; the ultimate objective is 2.5 million acres.

To some extent, United States aid is replacing French.[8] However, the closing of a few U.S. air bases, at the request of the Moroccan Government, has cut off a huge injection of Western funds. The flow of aid and surplus commodities from the United States in 1960 fell short of the annual pre-independence total of capital investments and loans from overseas. Morocco has also turned to the Soviet bloc for credit and military assistance and is skillfully playing one bloc against the other in order to get the largest possible amount of sorely needed assistance.

External Relations

This policy of taking help from both sides in the cold war has paved the way for a rather unexpected international role for traditionalist Morocco—as a close associate of the ultra-Africanist states of Guinea, Ghana, and the U.A.R. in the so-called Casablanca Group. It should be remembered that Morocco, although a traditionalist power, has a powerful and articulate left bloc that presses the government toward a form of neutrality, officially called "non-dependence." Also, Morocco is sympathetic to the anti-Western expressions of this ultra-Africanist bloc.

Anti-Western sentiment has been heightened by the protracted Algerian War, in which all Moroccans have sympathized with the Algerian nationalists and aided them in one way or another. The presence of several American air bases has been an added irritant, despite the U.S. agreement to withdraw entirely by 1963. Another important factor was the West's support of the French creation of an independent state of Mauritania. Ghana, Guinea, and the U.A.R. backed the Moroccan claim to Mauritania, and the Russians, seeking a special advantage, shrewdly vetoed in 1960 the admission of Mauritania to the United Nations. Feelings against France and the West over Mauritania have been intensified by French policies in Algeria and aspirations to hold on to the Southern Sahara, in order to stake out a monopoly over the rich minerals there. French testing of atomic bombs over the Sahara has further inflamed feelings.

North Africa's leaders of the Maghreb—Tunisia, Algeria, and Morocco—have projected a federal union in past meetings. Once Algeria gains full independence, this can become a reality, provided political rivalries and foreign-policy disagreements can be compromised. Tunisia, under the highly Westernized government of President Habib Bourguiba, has followed a more pro-Western policy and has served as a moderating influence in the explosive political atmosphere of North Africa.

In the slums of Casablanca and among the growing army of unemployed, the shadowy Communist Party is gaining strength. But the Communists have no prospect of gaining political power in the near future. Ben Barka and the leftist neo-Istiqlal probably would reap the benefits of any weakening of the modernizing traditionalist government.

Ben Barka's political philosophy has stirred much speculation. The conversation I had with him in 1956 and the comments of others who know him better confirm the accuracy of Charles Gallagher's opinion that he propounds a "socialism of underdevelopment." Ben Barka speaks of economic independence, nationalization of some industries, planning, and self-help—but not of renouncing foreign aid.

As Morocco rapidly modernizes, its future will be decided by the coming showdown between the moderates surrounding the palace—Westernized forces led by the Istiqlal—and the dissatisfied urbanized ultra-Africanists, growing in number, headed by the neo-Istiqlal.

The Ancient Ethiopian Kingdom

Ethiopia's king, who claims 312 predecessors on the throne, traces his lineage all the way back to the Biblical King Solomon. Legend would have it that the Queen of Sheba came from Ethiopia. Because of this long history and protracted periods of isolation from the influences of the major civilizations, tradition weighs heavily on the lives, customs, and politics of Ethiopians. In Addis Ababa, the capital, and in coastal Eritrea, a former Italian colony federated with Ethiopia, modernization has gone far; but in the hinterland, nearly all the people live in the rigid mold of a Byzantine culture.

His Imperial Majesty Haile Selassie is the absolute monarch of his subjects, variously estimated at between 12 and 19 million,[9] who regard him with great awe as "the elect of God." The symbol of centuries of tradition, he nevertheless has introduced many Westernizing changes in his country. He wants additional reforms yet is fearful that the political forces they would set in motion might undermine traditional authority. Innovations already instituted have created a new restlessness among the younger generation and some army officers. A Westernized, educated elite, eager for faster modernization, has emerged, but it is held in servile status by the traditional aristocracy around the monarch.

With a large and growing population, abundant resources, and large tracts of rich soil, plus her ample area and strategic location, Ethiopia has the potential to become one of the most prosperous and powerful nations in Africa. However, these great potentialities are largely untapped. Although Haile Selassie has done much to introduce reforms, the immense weight of traditionalism, which benefits primarily the aristocracy and the priestly class, slows progress.

The King of Kings

Haile Selassie, the "King of Kings" (*Negusa Nagast*), is virtually the proprietor of all property and the supreme lawmaker, as well as head of the clergy of the official Coptic Church of Ethiopia. All who come before him, even members of his own family, must prostrate themselves to demonstrate their loyalty and to beg for his favor. Haile Selassie was crowned Emperor in 1930, after a series of revolts and palace intrigues that displaced the daughter and grandson of the previous monarch, Menelik II. The new Emperor's claim to the throne was based on the fact that he had been declared regent and crown prince under the Empress Zauditu, daughter of Menelik.

Medieval in character, Ethiopia has both an aristocracy and a class of serfs. The priests, the military, and the landed aristocracy make up the privileged class which for centuries has dominated the millions of *gabars,* or serfs, who are forced to turn over a portion of all they produce to those who own their land. According to Ethiopian legend, when Menelik I returned from a visit to his father, King Solomon, he divided the land three ways—for the Crown, the Church, and the laity. Ever since, most of the land has been used to pay state officials and members of the clergy. From the hapless *gabars* who till the land is collected the tribute of rent. The land does not always remain with the office but is sometimes handed down from father to son. Even priests have been able to pass land on to their families.

As in the feudal systems of Europe, military service is an obligation of the land, unless it is owned by the Church. Different types of military service, such as fusilier or muleteer, were attached, in times past, to various portions of land. Not all land today falls under this *gabar* system. In certain sections, the land is communally owned, and the community or tribe parcels it out to families.

The Amhara race, which migrated centuries ago from the north and subdued the other tribes, dominates Ethiopian society. Amharic is the official language of the government. It is also the language of instruction in the schools through the fifth grade, after which English becomes the medium. As a consequence, a child of non-Amhara origin must learn a second language upon entering school, and a third language if he is to progress very far. This has made the Ethiopians facile at language, and has earned them a reputation for unusual linguistic ability.

Despite the fundamental pattern of rule by the Amharic landed

aristocracy, a broad social tolerance prevails. Moslems and ani-
mists are not persecuted. Christian missionaries from the Western
world are permitted to carry on their teachings, provided they do
not try to convert Coptic Christians.

Of the several other racial groups in Ethiopia, the most important are the Galla (who nearly defeated the Amharas), the
fierce and primitive Danakil, the Gurage, the Sidamo peoples of
the south, and the Somalis, who spill over from the coastal
Somali regions. All of these groupings break down into many
hundreds of tribes. An ancient Jewish tribe exists in one corner
of this vast country, as living proof of the Biblical origins of
Ethiopia.

Reforms

Emperor Haile Selassie has effected numerous reforms in his
kingdom—in agriculture, banking, trade, education, and government. At the same time, he has maintained a highly personal rule,
under which the favor of the Emperor is all-important to the
accomplishment of anything significant. The privileges of the
aristocracy and the Church, which control the land and the government, have not been significantly diminished. While his supporters proclaim Haile Selassie to be the "modernizer of Ethiopia," his critics assert that his rule is characterized by bribery,
incompetence, and excessive private influence.

As an energetic new emperor, he began his reign by proclaim-
ing the first Ethiopian constitution, in 1931. It created a two-
chamber legislature, giving the people their first, although limited, voice in the government. Initially, representation was indirect in the lower house, but it has since been made direct,
based, however, on a property franchise. The upper house (the
Senate) is appointed by the Emperor. Serious debates on legislation take place under the leadership of the prime minister and his
cabinet, composed of the various government agency ministers.
But all laws must bear the Emperor's signature, and there is no
way to override his veto. Thus, the representative legislature is
only advisory. No serious opposition to the government is permitted, and no Western-style political parties are allowed to func-

tion.[10] Elections receive little publicity, and very few people know what is going on. According to one American observer, "The mass of the electorate is profoundly ignorant of both the purposes and procedures of elections."[11]

Of perhaps greater lawmaking significance than the legislature is another constitutional agency, the Crown Council, a private cabinet consisting of a group of close advisers to the King, primarily princes and elder statesmen. This agency brings together the powerful chieftains of various areas, giving them some sense of power and participation in the national government.

Regional and local government is even more authoritarian than the central government. Provincial governors are appointed by the Emperor, who also takes part in appointing their underlings, thus having a hand in the government of even the most remote regions. Virtually no local representation exists.

All Ethiopians are held to have the right of direct access to their Emperor to express grievances and to ask for favors. In practice, of course, this right cannot be extended to all. Nonetheless, the Emperor conducts daily public hearings, which give a personal stamp to his rule, and the right of access is deeply cherished by all Ethiopians.

Ethiopia is governed by a complicated legal system, which employs two codes of law. The older is Semitic in origin and Mosaic in character—based on the principle of "an eye for an eye." The second, the Fetha Negast, was compiled in the ninth and tenth centuries from old Roman canon law and was greatly influenced by the decisions of the Nicene Council. It embraces both religious and secular matters—dealing with, for instance, duties to the Church as well as punishment for murder. Ethiopians are extremely fond of litigation, so that going to court is almost a national pastime. Numerous levels of appeal exist, up through the governor of a province to "the mouth of the King" (*Afa Negus*), and finally to the Emperor himself, who sets aside two days a week for judicial hearings.[12]

The customs of minority groups are broadly tolerated. Moslems, for example, are permitted to utilize their own courts for most civil cases, and Westerners enjoy a form of extraterritoriality whereby the appropriate consul is allowed to sit with an Ethiopian judge in a special court.

Potential Development

Much of the greath wealth of Ethiopia is untapped, especially in agriculture. Ethiopia has more arable land than any other territory or state in East Africa. The highland regions are excellent for growing grain and coffee, and there are vast tracts of pastoral land. According to studies of the United Nations Food and Agriculture Organization, Ethiopia could produce enough grain to feed its own population and still export a substantial amount. Yet Ethiopia imports millions of dollars' worth of food every year. The FAO also concluded that a major meat industry could be supported by the pastoral tribes, which have abundant land, provided rinderpest and other cattle diseases, which now take an annual toll of millions of animals, are overcome.[13]

Ethiopian agricultural techniques are amazingly backward, even for Africa. Such a simple instrument as the scythe has only recently replaced the sickle. Plowing is done with a very inadequate, metal-tipped, wooden instrument, and little traction power is used, despite the availability of draft animals. Seeding and weeding are done in ways that sharply limit the crop yield. With the help of the FAO and U.S. Point Four experts, the government has launched a vigorous program to introduce modern methods. For several years, Oklahoma A & M College has been building an agriculture extension and training program there that is regarded as one of the best in Africa. Yet a great deal remains to be done. The FAO recommended creation of small centers for training in the use of machinery in several parts of the country, and pushed for adoption of some cooperative farming methods, but only a few of its suggestions have been acted upon. Irrigation might accomplish a great deal, particularly in the Lake Tana region in the north. The capital needed for such projects could be found, but the Ethiopian Government has been lethargic. Improved methods of processing and marketing coffee, the chief cash crop, have been suggested; yet the ancient methods continue almost unchanged.[14] Government initiative is handicapped in general by a basic unwillingness to delegate authority. The head of a government department would lose prestige if he delegated authority, and his underlings, in turn, would lose face if they sought such authority.

Industrially, too, Ethiopia has great potential. It has iron, coal, gold, and platinum, and a little oil has been discovered. Copper, asbestos, potash, and sulphur deposits are known to exist. The most significant industrialization has been in food- and fiber-processing. Foreign capital from Greece, Holland, and England has helped develop sugar-refining and tobacco- and cotton-processing plants. Very little Ethiopian capital is invested in business ventures, since wealthy Ethiopians traditionally look with disdain upon those who make their living from commerce. Most Ethiopians with a little extra cash bury it or put it in a savings account rather than invest it in a new enterprise.

Since World War II, the government has increasingly undertaken economic enterprise. It took over a cement plant and a cotton factory from the Italians, and it made tobacco-processing a government enterprise. The country's total industrial sales, excluding mining and construction, were, in Ethiopian dollars, $44.6 million in 1954, compared with $28.1 million in 1951, indicating a rapid growth over that period. In the same period, industrial employment nearly doubled. No Western-style trade unions are permitted, although the government sponsors a labor center in Addis Ababa for training and vocational promotion. Wages are very low, even by African standards. Per capita income is between $60 and $80 a year. Working conditions are generally very poor, although an eight-hour day is observed.

Government policy encourages foreign capital to enter the country, and substantial and varied assistance has been received. In 1950, a "Statement of Policy for Encouragement of Foreign Capital Investment in Ethiopia" was published. It exempted new enterprises from profits taxes for five years from the start of production, waived customs duties for machinery imported for installation in new factories, and declared that, in general, Ethiopian capital participation would not be imposed on such enterprises.[15]

Ethiopia does not have the over-all economic planning of the more Westernized African states. Its programming is a patchwork, rather like that of the Middle East monarchies, where the public funds are scarcely distinguishable from the king's private purse. Social development remains a philanthropy of the monarchy, rather than a fundamental responsibility of the entire society. Government departments exist for education, trade, and finance, and an Economic Development Bank was created in 1951, with the help of a World Bank loan. But these agencies are not strong policy instruments, and they lack the unified direction of a long-range plan.

It would be incorrect to leave the impression that no progress has been made under Haile Selassie. Actually, there has been significant economic improvement. Education has been expanded on all levels. A University College has been established in Addis Ababa, and government-supported private schools now outnumber the traditional Coptic Church schools, whose curriculum is rote memorization of ancient texts and whose graduates are virtually illiterate in a modern language. In 1958, 11 per cent of the budget was expended on education, as compared with the 20 to 25 per cent allocated by some other African states.

Multinational Influences

Because of its special status as a nation with a long history of independence, Ethiopia has always been wary of the big powers. By employing technical personnel—to run the banks, hospitals, schools, and industries—from numerous foreign powers, Ethiopia has, from the beginning of this century, attempted to avoid being dominated by any one power. Russia and Sweden have been nearly as important in providing assistance as the European colonial powers. Great Britain's influence skyrocketed after World War II, because the British helped liberate the country from the Italians and then extended a great deal of both technical and financial help to get Ethiopia on its feet again. Between 1942 and 1945, the British granted Ethiopia some £3.25 million. The United States extended substantial aid, first under Lend-Lease and then in grants and credits from the Export-Import Bank and ICA. Sweden has helped underwrite the salaries of Swedish nationals employed by the Ethiopian Government and the purchase of school and hospital equipment from Sweden. The World Bank has extended several loans for improving Ethiopian communications, as the Italian-built roads needed repair badly and the French-built railway was at the point of collapse.

Even before the Revolution, the Russians were interested in Ethiopia.[16] Now their interest is far greater. The U.S.S.R. has built and staffed an impressive hospital in the capital. During a state visit to the Soviet Union in 1960, Haile Selassie surprised the world by entering into trade agreements with the Soviets and accepting long-term credits of $100 million from them.

The United States has launched one of its most extensive African technical-assistance programs in Ethiopia. Started in 1952, Point Four has gradually expanded its programs in agriculture, water resources, education, public health and sanitation, commerce and industry, and public administration. The primary objective is to train Ethiopian personnel to take over the administration of their country's development. By 1961, 146 American technicians were working in Ethiopia, and a total of $72.5 million in economic aid had been extended. Despite her agricultural potential, it has been necessary to provide Ethiopia with substantial shipments of grain. In 1959, the United States granted Ethiopia (under Public Law 480) 46,000 tons of surplus grain to make up for losses resulting from drought and locusts. In 1960, the Development Loan Fund lent Ethiopia $2 million for improving agriculture and industry through private enterprise. However, U.S. aid has been concentrated mainly in agriculture.

The Emperor's great pride is the country's unusually large and well-equipped army and air force. His confidence proved well placed in 1960, when the army's loyalty to him was the deciding factor in putting down an abortive revolution. Haile Selassie has been very careful not to permit any single outside power to gain paramount influence in the armed forces. Following World War II, Britain re-equipped the Ethiopian forces, and the U.S. helped to train a new air force, in addition to equipping three divisions and a small navy. More recently, the Ethiopians turned to a neutral power, Sweden, for direct assistance in training. She has continued to take military aid from several sources.

Officially, Haile Selassie has followed a neutral and pan-Africanist foreign policy. This is a new position for Ethiopia and dates from the recent rise to prominence of other independent African states. A generation ago, Ethiopians did not consider themselves African. Today they take pride in their important role within the African bloc. The Emperor attempts to stay aloof from the maneuverings between the Westernized nationalists and the ultra-Africanists, but his basic pro-Westernism finds the greatest accord with Nigeria and the Monrovia Group.

A difficult international problem was solved in 1952, when the U.N. approved the federation of Eritrea and Ethiopia. This gave Ethiopia access to the sea and re-established her rule in an area which Italy had dominated for more than half a century.

Ethiopia's relations with Somalia and French Somaliland are very strained, and the intermittent border clashes could develop into more serious conflicts. The Somalis are fearful that the Goliath on their borders has expansionist designs. This unease is aggravated by the fact that the borders are poorly defined and Somalis live on both sides. More than 500,000 Somalis live at least part of the year within Ethiopian borders, in the Ogaden region. Among the Somalis, there is a growing pan-Somali movement that would unite them all in one nation. Thus, any defection by the Somalis in Ethiopia could set in motion strong forces. Over 30 per cent of the Ethiopian population are Moslem, and pan-Islam is a considerable political force throughout the "horn of Africa." The Coptic rulers of Ethiopia are deeply distrustful of Egypt's political influence, and this adds fuel to the smoldering dispute.

The Crack in the Mold

The hard mold of Ethiopia's centuries-old traditionalism is cracking. The authority of the Emperor is still enormous, but it must inevitably decrease with the rise of an educated professional class in business and the army.

The abortive palace revolution of 1960 was led by dissatisfied elements within the King's own imperial guard and supported by the more Westernized younger men in and around the gov-

ernment. Even Crown Prince Asfa-Wassen appeared to be impli-
cated at first, when the rebels declared him head of the new government. However, upon Haile Selassie's return to Ethiopia from
a state visit abroad, where he had been at the time of the attempted coup, the Crown Prince was declared to have been an
unwilling prisoner of the rebels.

To his people and to most of the army, the old monarch is still
the leader who guided them to final triumph over the Italians in
World War II. His lonely exile from 1936 to 1942, as a prophet
crying in the wilderness against rising Fascist aggression, added
to his prestige. Thus, despite the cumbersome antiquity of the
regime, the King still occupies his throne. But the forces of
change, which he himself has done so much to bring to Ethiopia,
are steadily undermining the traditional forms of power and
privilege.

No other country in Africa has a pattern of traditionalism so
deeply ingrained as that over which the Lion of Judah presides.
Nonetheless, the highly personalized and often inept system of
rule by the Emperor and his followers, who have little vision of
what might be done with the vast resources at their command,
cannot withstand the pressures for progress. The rise in education and commerce is creating an educated elite and a populace
with growing appetite for the boons of modern life. Despite his
reforms, the Emperor has shown little desire to establish a constitutional monarchy. Nor does he permit the existence of rival
political factions. A peaceful transfer of power to educated, Westernized leaders appears to be unlikely in Ethiopia. The alternative is a drastic, sudden change, the frequent fate of monarchy. In
some Western circles, there is the naïve notion that the regime's
extraordinary antiquity gives it stability. Actually, the deeply
rooted traditionalism gives it a rigidity that makes it dangerously
incapable of adapting to the winds of change.

In the powerful neighbors to the north, the U.A.R. and the
Sudan, military regimes have initiated sweeping social reforms
more in the pattern of ultra-Africanism than Westernized nationalism. Perhaps, similarly, the Ethiopian Army contains restive
leaders who hold the key to the future of the ancient Kingdom
of Sheba.

2.

Westernized Nationalist
Patterns in Transition

The major political force in postwar Africa has been Westernized nationalism. All over that continent, the converts to Western ideas—the lawyers, the doctors, the successful businessmen—have molded political organizations and, by violent and nonviolent means, have pressed to obtain the political power held by colonial powers and traditional chieftains. They have been remarkably successful. The vast majority of Africans now live under governments run by these men. The political culture, as well as the governmental structure, reflects the basic Westernized nature of these states.

However, each of these countries has traditionalist and ultra-Africanist groups who produce political opposition and, increasingly, outright conflict. The stability and progress of Africa's new nations depend upon their ability to cope with revolutionary influences and to provide for peaceful, rather than disruptive, means of change.

Most Westernized nationalist governments in Africa have highly centralized political authority. Virtually all have one-party systems led by a single, dominant personality, who is usually both head of state and chief minister. Western democratic institutions have been adopted, but they often fail to function in the same way. Only Nigeria departs significantly from this authoritarian pattern. When it achieved independence in 1960, Nigeria had already developed a functioning multiparty system within a federation that allowed for a high degree of political freedom.

In all these new countries, the public sector has assumed the major initiative in economic planning. However, the investments of overseas nations are respected, and very little nationalization of property has taken place. The major colonial relationships of trade, currency agreements, banking, and investment have continued intact. Although new trade has been developed with previously excluded areas such as Eastern Europe, the former mother power maintains its dominant trading position. Educational systems are continued along former lines, with intensive expansion on all levels and numerous teachers from the West.

Many former colonial-service officers are hired by the new African governments, although Africanization of the civil services is being pushed very rapidly in all but the most technical fields. Control of the armed forces has been transferred to the new political leaders, but in many cases the military retains a number of officers from the former colonial power. Young African officers and officer candidates receive training at institutions like the Royal Military Academy at Sandhurst in England. Mutual-defense arrangements with the former colonial power have been continued by new British Commonwealth members, and a few formerly French territories.

These major similarities of Westernized nationalist governments should not be permitted to leave the impression of uniformity. There are many important variations in the form of government, the policy of leaders, and the ideology of their parties. Nevertheless, these Westernized nations fall into three broad patterns: 1) The West African Commonwealth has a background of British colonial rule and has patterned many modern social institutions on the British model; close cultural and economic ties within the Commonwealth are continued. 2) The East African Commonwealth is distinguished from the West African states primarily by the influence of racial minorities, especially white settlers, on its development under British rule. 3) The French-speaking states in West and Equatorial Africa have been greatly influenced by the distinctive nature of French colonial rule; the member nations maintain varyingly close relationships with their counterparts and with France.

The major tendencies in Westernized nationalism and the particular problems within each of these areas are discussed in the following analyses of three states—Nigeria, Tanganyika, and the Ivory Coast. A fourth, Liberia, represents a special kind of Westernized state; because it is the only state in Africa having special ties with the United States, Liberia is becoming increasingly a center of American influence in Africa.

Westernized nationalism is going through a rapid transition at varying speeds and in different ways, toward the more highly Africa-conscious form of nationalism called ultra-Africanism.

NIGERIA: WEST AFRICAN COMMONWEALTH POWER

Nigeria is one of the most powerful and important states of Africa. Its population (between 35 and 40 million) is greater than that of any other African state; one-sixth of all Africans live within its borders. With its large territory and substantial resources, Nigeria may one day be the greatest power in West Africa, if it can unify its numerous tribal and political groupings. This multiplicity is both a great strength and a disturbing weakness. A delicate balance of power has been struck among the three major tribal groups that permits none to dominate and a democratic political process to exist. The uneasy alliance of an essentially traditional with a primarily Westernized party makes for a shaky government.

On October 1, 1960, in a colorful ceremony, Her Majesty's Government of Great Britain granted full independence to Nigeria. Constitutionally, the new Nigeria appeared to be highly Westernized. It had a duly elected National Assembly, a cabinet, and a prime minister functioning in the parliamentary tradition of England. In addition, its thriving economy was moving forward by leaps and bounds. Since independence, very little anti-Western propaganda has emanated from the political parties or the press. Although the new government made clear its intention to pursue its own neutral path of "nonalignment" in foreign affairs, this powerful West African state remains a major member of the British Commonwealth.

Regional Divisions

The first independent Nigerian Government was voted to power in the December, 1959, all-Nigeria elections. It consisted not of one monolithic nationalist movement but of a coalition of two of the three major regional parties. Ideology is a minor source of disagreement among parties, while tribal rivalries are the determining force in Nigerian politics.

The strongest political party is the predominantly traditionalist Northern Peoples Congress (NPC), based in the northern region of the Fulani-Hausa tribe, from which Prime Minister Balewa was chosen. Balewa put together an uneasy coalition of his NPC and the National Council of Nigeria and the Cameroons (NCNC), a predominantly Westernized party based among the Ibo tribe of the eastern region. Many observers had believed that the popular and colorful leader of the NCNC, Dr. Nnamdi Azikiwe, would not take second place to anyone; but "Zik" surprisingly accepted first the presidency of the Federal Senate and later the governor-generalship of all Nigeria. An opposition was formed by Chief Obafemi Awolowo, leader of the Action Party of the western region, where the Yoruba tribe is dominant.

Minor parties and ethnic groups play an important role in the maneuvering among the three large parties. In the 1959 elections, the Northern Elements Progressive Union (NEPU) was allied with the NCNC, the United Moslem Party of Lagos Federal Territory gave important support to the NPC, and the Middle Belt Congress of the northern region joined forces with Awolowo. These numerous small ethnic groups create a political mosaic whose complexity is best indicated by the fact that there are 248 distinct languages in the country. The minor tribes enable the three major parties to break out of strictly regional areas and to become, to some extent, national parties. Both the NPC and the NCNC have parliamentary seats in Awolowo's Western Province. Similarly, Awolowo has won a following in the north and the east.

Sir Alhaji Abubakar Tafawa Balewa, Prime Minister of Nigeria, is a restrained, intelligent man, skilled in parliamentary maneuvers, but he is not the real leader of the NPC. Behind him stands Sir Ahmadu Bello, the Sarduana of Sokoto—six feet of haughty bearing and every inch the traditional nationalist ruler. As the chief in the feudal hierarchy of the north and Prime Minister of the Northern Province, the Sarduana is both supreme secular authority and traditional religious leader of Nigeria's Moslems. Islam is the dominant faith of the Fulani-Hausa people of the north, whose culture and civilization can be traced back to North Africa and the kingdoms of the Middle Ages. The Hausa Kingdom, with a history going back to the thirteenth century, was conquered by the fierce Fulani in the nineteenth century. This was a holy war for the Fulani, who were Moslem, and they imposed their faith on the Hausa. A people proud of their civilization and history, the Fulani-Hausa look down upon the "barbaric" tribes of the south who, they say, "were eating their grandmothers when we were civilized." Hausa is the principal language of the north, although the taller, fairer Fulani constitute the ruling class of this day.

The basis of the NPC's power in the north is the religious loyalty of the people to traditional values and habits of life. Rigid customs bind them to their ruling emirs. The emirs, although they have lost much of their power, still retain great civil and religious authority. Many continue to act like all-powerful lords, despite the elections by which the humble people now ratify their authority.[1] However, a progressive, educated group of young emirs and political figures is slowly emerging in the north. This group persuaded the NPC conservatives to agree to the coalition with the NCNC in the south.

A highly progressive but small party, the NEPU, is making a frontal attack on traditionalism in the north. It proposes such radical ideas as suffrage for women, who are still given only second-class civil status by Moslem custom. The NEPU won eight seats in the 1959 elections, but it has a long way to go before it can break the grip of traditionalism. The position of this Westernized party is made more difficult by the fact that the traditionalist NPC is a member of the governing coalition. However, the NEPU leader—Mellan Aminu Kano, who won the East Kano seat of the capital city of Kano by a big majority—is a new and promising voice from the north.

In political issues among the three major parties in the 1959 election, the largest ideological gap appeared between the NPC's conservative traditionalism and the NCNC's radical progressivism. Zik stood for rapid educational reform and a foreign policy of neutrality. The NCNC showed little interest in educational reform and advocated a close association with the West. But Balewa, with great political finesse, put these differences aside and joined with the NCNC in forming a government.

The NCNC was the second-largest party in the 1959 elections; it won 90 seats, the NPC 142, and the Action Group 73. Most of the NCNC seats were won in the eastern region, the center of the Ibo tribe's power. However, the NCNC also showed strength in the western region, where for many years it has won support from turbulent centers of population like Ibadan and Lagos. (Although located in the west, Lagos is a separate federal territory with three seats.)

In the early days of Nigerian nationalism, the NCNC showed promise of becoming a transtribal movement. Zik was first among contemporary nationalists to raise a vigorous voice for independence. Educated in the United States and an empire-builder in his own right, he published a string of newspapers, avidly read by Nigerians for their anti-British editorializing. Thus he was remarkably effective in mobilizing public opinion. He began a number of other business enterprises, not all of which succeeded, but his first love was politics. As the heir to the mantle of Herbert Macauley, founder of Nigerian nationalism, Zik dominated Nigerian politics. His influence reached far beyond Nigeria into other parts of West Africa, where an ambitious young teacher named Kwame Nkrumah, inspired by his influence, sought his help in furthering his education in America.

The 4-million-odd Ibos, mostly settled in the Eastern Province, home base of the NCNC, are a highly aggressive and agile tribe. Although less educated and developed than the people of the west, they are great traders. A historically unified group, they have no traditional chieftain hierarchy and are extremely individualistic. Their effervescence has made them naturally political. Free of the restrictions of many traditional tribal systems, they adapt quickly to modern living. In all probability, the Ibos will provide Nigeria with most of her political leadership for many years to come.

After independence, Azikiwe was elevated to the post of Governor-General and became an elder statesman in Nigerian politics. Although his influence continues to be felt, his retirement has changed the character of the NCNC. Control passed into the hands of less fiery, "careerist" leaders like Chief Ekotie Eboh, T. O. S. Benson, J. M. Johnson, and Raymond Njoku, who formed the coalition with the NPC after the 1959 elections. There are varying views of Zik's own role in this unexpected alliance. According to the Nigerian political analyst Babatunde Williams, Zik was negotiating with Awolowo for a coalition when word reached him that the careerists had thrown their support to the NPC. The radical wing of the NCNC was much embittered by this alliance with the traditionalists. But the more reflective members realized that this might be the only way to win wholehearted northern participation in the federation. Their leader's acceptance of the governor-generalship seemed to place his authority behind the compromise.[2]

Chief Awolowo, leader of the opposition party, the Action Group, is widely regarded as one of the most competent and intelligent leaders in Nigeria. He passed the bar examination in England and was a trade-union adviser before entering politics in 1948. Awolowo's power base is the Yoruba tribe of the Western Province, the most advanced and urbanized part of the country. The Yoruba possess a higher standard of living and more Western goods than the other tribes, and therefore consider themselves more civilized. Their pride incites both resentment and jealousy in the other tribes. Leaders of the Action Group are of the middle class and are well educated. Some are intellectuals from the universities who have been attracted by Awolowo's own intellectual leanings. If there is a weakness in the Action Group, it is its higher-level, reasoned appeal, which goes over the heads of the illiterate peasants. However, forming the opposition, Awolowo has shifted from the pro-Western moderation of the 1959 election to a more radical program of economic and educational Nigerianization. In foreign policy, Awolowo has swung full circle, and now opposes close identification with the Commonwealth and the West. He prefers the nonalignment policy of Ghana. But, like his party, he retains essentially a Westernized rather than an ultra-nationalist outlook. This could change as ideological lines solidify in the post-independence struggle for power. By the middle of 1961, Awolowo was speaking increasingly in the language of the pan-Africanists of Accra.

During the 1959 elections, Awolowo advocated separate regions for minority tribes, a platform that won him an alliance with the Middle Belt Congress of the Northern Province. Thus, he invaded the domain of the northern empire, depriving the NPC of twenty-seven seats. In the campaign, Awolowo used a helicopter to fly over the Northern Province. This incensed the emirs, because the flights over closed courtyards exposed Moslem women to view. This, plus the fact that the Action Group took the seats that would have given the NPC an absolute majority, made an alliance between it and the NPC impossible. Nevertheless, the Action Group enlarged its representation in the House from twenty-seven to seventy-three seats to become a powerful opposition.

Although some threats were made against the Action Group in the first few months of independence, the government made no attempt to hinder effective opposition by Awolowo. Only in sections of the Northern Province are there any real curbs on peaceful opposition.

Ultra-Africanism has not developed into a mass movement, although at one time, dissatisfied ultra-Africanist elements were associated with the NCNC. The Dynamic Party (an offshoot of the NCNC led by Dr. Chike Obi) advocates socialism and a "benevolent dictatorship" to achieve drastic reform. Obi, a senior lecturer in mathematics at Ibadan University College, allied his party with the NCNC and won the seat vacated by Zik in 1959. He was then in a strategic position to revive some of the former radical sentiments of those in the NCNC who had become disenchanted with the coalition. However, Obi's maiden speech in the House was such a slashing attack on the government that the NCNC withdrew its sponsorship of him, and he was forced out of his seat. In this speech, he opposed membership in the Commonwealth if it "put a brake on the course of pan-Africanism

and the union of West Africa."[3] He was especially critical of
the lack of military preparation and the failure to create a
ministry of scientific and industrial development. These have
proved to be appealing concepts among the youth of Nigeria.
The Pan-African Youth Movement is already echoing them.
Some day, Obi may be back in the Assembly with added support.

The Nigerian Socialist Group is another advocate of militant
pan-Africanism. It has support among younger leaders and even
among ministers in the eastern and western regions.

Constitutional Federal Development

Nigeria is a genuine federation, with three self-governing regions and the Federal City of Lagos. This federation is largely
the outgrowth of the British Colonial Administration.

Nigeria was not unified politically until 1914. The British employed separate administrative units from their first entry into
Lagos in 1861 and their final conquest of the Northern Province
in 1900. Lord Lugard, "the conqueror of the north," is the historical father of modern Nigeria. He brought the north into
Nigeria and ruled the colony as a unified whole as its first Governor-General.

Modern constitutional development did not actually begin
until after World War II. Before that, the British believed they
had indefinite time in which to build a modern state, and they
did not attempt seriously to prepare the colony for self-rule until
the 1946 Richards constitution. This laid the foundation for a
federal state and brought the Northern Province into the Legislative Council for the first time, although the emirs in the north
were very distrustful of the ultimate effect of association with the
southern regions. Then, in 1951, the Macpherson constitution
transformed the regional assemblies from advisory bodies into
truly autonomous authorities, and the federal house from an
appointive into an elective group.

Pressure from the southern parties drove the British to create
a rapid series of new constitutions, culminating in the agreements reached at the London conferences of 1957 and 1958. Regional self-government was granted to the Eastern and Western

provinces in 1957, but the Northern Province held back out of fear of southern domination, pleading that it was not yet ready. Finally, northern intransigence was overcome in the 1958 conference, and the NPC agreed to independence from Great Britain at an early date (1959). The way was then open for appointment of the first all-Nigerian government on August 30, 1959, under Prime Minister Balewa. After the first all-Nigeria elections in December, 1959, the British concluded that the country was sufficiently prepared, and October 1, 1960, was set as the date for independence.[4]

The Nigerian Government that emerged from this rapid constitutional transition was a fusion of the British parliamentary system with federal principles. Perhaps the best comparison is India, although the latter is far more complex and plural in nature than Nigeria. Each region of Nigeria possesses its own government, with a governor, prime minister, cabinet, and legislative branch. In the north and the west, the upper house for chiefs is more important than in the east. Each region has considerable powers of its own in the areas of taxation, education, social welfare, and police powers.

The Federal Government has upper and lower houses, and the lower House of Representatives is the prime legislative authority. From it, the Governor-General chooses the prime minister, who in turn appoints his ministers. At the time of independence, Nigeria decided to remain within the Commonwealth. Thus, all law and authority stems from the Crown of England, although the locus of power has shifted to Africa.

The British Colonial Service has played an important role in the administration of independent Nigeria. For many years after independence, all the ministers of the various government departments were African, but their immediate assistants were British. In all former British colonies, this system has worked surprisingly well. Colonial officials who could adjust to living in an African state and working for African employers stayed on as civil servants in the new countries. In Nigeria, the nationalist parties have exerted tremendous pressure to Nigerianize the government service, partly for patronage reasons and partly because of public opinion. Most Africans are eager to see an African government run by Africans. Rivalry for government posts exists among the educated elite, for the jobs pay comparatively well and provide security. The other parties have accused the NPC of packing the civil service with the intent of extending its power and influence at the expense of the southern regions. But Prime Minister Balewa has replied that the north is merely trying to catch up with the south, where the bulk of civil servants have been drawn from in the past. Of course, the temptation to use the civil service as a political tool is strong in every country.

The sudden influx of Africans into the extensive Nigerian government structure has made the maintenance of high standards of efficiency and honesty a difficult matter. The liberal use of "dash," or bribery, is a major challenge here, as in the other new African governments.

Economic Boom

Few countries in Africa—or in the world—have made such impressive economic strides as has Nigeria. If this pace can be continued, Nigerians will enjoy one of the highest standards of living in Africa, and Nigeria will have power and influence throughout West and Central Africa.

In the 1948–59 period, exports doubled in tonnage, and imports trebled. Port and railway facilities have been vastly expanded to open up the great hinterlands for development. In 1960, $14 million worth of oil was exported. Construction of a refinery could make Nigeria self-sufficient in oil products, since the Niger delta swamps contain reserves of perhaps a billion barrels. Some interest has been shown in developing the extensive iron ore, lead, and zinc deposits. Already, tin and columbite (needed for jet-engine alloys) are being exported. Prime Minister Balewa is attracted by the idea of building a steel industry with a huge hydroelectric plant on the Niger River.

Some industrialization is deemed possible because there is ample power to be found in coal, water, and oil; the question is just how much. Economists believe that the large, growing population provides a considerable consumer market for secondary manufacturing. However, the Nigerian economy is primarily agrarian, and her prosperity depends largely on the export of cocoa, groundnuts, cotton, and rubber.

In 1954, the seven-year Nigeria Development Plan was adopted, entailing an expenditure of £330 million. Three quarters of the capital was to come from domestic sources. The Colonial Development and Welfare Program was to provide £15 million, and the United Kingdom another £10 million.[5] The World Bank made a loan of £10 million, primarily for railway improvement. Private foreign capital investment has been running at a higher rate than expected, and government planners are looking to the development of an internal capitalization program to supplement government spending. By 1960, government expenditures for all purposes totaled £75 million; in 1945, they had added up to only £10.7 million.

The Balewa government is aware that Nigeria's future prosperity depends upon expansion of crop exports. This requires improved communications and agricultural methods. And improved agriculture can best be realized by expanding education and employing foreign technicians for a number of years. Outside capital could be most helpful in developing a more adequate communications network, but increasing peasant crops in an area of good, arable land is primarily a domestic task. Nigeria needs to establish easier credit and improved cooperative marketing programs and to persuade the peasant to modernize. Rising peasant production will in turn bring about the rapid growth of the internal consumer market which new, secondary industries could supply.

Nigeria has more nationals studying abroad—more than 3,000 —than any other African country. A former English teacher, Prime Minister Balewa gives high priority to the expansion of education. The ambitious goal of universal primary education was adopted in 1954. By 1957, 2.5 million children were attending primary school. The first class to be graduated under this program, in December, 1960, more than doubled the number of primary-school graduates for the preceding year. Higher education is also being pushed. A new university has been established in the Eastern Province, to supplement the University College at Ibadan, and a third university is planned for Lagos. A university degree is a prize avidly sought, for it guarantees a well-paid government job and membership in the new Nigerian elite. With this new vocational goal, emphasis in higher education has shifted from classical studies to scientific and practical training.

A Pro-Western Alliance?

Nigeria's continuing close relationship with Great Britain is apparent in every important aspect of life. Most of her trade is with Britain. Banking, finance, and industry are still in the hands of the English. British subjects staff the high levels of the civil service and the army. The present government has actively promoted this policy of having the British "walking alongside" in the development of the country.

The Commonwealth tie explains Nigeria's foreign policy, which is a moderate version of "positive neutralism." Nigeria shuns the extreme, passionate outbreaks of anti-Western sentiment that are typical of the Ghana-Guinea axis. Moreover, Balewa has approached trade and aid agreements with the Communist bloc very cautiously, because he is wary of the Soviet Union's use of economic aid as a political device of penetration. Soon after Nigeria became independent, the Prime Minister announced that his policy would have the objective of preventing Africa from becoming a battlefield in the ideological war.

Nigeria has assumed a leading role in behalf of African interests at the United Nations. Her ambassador to the U.N., Jaja Wachuku, was made Chairman of the U.N. Conciliation Commission for the Congo, established in 1960 to attempt to restore to the Congo a representative and stable government. As the giant of West Africa, Nigeria has immense influence, and this will grow even greater if she can persuade enough of the new African leaders that more is to be gained by moderation than by extremism during the years of crisis ahead.

Relations between Nigeria and ultra-Africanist Ghana and Guinea are strained. Nigeria naturally seeks allies among the more Westernized governments like Liberia and the French Community–oriented states. Nigerian leaders accuse Nkrumah of utilizing pan-Africanism to serve his goal of ambitious expansion. They are critical of the "utopianism" of Nkrumah's aims of West African unity. These verbal battles have grown more intense, and could become serious if conflicts break out over boundaries between the smaller states.

Too close identification with the West could prove dangerous for the Balewa government. The signing of a mutual-defense pact with Great Britain in late 1960 aroused passionate reactions from Awolowo's party and student groups. Animosities against whites flared up in Lagos at the time of Patrice Lumumba's death in the Congo. Ultra-Africanism is weak in Nigeria, but if tribal disunity prevents rapid progress, and if African relations with the Western world deteriorate because of crises like that of the Belgian Congo, Dr. Obi's Dynamic Party and the Pan-African Youth Movement might possibly swing the left wing of the NCNC to Awolowo's Action Group. In this way a radical shift could occur in the character of the government. The great danger is that a shift too far toward a powerful, modern, centralized government might arouse secessionist sentiment in the traditionalist north, causing a radical counteraction in the south. National unity rests on a delicate balance of power that permits democracy to exist—but at the price of possible disunion.

Despite these dangers, Nigeria has one of the brightest prospects in Africa.

TANGANYIKA: COMMONWEALTH AND RACE

African nationalist movements in East Africa have been delayed by special conditions. Their contacts with the West have been more recent, and so their economies less developed. Yet, Western influence on East African patterns of life has been greater than in West Africa. African indigenous culture was weaker when the European nations conquered the Africans in the nineteenth century, and the West completed its domination by promoting the influx of white settlers, whose interests and values became paramount. Most of them looked upon the African as a savage who provided cheap labor for their large plantations. At best, they believed, it would take several centuries of civilizing influence before Africans could become the equals of whites.

But then the equalitarian mass nationalist movements of the

West Africans gripped the imagination of East African peasants, who flocked to the banners of independence raised by Julius Nyerere, Tom Mboya, Dr. Hastings Banda, and others. Now the once arrogant settlers, who formerly controlled the best land and ran the banks and industries, are seeking ways to make peace with the African nationalists, in the hope of keeping a place for themselves in the rapid development of independent Africa. More moderate Westernized nationalist opinion is ready to forget, if not forgive, the past, and to work together with whites in a spirit of "nonracialism." This attitude is best expressed by Julius Nyerere, first Prime Minister of Tanganyika.

In his country, both Europeans and Indians continue to exercise great influence as technicians, teachers, and entrepreneurs in a predominantly African state. The British, who for fifty years ruled this vast East and Central African region, are hoping that the territories of Uganda, Kenya, Nyasaland, and Northern Rhodesia will be inspired by the moderate Commonwealth orientation of Nyerere and his followers. However, the emerging influence of Kenya's more race-conscious Africans, like Jomo Kenyatta, who have chafed under "white supremacy," and the deadly struggle between white settlers and Africans in the Central African Federation on the southern border of Tanganyika, are storm clouds on the horizon.

Nevertheless, from Tanganyika's dry plains has come an unexpected wind of change that has brought fresh prospects for progressive and peaceful transition in multiracial East Africa. A few years ago, this would not have been thought possible.

When I was in Uganda in 1952, Tanganyika was considered the most backward of the three territories of British East Africa. Shortly thereafter, I met Julius Nyerere for the first time at the United Nations, where he had come as a petitioner to protest British suppression, in several districts, of his political party, the Tanganyika African National Union (TANU). He was given a sympathetic hearing, and the interest shown in TANU by the next U.N. visiting mission undoubtedly accounted for much of the rapid progress that followed. When I visited Tanganyika in 1959, I was scarcely prepared for the tremendous, quiet progress that had been made. One of the most astute British observers of the African scene, John Hatch, summed up the significance of these changes:

> The Tanganyikan achievement is the most important single occurrence in postwar Africa. It proves the possibility of three racial communities learning a common loyalty to a single nation, placing that loyalty above their immediate communal interests and discovering that their individual freedom and the welfare of their communities is best served through this united purpose. This lesson directly challenges the black and white racialism of the Continent and by its obvious success, is fast undermining them.[6]

There is certainly much ground for optimism about the future of Tanganyika, a former United Nations Trust Territory and the first British East African territory to gain independence. However, deep-seated racial animosities lurk like sharks beneath the calm surface. Also, Tanganyika is seriously lacking in economic assets.

The Non-African

Tanganyika is an immense territory of some 362,000 square miles, with a great variety of mountains, great plains, and forests. It borders the Indian Ocean on the east and the second-largest lake in the world, Lake Victoria, on the northwest. Its population, surprisingly small for such a vast region, numbers about 9 million, according to the 1960 census. Only small areas are arable, which limits the population. Rainfall is scanty.

Non-African penetration in East Africa goes back to the Greeks and Phoenicians. Relics of the Arab period, 1100–1300 A.D., during which coastal towns thrived on the inland trade, are found all along the coast between Mombasa, in Kenya, and Dar es Salaam, the capital of Tanganyika. These were partly destroyed by the Portuguese, who first arrived in the thirteenth century and built their forts along the coast. Over the centuries, the Portuguese and the Arabs fought periodic battles for control, and finally the Arabs, under the Sultan of Zanzibar, prevailed. East Africa was invaded again in the nineteenth century, this time by the leading European powers. Following the explorations of Dr. Karl Peters, the Germans took control of Tanganyika in 1885. In

World War I, the British drove the Germans out and turned the
colony into a mandate territory under the League of Nations,
and Tanganyika became a trust territory under the United Nations in 1946.

Because of these numerous influences, Tanganyikan society has
a multiracial upper stratum. Non-Africans account for only 1.5
per cent of the population, but they dominate the country's economic and political life. According to the 1957 census, there
were 20,598 Europeans, 71,760 Indo-Pakistanis, 4,776 Goans,
19,000 Arabs, and 2,257 Coloreds.[7]

The Goans, although Asiatic, are Catholic. The product of
early Portuguese influence, they have become, like the Indians,
the traders and merchants of the economy. The Africans regard
the Indians with great distrust because of their sharp trading
practices and their clannishness. The European population is of
mixed origin. When the British took over from the Germans,
they appropriated some of their lands and industries, but not all.
Half the European population is British. (Next door in Kenya
the vast majority are English, with an unshakable loyalty to the
Queen.) The settlers are industrious coffee- and sisal-plantation
owners and cattle ranchers. Arabs are found mainly in the coastal
towns; like the Indians, they are traders, but they have not
prospered.

"We have the land, the Asians have the money, the Europeans
control the government." This has long been the African way of
describing race relations. Now that the Africans have taken control of the government, the non-African minorities are trying
desperately to find a basis of accommodation with the Africans.
They hope to keep their land and to continue in their leading
role in Tanganyika's economic and financial life. Resentment
over past expropriation of their land by white settlers lies at the
root of much of African racial bitterness and political feeling.
The nationalists have not forgotten the racial discrimination en-
forced by British and German settlers and officials in hotels,
restaurants, schools, and medical facilities. Among the leaders of
all races, there is hope that this racial conflict is a nightmare of
the past, but wishful thinking cannot dispel it. Much hard work

in building confidence remains to be done if racialism is to be minimized in politics.

TANU and Nyerere

Julius Nyerere is regarded by the British officials who gradually handed over power to him as the greatest of the African nationalists. This slight, soft-spoken, but very determined young African asserted that he would establish a "no-nonsense government" with no victimizing of minority races or outbreaks of tribalism. This he did. But when Nyerere resigned in early 1962, some observers thought that he had lost the internal struggle with the ultras and racialists within TANU. This is too definite a conclusion, though. By turning over the government to his young and more radical lieutenant, Rashidi Kawawa, Nyerere could concentrate on building and educating TANU into a progressive and enlightened force, for the future of Tanganyika depends far more upon TANU than upon Nyerere. But he has set himself a tremendously difficult task. In the revolutionary climate of East Africa, the moderate, Westernized philosophy of Julius Nyerere faces great odds.

Nyerere is an unassuming man with the ascetic nature of Mahatma Gandhi and the organizing genius of Kwame Nkrumah. He knows the peasant masses and how to arouse their passionate support, but at the same time he possesses an astute insight into the Western—particularly the British—mind. Like many other African nationalists, he has studied abroad. After a teacher-training course at Makerere College in Uganda, he took an M.A. at the University of Edinburgh (1952). He taught for several years at a Catholic secondary school near Dar es Salaam, until finally the headmaster asked him to choose between politics and teaching.

TANU swept the 1959 and 1960 elections, encountering no serious opposition. The United Tanganyika Party, based on multiracial ideas and given quiet British official support, was buried in the 1959 elections. To the left of TANU, the Tanganyika African National Congress tries to whip up feeling against Nyerere's conservatism and "collaboration" with members of other races in government. Its leader, Zaburi Mtemvu, is a disgruntled former member of TANU; he has little support, but Mtemvu preaches a dangerous brand of racialism that, under certain conditions, might catch fire.

Neither tribalism nor religious differences broke up the solid front of the TANU of "Bwana Julius" in its early rise to power. A unique feature of Tanganyika is the good feeling between tribes. There is certainly rivalry, as between the Masai and the Chagga, but nothing to compare with the distrust between tribes in neighboring Uganda and Kenya. One reason for this is the great number of tribes—approximately 120—none of which has ever been dominant. The largest tribe is the Sukuma, in the Lake Province, who number more than a million and who have excellent relations with their neighbors. Also, the TANU leaders have learned from the West African experience of clashes between traditionalists and modernists. A conscious effort has been made to suppress religious and tribal antagonisms, and Nyerere used all his authority to promote unity. But after independence, tensions became more serious.

Nyerere propounds a highly sophisticated political philosophy that combines the Commonwealth orientation of Balewa with the pan-African socialism of Nkrumah. His primary aim is rapid economic and social development, planned and controlled by a powerful central government. He denies that this necessitates authoritarian rule, and believes that African democracy is a product peculiar to African soil. However, there is little room for opposition to the government party in Nyerere's democracy.

In an address to an American audience on this subject, he said: "The presence of an organized opposition as a visible symbol of democracy is not, in fact, universal. It is, rather, the Anglo-Saxon's symbolic demonstration of his own democracy and implies the existence of a class struggle."[8]

He argued that African society is entirely different, that it is possible that for some time to come there may not exist in Tanganyika the basic differences that produce a multiparty system. As long as the people elect representatives and have the opportunity to "shout against" the government if they choose, he contends, the essence of democracy is preserved. Like many West African leaders, Nyerere believes that to preserve unity and make progress, criticism must take place within a single party.

In Nyerere's view, the African's loyalty to the nation is simply an extension of his loyalty to the community. This means that conflicts between the individual and the state, so typical of the individualism of Western society, are not apt to arise in the "communitarian" African society.

Within TANU, there is opposition to Nyerere, based on ideological and personality differences. The powerful cooperative and trade-union movements have long been grumbling. If their demands for rapid economic progress and equalization of opportunity are not heeded within TANU, they may seek other avenues of expression. A split has developed within the Tanganyika Federation of Labour, with the railway workers leading a strong dissent against the government.

Prime Minister R. M. Kawawa, at the time he was leader of the Tanganyika Federation of Labour, expressed skepticism about nonracial politics while Europeans and Indians still monopolized most economic opportunities. In an article on "Africanisation," he wrote:

> To ask the indigenous Africans to forget the agony of their past is to ask them to ignore the lesson that their experience has taught them. Asians and Europeans are crying in Tanganyika for non-racial parties, but just how practical is this? Those non-racial political parties which have been formed in Tanganyika have never succeeded, for they never aimed at emancipating the African, but only at deluding him into satisfaction with the lowest rung.[9]

Under Kawawa, Africanization is apt to be pressed more vigorously. The resignation of the European Minister of Finance, Sir Ernest Vasey, was one of the first steps in this direction. But Kawawa has clearly placed himself behind Nyerere's policy of "no nonsense" in race relations.

The Transition

In September, 1960, the British Trusteeship Government created what it called "responsible government," meaning internal self-rule, for Tanganyikans. A 71-member elective legislature was formed, with a very limited power to nominate additional members. Of the prescribed seats, 11 were reserved for Asians and 10 for Europeans. TANU let it be known that this racial alloca- tion was only temporary and that it would shortly press for nonracial representation. This would not exclude racial minori- ties from the legislature, as several European and Indian repre- sentatives could be and have been elected with the support of Africans.

A cabinet was formed, with nine out of the twelve members drawn from elected TANU members. Nyerere was made Chief Minister, with the Governor, Sir Richard Turnbull, retaining final executive authority. Two powerful African members of this first cabinet were C. G. Kahama, Minister for Home Affairs, who is a leader of the cooperative movement, and R. M. Kawawa, who heads the fast-growing Tanganyika Federation of Labour. A popular European settler, D. N. M. Bryceson, was made Min- ister for Health and Labour. An Indian friend of Nyerere's, Amir Jamal, was appointed Minister of Communications, Power, and Works. After conferences between TANU and the colonial sec- retary in early 1961, the British granted the new government full autonomy in May, and Nyerere became Prime Minister. Shortly thereafter it was agreed that independence was to be granted in December, 1961.

Once legislative seats reserved for non-Africans are vacated, the fate of European and Indian representation in the govern- ment will depend upon the will of Nyerere and upon TANU. Non-Africans are excluded from TANU, although Nyerere has told many observers, including the author, that he intends to eliminate this restriction as soon as African political control is consolidated.

The United Nations can claim credit for removing several roadblocks in the way of this rapid constitutional advance. In 1954, a U.N. Visiting Mission stirred up a great deal of hos- tility among the settlers by calling for abandonment of the racial- parity system and introduction of a more representative legisla- tive council. In addition, the U.N. Trusteeship Council pub- lished a report of the mission that estimated the territory might become independent within twenty to twenty-five years. Iron- ically, this was criticized by the settlers and some British authorities as being too precipitate. Nevertheless, these suggestions set in motion the steps toward reform which resulted in far more rapid changes than even Nyerere had thought possible.

Despite the misgivings of some settlers, all groups adjusted to the accelerated pace, so that Tanganyika moved a good distance toward Nyerere's primary goal, "to assure that every citizen, whatever his color, can feel confident and safe about his future in Tanganyika."[10]

Poverty and Progress

Continued harmonious relations depend to a great extent on the rate of economic advance. "In a developing country there is more than work enough for everyone with a skill who is willing to work," one of the leaders of the Indian community, a minister in the new government, told me.

Tanganyika has considerable untapped resources, yet it is not a wealthy country. It lacks the vast mineral wealth of neighboring Congo or the fertile soil of Uganda. Its wealth lies primarily in the arable land, suitable for a variety of tropical crops, such as sisal, coffee, cotton, tea, tobacco, pyrethrum, sugar, and cashew nuts.

Cash-crop cultivation must be greatly expanded, especially by African farmers. Virtually 95 per cent of Tanganyika's African population is engaged in agriculture. Thus, prosperity for the average family depends on the improvement of farming methods and the types of crops raised. Tanganyika's most important crop, sisal, is grown almost entirely by non-African planters. Pyrethrum, used in insecticides, was exclusively a settlers' crop until the late 1950's, but is now being promoted as a crop for African cooperatives and small growers. In recent years, African production of coffee and cotton has increased remarkably, both in yield and in quality, under the direction of government agriculture officials.

Three major areas of concentration have been selected for government development—land, credit, and education. Vast areas of land can be reclaimed for cultivation and settlement. Surveys have been made for projects using the great waters of Lake Vic-

toria in the Lake Province region. A German plan for a vast irri
gation system in Sukumaland, which is lower in elevation than
the great lake, is being revived. A highly successful water-develop-
ment project has been carried out at Makonda, in the Southern
Province. Ten thousand gallons an hour are pumped to supply
an area of 380 square miles, where people formerly had to walk
over a 1500-foot escarpment for eight hours to fetch water. The
FAO has undertaken a survey of the Rufizi Basin in the south-
central region, which could bring hundreds of square miles into
cultivation.

Measures have been taken to establish more effective systems
of land tenure through village councils. Such programs are indispensable, if significant amounts of credit and capital are to
become available to the African farmer. Nyerere intends to push
ahead rapidly by expanding existing government credit agencies such as the Local Development Loan Fund and the African
Productivity Loan Fund. By 1959, 452 programs of community
development, such as water supply and roads, were under way.
The African Productivity Loan Fund, begun by an American
ICA grant, has helped finance improved farming methods for
numerous small African growers.

African farmer cooperatives have made phenomenal progress
in Tanganyika. By 1960, one-fourth of all commodity exports
(more than $28 million in value) were produced by cooperatives.[11]
The Kilimanjaro Native Cooperative Union, one of the most
successful, processes and markets its members' coffee. Another
fast-growing cooperative union has sprung up in the Lake Province, where African farmers operate several cotton ginneries
that net additional returns to more than 100,000 members.[12] One
of the most remarkable new cooperatives is the Meru Cooperative
Union near Arusha. A smaller, less developed tribal cooperative,
it has heightened greatly the amount and quality of its members' produce, under the direction of an American adviser. Part
of the surpluses earned go into a fund for overseas scholarships
for young members of the tribe. African cooperatives have been
in the forefront of this self-help approach to training new leaders
in cooperative practices and other essential professions of a developing society.

The Tanganyika Agriculture Corporation has had some success in applying cooperative principles to resettlement projects
in newly opened areas cleared of the tsetse fly. The corporation
supplies the machinery and supervision and then buys the crops;
the new settlements supply the labor and the land. At Urambo,
in the Western Province, 200-acre units brought into production
now earn over $1400 per year. In the southern highlands, a
project is under way to grow wattle, used for tanning leather.[13]
Programs of this type can be expanded substantially to provide
a rapid rise in African productivity and prosperity.

Mineral wealth is apparently limited in Tanganyika, although
much territory remains to be thoroughly explored. The famous
Williamson Diamond Mine at Mwadui exported $12,292,000
worth of diamonds in 1958. This mine, famous for its gem diamonds, yielded the largest diamond in the world. On the death
of Williamson, the government of Tanganyika bought a one-
half ownership of the mine from De Beers. A large coalfield at
Songes cannot be brought into production until a rail line is
built. Deposits of gold, iron ore, and niobium are under development.[14]

Like all the new nations, Tanganyika has promising development plans. The new African ministers and their European and
Indian associates fully intend to generate enthusiasm among all
the people for the new development programs in education and
productivity. Nyerere and the TANU leadership, while envision-
ing large possibilities, have a realistic view of their limitations.
One of the African ministers informed me that additional capital and resources for progress will have to come from within
Tanganyika, and not from outside. As head of the government
and party leader, Nyerere misses few chances to urge his people
to greater efforts. The party slogan is *"Uhuru na kaze"* ("Freedom and hard work").

Fulfillment of Tanganyika's development programs has been
made difficult by the drop in world market prices for sisal, coffee,
and other commodities. This caused the government to cut its
capital expenditures for 1959–60 by some £2 million.[15]

African leaders are looking at what can be done at home before
going abroad for help. They believe that additional capital

can be derived from increasing export-import levies and other taxes. This would mean cutbacks in consumption, which can be politically dangerous. Outside aid may ease the strain. England's Colonial Development Fund, in late 1960, announced a loan of $3 million, and in 1961 the United Kingdom agreed to a further loan of $11.2 million for Tanganyika's Development Program, plus additional sums to help compensate overseas officers. This helps, but it is only a trickle of the stream of capital which Tanganyika must find. A World Bank mission surveyed the prospects of Tanganyika in 1960. Development programs like the Rufizi River Basin project surveyed by the FAO will cost £80 to £100 million. With a total national budget of only £21 million, Tanganyika is hard-pressed for capital.

Tanganyika's educational system lags behind those of other East African territories. Middle and secondary schools especially need development. In advanced areas like Moshi, the population is virtually 100 per cent literate, but among less prosperous tribes, illiteracy is very high. At the present rate of progress, 450,000 children will be in the primary grades by 1964, and 1 per cent of that number will be in secondary school. Support for expanded education programs is being vigorously explored by the new government. A University College of Tanganyika is under development, to supplement the overburdened East African facilities.

The United States, which has taken a keen interest in Tanganyika's future, has loaned it $1.9 million from the Development Loan Fund for improvement of its road system. Technical workers and a Peace Corps team are now at work on a road survey.

However, by the middle of 1961, Tanganyika had not received the substantial capital aid indispensable to rapid development. Dramatic gestures of support like the Peace Corps are invaluable, but they cannot substitute for vitally needed capital.

East African Federation

The destiny of Tanganyika is interwoven with that of the other British areas in East Africa: Kenya, Zanzibar, Uganda, and perhaps Nyasaland. The East African High Commission provides close financial, communications, and customs ties. All the African leaders in these territories have expressed their desire to continue these functional links and to initiate political federation. Already, close political liaison connects the nationalist movements of these East African areas through the Pan-African Freedom Movement of East and Central Africa (PAFMECA). An East African Federation is the major political goal, once all have gained independence. Although many obstacles lie in the way, this proposed union may be more realistic than federation schemes in other parts of Africa. The pre-independence economies of these East African areas have been tied closely together, and British policy has long encouraged closer union. It is, of course, the British hope that after independence the entire region will continue its close associations with the Commonwealth.

Foreign policy has not been clearly formulated at this writing, but Nyerere's statements over a period of time indicate clearly that an official policy of neutrality within the Commonwealth will be pursued. Nyerere has participated actively in the All Africa Peoples conferences organized by Nkrumah. The influence of the new leaders of Kenya and Uganda will be substantial, and the East African countries will continue to cooperate closely on external affairs, because of their customs and currency union. It is likely that the foreign policy which will emerge will be pan-African and nonaligned, between the views of Nkrumah and Balewa.

Optimism over East Africa under the leadership of Julius Nyerere and other Westernized nationalists should not obscure the fact that Tanganyika is not free from the explosive forces of African nationalism which we have noted in other parts of Africa. Tribal conflicts in Uganda can arouse traditionalist forces elsewhere. Also, there are many indications that racial hostilities in Kenya are not subsiding, despite progress toward self-rule and changing attitudes. Many Africans and whites have not forgotten the bitter days of Mau Mau. Yet there is a chance that Mboya and Kenyatta can hold race hatred in check. If these rational leaders fail, Tanganyika and all Africa will be rent by racial conflicts.

Beneath the surface of vastly improved race relations lurks the danger of counterracialism. This can be whipped into black chauvinism by extremist ultra-Africanists who seek power by attacking Westernization. Communist influence is bound to grow as the Communist bloc is allowed to open direct relations with East Africa. Communism does not hesitate to exploit racialism. A degeneration of race relations in Southern Rhodesia or South Africa, which would implicate the West in the eyes of African nationalists, could inflame passions. The greatest hope for unity and harmony lies in concentrating on achieving rapid progress in the programs first laid out by Nyerere. The West should avoid becoming involved in the defense of the settlers' interests. The speedy betterment of life for all East Africans must be the primary goal. Thus development rather than racialism must be made the focus of concentration.

Tanganyika is an experiment in social development which we cannot allow to fail. In speaking of the Commonwealth and race relations, the President of TANU said:

> Here in Tanganyika we believe passionately in accepting peoples as they are, as human beings. We believe it is wrong to say that individuals are good or bad because they happen to belong to a particular country. We believe it is equally nonsensical to judge them by the colour of the skin. It is not always easy to overcome the prejudice of human beings; but here in Tanganyika we are trying and we shall do it and nobody is going to get unfair treatment because he is of a different colour from those who happen to be the majority.[16]

Finally, America and the West might well ponder the challenge in the following statement by Nyerere: "Tanganyika has become an example to the whole of Africa. As a matter of expediency alone, not only as a matter of morals or ethics, we must recognize this."[17]

THE IVORY COAST AND THE FRENCH COMMUNITY

Under the leadership of its lively and eloquent President, Félix Houphouet-Boigny, the Ivory Coast has become one of the most important ideological centers and commercial capitals of what is broadly known as French-speaking Africa. Using his powerful political appeal, Houphouet-Boigny has molded a coalition of Westernized African states, called the Brazzaville Twelve, in opposition to the ultra-Africanist Ghana-Guinea-Mali group. These pro-French states, led by the Ivory Coast, are all in orbit around France, although not all are members of the French Community.

The Brazzaville Twelve include the West African states of Ivory Coast, Dahomey, Niger, Upper Volta, Senegal, and Mauritania; the Equatorial African states of Chad and Gabon; the Central African Republic; and the Congo Republic (Brazzaville). The Malagasy Republic, formerly known as Madagascar—an island off the coast of East Africa—somewhat reluctantly joined the group under the leadership of its extremely pro-French President, Philip Tsiranana. Cameroun, former French Trust Territory, became the twelfth member. The group was so named because its first meeting was held at Brazzaville, in December, 1960. At its third meeting, the official name was chosen: The Union of African States and Malagasy.

Despite the severance of direct political ties with France—and the weakening of links to the French Community, as well—French culture, economic aid, and trade remain major connecting ties. Among the African intellectuals and political elite, French philosophy, art, and literature are extremely influential. *Présence Africaine,* which is edited by the Senegalese Alioune Diop and reflects the African response to the challenge of French culture, is one of the most influential journals in West Africa. All of these new, French-speaking republics have adopted French political forms, with a president and an elected assembly. However, in most of these countries, the typical African one-party system prevails, rather than the French pattern of multiple parties.

Each republic is different, but all share a common ideological orientation and political structure. The Ivory Coast is the most important and representative of this group.

Origins of the RDA

Ivory Coast politics is presided over by the man who led a political movement that once dominated virtually all of French

West Africa. At that time, the French regarded him as the
most dangerous of all African politicians. He was allied with
the Communists and fomented rebellion in many territories.
Some years later, he was lionized by the French and made a
member of French cabinets, and even Minister of State (1957–59).
Born on October 18, 1905, in Yamoussokro, a village of the
Ivory Coast, Félix Houphouet-Boigny was the son of a great
family of Baoulé chieftains and thereby marked for leadership.
He received the training of a Westernized nationalist, graduating
as a medical assistant from a medical school in Dakar in 1925.
For fifteen years, he practiced medicine; meanwhile he also grew
cocoa and gradually became prosperous. He was led into politics
by the highly discriminatory price differential imposed in the
French market, to favor the French cocoa planters. Few political
movements in French West Africa have agrarian roots, but
Houphouet-Boigny managed to persuade his fellow African
planters to form a union, the Syndicat Agricole Africain (SAA)
in September, 1944.[18] The SAA became the financial center of a
common front with the more radical urban areas in the formation of the Parti Démocratique de la Côte d'Ivoire (PDCI). This,
in turn, became the Ivory Coast Section of the interterrito-
rial movement, Rassemblement Démocratique Africain (RDA),
launched in 1946. Throughout French-speaking Africa, Houphouet-Boigny found support for the RDA. Movement and organization across territorial lines was facilitated by the centralized
pattern of French rule, which treated the territories within West
Africa and Equatorial Africa as unified administrative units. New
and more radical leaders—like Sékou Touré of Guinea—emerged
in other territories to support the RDA, and a decade of protracted struggle began between French colonialism, which supported the interests and investments of the French settlers, and
the new, mass-based, nationalist parties.

By the middle 1950's, Houphouet-Boigny had become less
radical; in the left wing of the RDA he was known as an apologist
for France, particularly when he accepted a post in a French
cabinet. For nearly a decade, Houphouet-Boigny tried to strad-
dle French and African politics, living in Paris and going only
occasionally to Abidjan.

French Policy

France pursued a policy of assimilation of her overseas territories as late as 1956. The objective was to absorb into a Greater France the peoples and cultures of other continents. Independence was an unthinkable concept to French administrators; African nationalists who proclaimed this goal in "free" elections were clapped into jail.

Assimilation is now recognized as unrealizable. It was broken on the rocks of alien African culture which the French had assumed to be inferior to their own. The renaissance of African life and culture, propelled by the driving force of nationalism, proved to be much more vigorous than Western colonial powers had realized. Exaggerated notions of the weakness and primitiveness of African culture have often blinded the judgment of the colonizers. What is remarkable about formerly French West Africa is that so much interchange with France has survived the failure of assimilation.

In the Ivory Coast, as in other parts of West Africa, there were well-advanced kingdoms before the arrival of the French. Early European travelers have left records of the kingdoms of Krindjabo, Bettie, Indenie, and Boundoukou in the southeastern and northern sections.[19] Quarrels and warfare among these kingdoms weakened them, and after the introduction of slave trade on a large scale—first by the Portuguese and then by the French—their decline was rapid. French control over the tribes of the Ivory Coast, which began about 1887, was always uneasy. The revolts of 1906 left only a narrow coastal strip under French control. However, through the application of severe measures, the French re-established sway, only to face another revolt in 1916. Once again, superior technology prevailed, and French control was restored in the Ivory Coast.

The French conquerors had little respect for tribal institutions. Many hereditary chieftainships were abolished, and the people were ruled directly by a centralized administration. This policy of the French was, of course, fiercely resented by the Africans. However, it has in recent years provided the nationalist movement with a significant advantage; Houphouet-Boigny has had nothing like the trouble with nascent tribalism that has plagued Nkrumah in neighboring Ghana.

In the years immediately after World War II, with the exception of a short-lived period of reform in 1945–46, the French treated any opposition to assimilation as treason. Their tough policy evoked violent and radical African reactions.

From Radicalism to Collaboration

The RDA's rise to power in the Ivory Coast and other parts of French West and Equatorial Africa was marked initially by moderation. This was followed by a swing to extremism, violence, and Communism, and, finally, by fragmentation and conservative consolidation. In its initial phase, the RDA pulled together a great coalition which included a few Europeans, a small contingent of African bourgeoisie (coffee and cocoa planters), peasants, young intelligentsia, Moslem Dioulas, and trade unionists. Its peaceful tactics were highly successful. However, by 1948, Communist influence had grown under leaders like G. d'Arboussier, who had decided to transform the bourgeois movement into a militant, revolutionary arm.[20]

France's brief period of toleration for nationalism turned into repression as alarm spread among the small but highly influential bloc of French planters and businessmen. In the face of such opposition, the nationalists sought allies among the political parties in Continental France. The only party willing to give unqualified sympathy and support were the Communists; as members of the earliest postwar governments of France, they were in a strategic position to assist. Moreover, French political parties could not be outlawed in overseas territories, although native parties could be. The Socialists were the only other French party to take a direct interest in African nationalist organizations. They managed to gain considerable influence in Senegal through the poet-politician Léopold Sédar Senghor and the Bloc Démocratique Sénégalais (BDS), later the Union Progressiste Sénégalaise (UPS).

Through the RDA, the Communists gained extensive influence. This led to the resignation of more moderate leaders such as

Etienne Djaument of the Ivory Coast, who were close to the French administration. Repressive countertactics against the RDA resulted in mob action and numerous arrests, further inflaming the ultra-nationalist elements of the party.

In these early years, Houphouet-Boigny was often called a Communist by his adversaries, but such accusations were unfounded, and he himself stated on many occasions that the alliance was one of convenience. However, because of the intense fear of Communism, such charges sharpened the repressive measures of the French and at the same time badly split the moderates and the radicals of the RDA. Houphouet-Boigny, who as leader of the RDA had become virtual ruler of French West Africa, began to lose power and support, which weakened his bargaining position with the French. A shrewd political strategist, he gradually turned on the radical and Communist-influenced elements and systematically drove them out of the RDA. By 1954, the RDA was transformed, and its strength was increasing. With the 1956 elections (promulgated under the Loi Cadre, whose constitutional revisions granted internal autonomy to overseas territories), the RDA in the Ivory Coast was restored to grace.[21] However, Houphouet-Boigny's influence had waned in other areas of French West Africa such as Guinea, where the powerful trade-union leader Sékou Touré had refused to follow the RDA's leader on the road back to moderation. Their differences soon brought a major ideological split, which does much to explain Guinea's departure from the French Community in the 1958 referendum on the Constitution of the Fifth Republic. Guinea voted an overwhelming "no," the Ivory Coast a massive "yes."

Following the referendum, major differences erupted between the Ivory Coast and several other French-speaking republics. The issue of West African federation versus federation with France divided Houphouet-Boigny from Léopold Sédar Senghor of Senegal. As a member of the French Cabinet, the Ivory Coast leader sharply opposed a closer union among West African states, since this would weaken French influence. Greater independence from France was the goal of Senghor and other West African leaders who formed the Parti du Regroupement Africain

(PRA). Senegal and the Sudan eventually formed the abortive Mali Federation, and Houphouet-Boigny barely managed to keep Upper Volta and Dahomey out of it. Although the Mali Federation broke up—because of quarrels between the two member republics—it started all the republics moving toward independence from France. In 1960, France finally conceded the inevitability of independence and amended the constitution of the French Community to permit independent states to remain within the Community. All the republics chose independence. Confronted with this overwhelming sentiment, Houphouet-Boigny did an about-face and led his country to independence. This shrewd reversal preserved his leadership in what remained of the RDA in West and Equatorial Africa, but his opposition to federation contributes to the Balkanization of French-speaking Africa. Since independence, much of his effort has been spent in attempting to pull former French territories into a closer union.

Houphouet-Boigny's opposition to a West African Federation is not simply the result of an affection for France, as many of his critcis have surmised. In a thorough study of the French West African economy, Elliot Berg concludes that Ivory Coast opposition to federation stems from a long history of subsidizing the other French West African territories. He says:

> The Ivory Coast position rests on a profound sense of economic grievance—that it has been, as its leaders say, the cow that the other territories never tire of milking. The basis of this sense of injury lies in the recent history of federal finance in the country.[22]

Thus, the Ivory Coast is willing to cooperate closely with other African states in customs unions and currency agreements—but so long as its per capita income is substantially greater than that of its neighbors (and only Senegal approaches it in development), political union is impossible.

One-Party Rule

When the Ivory Coast received complete independence in November, 1960, Houphouet-Boigny became president of the new state. His office is similar in prestige and power to the

French presidency. In addition, the Ivory Coast president is head of the administration and prime minister combined. No other Ivory Coast political leader approaches him in power. He can veto legislation, and a two-thirds vote of the National Assembly is necessary to override his veto, as under the U.S. Constitution. In addition, he is head of the armed forces and has complete control of foreign policy.[23]

There is universal suffrage in the Ivory Coast, and the president and the national assembly are elected simultaneously every five years. The first election was held in November, 1960, when Houphouet-Boigny was elected overwhelmingly, and his party, the PDCI (the Ivory Coast affiliate of the RDA), and its allies swept all seventy seats of the assembly. Since only one party is permitted, this victory surprised no one. The election actually amounts to a ratification or rejection of presidential policies.

The one-party system of the Ivory Coast is considered democratic by some observers, who believe that the single political party does permit the expression of opposite points of view within itself. Gwendolen Carter believes that the PDCI hierarchy is extremely sensitive to the wishes of the people and allows for "continuous interaction between groups striving for influence." However, prospects of violence between dissatisfied ethnic groups remain. Miss Carter maintains that, at the outset, the initial government of Houphouet-Boigny was benevolent and popular. It remains to be seen whether it will successfully resist the inevitable tendency of one-party systems to become more hierarchical and authoritarian for the purpose of repressing unreconciled differences. It is significant that the youthful leaders of the PDCI feel considerable dissatisfaction with Houphouet-Boigny's pro-French, moderate, anti-Guinea policies. Thus, ultra-Africanism bides its time within the party structure. The drift of events since 1958 has been increasingly in its favor.

Tribalism is not a serious problem among the peoples of the Ivory Coast, but bitter resentment is directed against the "outsiders" who have come in by the thousands from Dahomey, Togoland, and Nigeria. These feelings erupted in the violent riots of 1958, which resulted in many deaths and much destruction of property.

The total population of 3 million includes some 12,000 non-Africans—French, Lebanese, Syrians, and Italians. The African population consists of six major tribal groups: the Aznis-Ashantis-Baoulés in the southeast; the Kona-Kona and Krounen in the southwest; the Mande clan (including the Dioulas) in the northeast and northwest; the Voltaic clan, also in the northeast; the Senonjo clan in the north; and the Dans and Gouros in the center.[24] Regional representation is effected by general councils elected in four departments—North, Center, Southeast, and Southwest—which are in turn divided into a total of nineteen subprefectures. Chiefly powers, curtailed by the French, have been rendered largely ceremonial by the new government.

Rapid Development

Economic growth has been rapid over the last decade. Between 1947 and 1957, France invested $109 million in the Ivory Coast, through the Fund for International Economic and Social Development (FIDES). Much of this was longterm loans, but some was outright grants for social and welfare programs. FIDES (now FAC, the Fund for Aid and Cooperation) assists countries which have signed agreements of cooperation with France. This assistance, plus preferential trading agreements, constituted an important factor in the African republics' decision to retain close economic ties with France. Through FIDES, the French government poured a remarkable amount of public capital into the development of her sub-Sahara African territories, amounting to $2.14 billion from 1947 to 1958.[25]

Now that direct French control has ended, and the economic initiative has shifted from French enterprise to the African government, the prospect is uncertain that the same volume of capital will continue to flow into the Ivory Coast. Consequently, the major development problem for the new government is to find alternative sources of assistance without losing the good will of the French, who are jealous lovers. These may be found within the new European Economic Community, in which the Ivory Coast and the eleven other Brazzaville powers, plus Mali, have an associate status.

The Ivory Coast is the most prosperous of the formerly French sub-Sahara territories. Since 1948, the volume of exports—of which coffee and cocoa constitute 75 to 80 per cent—has more than doubled. Further, the quality of these products has been vastly improved, through better methods of processing and marketing. Wood and bananas have risen high on the list of valuable exports. Minerals have been discovered in quantity. Some 13 million tons of manganese have been reported at Grand Labou, and estimates are that 100,000 tons can be exported annually.

Transportation and harbor facilities are far ahead of those of most other former French African territories. Abidjan boasts an excellent harbor and one of the best airports in Africa, constructed with French aid. There are sixteen secondary airfields in the back country. A railway line connects the Ivory Coast with the Upper Volta, and the ocean port gives access to the West African interior. However, vast railway expansion is needed before the hinterland can be opened up at a desirable speed.

Education has made corresponding progress. Despite the high birth rate, the number of enrolled children of school age rose from 9 per cent of the total in 1947 to 28 per cent of the total in 1958. Almost one-fifth of the national budget is expended for education. But, despite substantial progress, the Ivory Coast has a long way to go to match neighboring Ghana, which in 1959 had 86 per cent of its school-age children enrolled.

Like Touré and Nkrumah, Houphouet-Boigny has initiated five-year plans for economic development. But there is less sloganeering about the virtues of socialism as against those of free enterprise. Among the younger intelligentsia, Marxism and the examples of Russia and China have made a deep impression. But there is much more wariness about receiving Communist aid than there is in the former British and the North African states. This is because the present RDA leadership is Westernized and the ultra-Africanists have been repressed. Nevertheless, tales of Communist contributions to economic well-being and independence filter across the borders from Ghana and Guinea, and inflame the imaginations of the young.

Close economic association with France is a key to the development plans of the Ivory Coast. Nearly 64 per cent of her exports

were to the franc area in 1959, and 73 per cent of her imports
came from there.[26] The European Economic Community has
opened up new opportunities for trade and investment for the
African republics of the French Community. Such heavy dependence on France and Europe is a source of dissatisfaction
to the ultra-Africanists, who feel that France has neocolonial
aims in keeping "French Africa" dependent upon her. Alternative sources of aid and trade exist, with America and the Sino-
Soviet bloc, but neither of them has been developed extensively
by the Houphouet-Boigny government. Until the middle of 1961,
the radical wing of the RDA had prevented the Ivory Coast
from formally re-entering the French Community after achieving independence in 1960, although certain agreements for close
political and economic cooperation with France were signed.

The Pull of Pan-Africanism

What, then, is the future of the Westernized nationalism of
Houphouet-Boigny and the Ivory Coast in the French-speaking
states of Africa? We have observed how rapidly this highly pro-
French nationalism has moved, since 1958, to a state of increas-
ing independence. Through the Brazzaville Twelve and the
Entente, the Westernized nationalists have attempted to create
broad associations for economic integration and to satisfy pan-
African sentiment.

The West African Council of the Entente—consisting of the
Ivory Coast, Upper Volta, Dahomey, and Niger—was formed
in 1959 to offset the influence of the Mali Federation. Led by
the Ivory Coast, the Entente meets twice annually and has a
permanent secretariat. The members have a customs union, and
coordinate their policies on taxation, public administration,
labor legislation, public works, transportation, and communications. This cooperation gives promise of healthy political and
economic growth. These small states cannot function with stability by themselves, but they may do so through close association, assisted from the outside. Now the Brazzaville Twelve have
carried this diplomatic and economic integration one step further
in the broader-based Monrovia Group.

The rift between the French-speaking states and the Casablanca powers is not as wide or as unbridgeable as it seems to be on the surface. The issues of Algeria, the Congo, and Mauritania, which appear to separate these two blocs, are merely passing disputes. Even the more fundamental conflict between the Westernized leadership of Houphouet-Boigny and the ultra-Africanism of Nkrumah and Touré appears to be dissolving. Three major factors are responsible.

First, the younger generation of African leaders in the Ivory Coast, as elsewhere, is intensely interested in the forced-march programs of Sékou Touré and is attracted to the militant Africanist slogans of Nkrumah. It should be remembered that the RDA was once a highly radical and anti-Western political movement. It could easily resume this identity as ultra-nationalism grows among the younger leaders, who can exert great influence on Houphouet-Boigny. Second, the pervasive influence of pan-Africanism works against those leaders who seek to perpetuate boundary and political differences derived from colonial days. Houphouet-Boigny and other Westernized nationalists cannot escape responsibility for supporting the anti-federation French policies which led to the Balkanization of French-speaking Africa. Economic unity holds much promise, but there is no logic in confining it to the French Community. The pan-African appeal to transcend the limits of French- or British-speaking areas contains a great deal of realism. Finally, France and her allies find it difficult to refrain from using the Brazzaville Twelve to damp the influence of the Casablanca bloc. But this is a dangerous game, for it strengthens the arguments of the ultra-Africanists that France is promoting "neocolonialism."

The French Community is in danger of falling apart completely in Africa, despite its radical reform. At this late date, there may be little to be done to preserve it as a formal structure.

In any event, it is more important to preserve the spirit rather than the form of French influence. Certainly the influence of French culture will continue for decades, and perhaps centuries. Mutually beneficial economic ties will not be allowed to lapse. Unfortunately, the historic inflexibility of French policy toward Africa may at any moment touch off a new wave of anti-Western

feeling that could destroy many valuable prospects and relationships in French-speaking Africa.

Ultra-Africanism, which is pulling the formerly French areas
away from France, cannot be overcome by Western intervention. Such a move would only intensify anti-Western feeling.
The most that can be done is to keep the channels of communication, aid, and exchange open, even in the event of radical change.

LIBERIA: THE AMERICO-LIBERIAN ELITE AND "NATIONAL UNIFICATION"

Except for those countries settled by whites, Liberia is the
most Westernized African state. Yet it is one of the most underdeveloped. This small West African state has a history of more
than a century of independent existence, dating back to its creation by former American slaves. It is dominated now by the
descendants of former slaves. These Americo-Liberians, as they
are called, formerly comprised a Western aristocracy with a culture "superior" to that of the indigenous populace. But in recent years, under the leadership of President William V. S. Tubman, substantial progress has been made toward assimilating
the indigenous Africans, who make up the vast majority of the
population, into the modern social system. However, from across
the borders of Guinea and the Ivory Coast come voices of the
new mass nationalism, disturbing the sleepy traditionalism of
the hinterland tribes.

The Americo-Liberians

The American Colonization Society was founded in 1820 "to
promote and execute a plan for colonizing with their consent
the free people of color residing in the United States, in Africa,
or such other place as Congress shall deem most expedient."
Two years later, the society landed the first group of colonizers
on a mosquito-ridden island off the west coast of Africa. The
colonists grew in number, and finally extended their dominion
to 43,000 square miles of tropical land. In all, some 13,000 American Negroes were brought to Liberia. Their number was increased by the slaves whom the British and American navies

captured from slave traders and then set free in Liberia. By 1960, there were 15,000 to 20,000 Americo-Liberians, plus 3,000 Americans and Europeans and another 3,000 Lebanese. The rest of the 2 million inhabitants are indigenous Africans. They live in the hinterland, and most of them are primitive, illiterate tribesmen. Some 28 distinct languages are spoken in the hinterland.[27]

The ruling Americo-Liberian elite live in the urban centers, make the laws, and are assuming increasing control of business and industry, which is dominated by the Lebanese and the Europeans. Because of their strong sense of color—most of them are mulatto—and their Western tradition, they have been compared to white minorities in other parts of Africa. This comparison is no longer valid, since considerable integration, even in social life, has taken place. Liberia's early history has created an unfortunate stereotype that is difficult to exorcise. Liberians have a special problem: The Americo-Liberian elite is extremely Westernized, and the indigenous majority is unusually primitive and traditionalist. The gulf separating the two is greater than that in any other West African state. It will not be easy to bridge.

The True Whig Government

Liberia has a highly centralized government, with the locus of power in one man, who heads the one political party. President William V. S. Tubman, a hard-working and effective man, is the leader of the True Whigs. This party, dominated by Americo-Liberians, has ruled Liberia for eighty years. Tubman has been President since 1944; he was re-elected in 1959, by 182,508 votes to 24 for Dr. W. O. Davies Bright. Among the limited electorate, "Shad" Tubman is unquestionably a popular man. However, serious opposition is not tolerated. Opponents like Dihdow Twi, who represented the tribal peoples, particularly the Kra, have been forced into exile by charges of sedition. Opposition to President Tubman also exists on the right, as some Americo-Liberians feel he is moving too rapidly in integrating the tribal peoples.

The electorate is limited to the 150,000 who can meet the

property tax, residence, and English-literacy requirements. The vast majority of Liberians are ruled from the capital, Monrovia, through appointed paramount chiefs, who are responsible to district superintendents. Thus, the True Whig Party does not have the popular base of the CPP in Ghana or the PDCI in the Ivory Coast. Nor do the True Whigs have the democratic processes that prevail in the CPP and PDCI. The Liberian government is less responsive to public opinion and more authoritarian, although in the paternalistic Tubman manner.

Liberia's painstaking imitation of American political institutions extends even to its flag, which has stars and stripes. Two senators are elected from each county for six-year terms, and the thirty-five members of the House of Representatives, three of whom represent the hinterland provinces, are elected for four-year terms. There is a supreme court, and the president appoints his cabinet, whose members head the major executive agencies. The government operates on an annual budget prepared by the president and approved by the legislature. Because of improved education at home and the increasingly numerous young Liberians who have been trained abroad, standards have been rising for the government administrative service. For many years, politics and government have been the major pastime of the leading Americo-Liberian families. Favoritism, nepotism, and corruption have been a major problem for Liberia. But Tubman's progressive administration has done much to eliminate them. Liberia has had both the advantages and the disadvantages of developing without colonial tutelage.[28]

National Unification Policy

In recent years, very rapid economic and social changes have taken place in Liberia. Thousands of indigenous Africans have left the tribal villages for urban life in and around Monrovia. However, the sharp cleavage between the tribal African and the Americo-Liberian remains the basic problem. Virtually all phases of modern life are controlled by whites and Americo-Liberians. They run the big plantations and mining industries, the banks, and the stores. They monopolize the professions, especially law and politics.

Tubman has launched a program he calls "national unification" to hasten the integration of the tribal peoples into all strata. In a major address, he called for the end of Americo-Liberianism:

> We must now destroy all ideologies that tend to divide us. Americo-Liberianism must be forgotten and all of us must register a new era of justice, equality, fair dealing and equal opportunity for everyone from every part of the country, regardless of tribe, clan, section, element, creed, or economic status.[29]

To promote unification, Tubman has appointed one indigenous African to the supreme court and several others to his cabinet. However, dissolution of the tribal system too hastily, without providing sufficient occupational pursuits for the uprooted Africans, as well as educational opportunities, could result in political unrest. For that reason, the unification policy seeks to preserve the major outlines of tribal society.[30]

In the past, the Liberian government has been accused of deliberately keeping indigenous tribes primitive in order to exploit them. Foreign concerns in need of cheap labor—primarily Firestone—were suspected of conniving in this policy. In fact, during the 1920's and 1930's, when the country was weak and dependent on U.S. loans, Firestone was often referred to as the real government of Liberia. For many years, Liberia's major industry was rubber, and the government granted to Firestone, in 1926, a million acres for its plantations. However, Firestone did not really prosper in Liberia until World War II, when the sources of rubber in Southeast Asia were cut off from the Western world.

Ironically, this little country created by former slaves nearly foundered in 1930, when some of its high officials were accused of complicity in slave trading. A League of Nations commission charged that these men had profiteered in a forced-labor system indistinguishable from slavery. After a severe reprimand from the United States, which continued in its historic role of protector against the colonial powers, Liberia initiated reforms.[31]

At the start of this century, certain foreign investment interests, working closely with a corrupt Americo-Liberian group, exploited the people and wealth of Liberia. Under Tubman, most of this has been eliminated. The economy has been diversified. The government is no longer dependent for its revenue and loans on the rubber industry alone. An educated, dedicated group of younger Americo-Liberians is taking over.

Education, once sadly neglected, has forged ahead. By 1958, the education budget was $2 million, compared to $83,000 in the 1940's, and 46,400 students attended elementary schools and 2,600 secondary schools. The University of Liberia has been greatly improved, and Booker T. Washington Institute, a trade school, has been expanded, with U.S. help. The Episcopalian Cuttington College and the Catholic Our Lady of Fatima College have more students and higher standards. In 1958, 447 Liberians were studying in the United States or Europe, many on government scholarships.

Liberia possesses fertile land in abundance and a hot, humid climate suitable for such crops as rubber, coffee, and palm kernels. Even more important, rich deposits of iron ore are under exploitation, and a new diamond industry is being developed. Until after World War II, the economy was dependent upon the fluctuating world market for rubber. Most of this was produced by the Firestone plantations, but in recent years a number of Liberian-owned plantations have been developed.

High-grade iron ore (60-80 per cent iron) is replacing rubber as the country's principal export. The American-owned Liberian Mining Company was the primary developer until the Liberian-American-Swedish Minerals Company was granted a concession in the Nimba range. The Liberian government owns 50 per cent of the new company's stock and now requires that a fixed percentage of stock in new enterprises be reserved for Liberians. These rich deposits are being carefully supervised to insure that much of the proceeds remain in Liberia for further development.

A great leap forward has been made by the Liberian economy since 1942, when the gross domestic product was $51 million. In 1958, it was $130 million. Long-range government planners estimate that, with rising ore exports, this should reach $300 million by 1968. Government participation in development is taken seriously by Tubman, who in 1951 announced a five-year development plan, revised to nine years in 1953. A target of $74 million of public investment was projected, on the expectation that the government would earmark 20 per cent of its revenue for the program. A substantial proportion of the target sum has been realized, with help from the United States particularly. Increased government revenues and outside aid are expected to double government expenditures during the next ten years. Continuing help from the United States and the United Nations is expected at an annual level of between $2.5 and $3.5 million.[32]

Liberia and America

Historically, a special relationship exists between the United States and Liberia. Although the U.S. treated Liberia almost like a forgotten stepchild during the nineteenth and early part of the twentieth century, she exerted her power at critical junctures to protect the little republic from being devoured by the European powers which had carved up the rest of Africa. Much of Liberia's trade is with the United States. In World War II, the U.S. inaugurated a new policy of public investment in Liberia. President Roosevelt initiated the construction of the Free Port of Monrovia, the country's first harbor with docking facilities for ocean-going vessels. Robertsfield Airport was constructed with U.S. funds for military purposes, and has since become an important commercial communications center. Export-Import Bank loans and Point Four technicians have helped expand Liberia's trade and improve the education system. From 1952 to March, 1961, American non-military aid totaled $92 million. This was substantially more than the amounts committed to Nigeria or Ghana, and was surpassed only by the programs in Ethiopia and Libya. Early U.S. aid programs in Liberia were not marked by success. One limiting factor, now abandoned, was the paternalistic policy of staffing ICA projects with only American Negro personnel. American aid has been directed particularly at raising educational standards; $4.9 million was spent on this by 1960. This has met with only partial success because of the Liberian government's view that the expansion of investment opportunities takes priority. In addition, there is a lack of recognition of the importance of raising qualitative, as well as quantitative, standards in Liberia.

Liberia is one of the few African countries to have a mutual-defense pact with the U.S. Some small-arms equipment has been granted to Liberia for border patrols.

Although Liberia is officially neutral in foreign policy, she has a pronounced pro-U.S. bias, and this is likely to continue, as long as President Tubman and his Americo-Liberians remain in power. But this policy could be changed by an upsurge of indigenous Liberian nationalism.

Liberia is surrounded by new African states whose governments and policies are sharply different from its own. The most divergent are Ghana and Guinea, countries based on mass peasant parties and led by ultra-Africanists who are increasingly critical of Liberia's pro-Western position. Although courteous relations have been observed, the militant Africanists do not disguise their distrust of the Americo-Liberian elite.

President Tubman attempts to play the role of conciliator between rival African states. Being representative of neither an ex-French nor an ex-British territory, he is a neutral third party to whom conflicting interests can appeal. He is skeptical of what he calls "utopian and unrealistic" concepts of pan-Africanism, but strongly in favor of close cooperation between the new African states. He attempted to promote a Union of West African States with Ghana and Guinea, shortly after Guinea obtained independence, but the ultra-Africanism of these two countries proved too much for him, and Tubman now seeks allies among the Westernized states.

Monrovia was the site of an important meeting of the Commonwealth and French Community states in May, 1961. All the Brazzaville Twelve attended, along with Nigeria, Sierra Leone, Togoland, Ethiopia, Somaliland, Tunisia, and the Sudan. Although invited, Morocco, Guinea, Ghana, the U.A.R., and Libya failed to send representatives. The major theme of the conference was "noninterference" in one another's affairs, and topics included the Congo, Algeria, and interstate cooperation. Many of the smaller states, among them Liberia, Togoland, and Sierra Leone, expressed a growing fear of possible expansionist designs by the more militant ultra-Africanists. All these Westernized and traditionalist leaders shared a special concern that their authority might be weakened by the infiltration of the more neutralist and socialist ideas of ultra-Africanism. Nigeria's prime minister played an active role at the Monrovia Conference in shaping a moderate, pro-Western neutralism, scorning the utopian pan-Africanists of Accra and plumping for increased communications and trade among the new African states.

Although there are ideological differences between the Monrovia group and the Ghana-Guinea coalition (the Casablanca powers), even greater differences exist within the broad-based Monrovia groups, such as those between Senegal and Ethiopia.

Liberia and Nigeria share a Westernized-nationalist outlook and seek to give a more moderate tone to West African politics. Their efforts have already won warm Western support. For a time, they may succeed in welding a Westernized coalition, but they are building on shifting sands. Ultra-Africanism is effective in reaching the pan-Africanist youth groups in all these countries. Furthermore, Liberia and Nigeria must first solve many internal political problems before there will be any real alternative to the Casablanca powers. Liberia, for her part, must heal the breach of race and culture that intensifies the traditionalist-modernist struggle between her peoples before she can provide continuous, effective leadership in West Africa.

3.

The Rise of
Ultra-Africanism

The third major stage in the development of African nationalism is strongly influenced by Western concepts, but essentially African in perspective. This is the phenomenon of ultra-Africanism, the reassertion of African culture after centuries of subjugation and assault by the Western World.

The upsurge of ultra-Africanism can be attributed in part to the need for counterpropaganda felt by certain African leaders. But to conclude that this is a counterfeit movement, manufactured only to serve the personal ambitions of a few African leaders, is to overlook the deep revolutionary forces astir throughout Africa. All African leaders and their followers feel the necessity for placing their political goals in a truly African center. Some, because of individual circumstances, reach the point of expression earlier than others.

In discussing Nigeria's role in the world, Akin Mabogunje, of the University College of Ibadan, seeks the motivation behind this new approach in these words:

> Out of these two concepts—Pan-Africanism and Negritude—has emerged the desire to project the African personality to the rest of the world. At the bottom of this desire is the dim feeling that the African, in rediscovering his lost dignity, has something special to teach or tell the rest of the world. Those who share this feeling are trying to give it shape and communicate it, whether in the field of international diplomacy or in matters of culture and religion.[1]

Professor Mabogunje is not sure that Ghana expresses the spirit of the new Africa:

> At present what is more evident is a striving to project something, and something that is still rather elusive. Ghana, for instance, is trying to remodel Western democracy to suit what she claims to be the African condition; and only time can show whether what is achieved affects the very substance of democracy or merely its trappings.[2]

Much of ultra-Africanism is still elusive, and doubtless time will reveal more precisely its concepts and practical expressions. Nevertheless, four major political concepts are common to the ultra-Africanist parties of the various new states:

1) Economic and cultural independence from the "neocolonial" West through African integration and diversification of trade and aid.

2) A state program to foster rapid economic growth through communal systems of ownership, production, and distribution.

3) A mass-based one-party system that provides for the expression of divergent viewpoints within the party but evokes and requires national conformity.

4) A pan-African outlook emphasizing the great cultural and racial heritage of the African people and the need to transcend national boundaries, derived from the colonial period, by pan-African political union.

Of course, certain Westernized nationalists share some of these goals, but they differ in more than emphasis. For a parallel in Western ideology, we might compare the advocates of a mixed economy and the proponents of democratic socialism: The former want to preserve the old order of capitalism; the latter seek to reconstruct it into a new system. In Africa, where not only an economic system but a whole culture is at issue, the struggle is not simply between classes, but between civilizations.

Much of Africa has arrived at ultra-Africanism, and because of the highly divergent conditions found in Africa, the brand of ultra-Africanism will be different in each country. Nevertheless, a common set of attitudes and aspirations is emerging. Among the educated younger generation is a restless hunger for identity

and substance. This spirit of seeking is well expressed by a young
African poet, Mabel Imoukhude Jolaoso:

> Here we stand
> infants overblown
> poised between two civilizations,
> finding the balance irksome,
> itching for something to happen,
> to tip us one way or the other,
> groping in the dark for a helping hand—
> and finding none.
> I'm tired, O my God, I'm tired,
> I'm tired of hanging in the middle way—
> But where can I go?
>
> (With acknowledgments to "Odu")[3]

In Ghana and Guinea, this search seems to have ended for
many of the educated elite and a wide cross-section of the illiterate population. Despite the denials of a few skeptics, a mass-
based enthusiasm supports the neo-African views of the two chief
prophets, Sékou Touré and Kwame Nkrumah. In Mali and other
French-speaking states, the attraction of this doctrine is growing,
while in the north, President Nasser of the U.A.R. promotes
through Africa his own brand of pan-Islamic ultra-Africanism.

GHANA: AFRICAN CHARISMA

The achievements of Ghana have exercised a charismatic influence throughout West Africa—and, indeed, all of Africa. Even
though Ghana is small—not much larger than Minnesota—and
has a population only slightly less than 5 million, she has been
the most influential state in sub-Sahara Africa for the last decade.

Ghana, formerly the Gold Coast, was the first African colony
south of the Sahara to gain freedom. Since 1951, when Kwame
Nkrumah was brought from prison and installed as leader of
government business, the peoples of Africa have looked to Ghana
for leadership in their emancipation. Ghana's leaders, particularly Nkrumah, have sparked a series of pan-African conferences

that have added momentum to the African drive toward independence. "Everybody in Ghana considers himself important; and everybody is seized by the importance of Ghana." These words of Ian Colvin are still true. Although Ghana has been surpassed by larger states and even more dramatic changes, it remains an ideological center—a kind of Massachusetts among former African colonies, who look to it for insight and direction.

Ghana's leaders have been acutely conscious of their role on the world stage. Nkrumah, in a now-famous speech delivered in 1957, on the new Ghana constitution, quoted Edmund Burke: "We are on a conspicuous stage and the world marks our demeanor." Nkrumah then went on to say:

> Never has this been truer than today. How we conduct ourselves when we become independent will affect not only Ghana but the whole of Africa . . . If we can make a success of our independence, we shall have made an incalculable contribution towards freedom and progress throughout Africa . . . We must show that it is possible for Africans to rule themselves, to establish a progressive and independent state, and to preserve their national unity.[4]

Although the Nkrumah Government has lost much prestige in the eyes of friendly Western observers because of its treatment of internal opposition, Nkrumah's popularity remains high across Africa.

Nkrumah's nationalism has moved from Westernized to the first stage of ultra-Africanist. This development has disturbed many Westerners and placed Ghana in conflict with other, more Western-oriented African states. However, many moderating aspects give this unusual little country a very special role. Although Nkrumah's pan-African, neutralist policies have taken on a more anti-Western tone, he still associates closely with the British Commonwealth and fosters economic and social programs with Western as well as with Communist nations. Moreover, Ghana's one-party government permits greater opposition to official policies than is found in most of the other new African states. A limited official opposition party is permitted in Ghana. Some Western circles have tended to idealize Ghana and, when all their expectations were not realized, to attack it. Before judgment is passed, what has happened in Ghana must be placed within the context of what has been happening throughout Africa. For Ghana is both unique and fundamentally African.

Revolution in the Gold Coast

The British were latecomers to the Gold Coast. The Portuguese, the Danes, and the Dutch preceded them by two centuries, engaging in trade for slaves, ivory, and gold. Christiansborg Castle by the sea was built by the Danes as a slave-trading fortress and later became the home of British governors. Now it is the residence of the prime minister. Nkrumah moved into these lavish quarters because he wanted to show his people that the stronghold of the imperialists had been taken.

The Gold Coast was at one time linked to Nigeria, under British rule, and was gradually transformed into a separate colony by 1856. Not until the turn of the century, and only after seven wars, were the warlike Ashantis to the north finally subdued. A British governor nearly lost his life when he arrogantly ventured to sit upon the Golden Stool of the Ashantehene, paramount chief of the Ashantis. His act sparked another uprising of the Ashantis, who believe the stool is a gift of the gods.[5] Stools are a sign of traditional authority in many parts of West Africa.

The Gold Coast was enlarged after World War I, when the British acquired the mandate of British Togoland. This was the result of the splitting up of the German colony of Togoland, a division that rent the powerful Ewe tribe into two factions, causing a pan-Ewe tribalism that now plagues the Ghana Government.

Great Britain ruled the Gold Coast through a governor who had supreme legislative and military power. An advisory council, made up of appointed chiefs, British trading interests, and British officials, represented the non-African, dominant minority. With the election of a few Africans to its membership in 1946, the council began its transformation into a representative legislature.

The Gold Coast was ripe for revolution in 1948, when a young man who had been studying for ten years in the United States and England returned. Kwame Nkrumah, the son of a goldsmith, was born in September, 1909, in the coastal village of Half-Assini. According to the tribal custom of the Akan, he was named Kwame because he was born on Saturday.

Nkrumah had been brought back to the Gold Coast by Dr. J. P. Danquah, who later became his principal political opponent. When the young, fiery orator found Danquah's party, the highly Westernized Gold Coast Convention (GCC), too moderate for his impatient spirit, he set up the Convention Peoples Party (CPP). He took with him many other young nationalists who were also dissatisfied with the sweet reasonableness of the lawyers and businessmen who led the GCC. Nkrumah denounced the deliberations of the British-created Coussey Commission, then considering a new constitution, and demanded "self-government now." He launched a "positive action" campaign which erupted in strikes and boycotts. Finally, in 1950, the aroused British imprisoned Nkrumah and several other young leaders, among them Kojo Botsio. But when the CPP swept the 1951 elections, the British Governor, Sir Charles Arden-Clarke, in a magnificent flash of insight, decided to free Nkrumah and install him as leader of government business. Events moved swiftly from that point, and in a quick series of steps, power was completely transferred to an all-African Government. Throughout the six years of transition, the African leaders demonstrated an administrative ability that amazed the British and silenced most skeptics. In 1957, Ghana became independent.

This virtually bloodless revolution was due primarily to Nkrumah's own positive-action philosophy. He describes it as a composite of Gandhian nonviolence, Christian humility, and Marxian economics—a mixture later adopted by many other nationalist groups in Africa. Nkrumah had long admired the struggle of Mahatma Gandhi, and studied it closely during his student days. He came to believe that similar tactics were suitable for Africa. An unorthodox and unafilliated Christian, he was trained in mission schools. He studied at the London School of Economics under Harold Laski, and views history in terms of economic determination and the class struggle. Timothy Bankole, once a close associate of Nkrumah and author of the biography *Kwame Nkrumah,* quotes him as saying, "I am a Marxian Socialist and an undenominational Christian." He also quotes a letter to the dean of Lincoln University in Pennsylvania from Nkrumah, in which Nkrumah affirms his Christian commitment and reports his attempt to adapt it to the lives and customs of his people.[6]

Nkrumah's policies reflect his non-violent, gradual socialism. After he achieved political power, his Marxist ideas seemed to move to the forefront of his thinking. His Marxism, however, is not the doctrinaire brand found in Eastern Europe, but a functional instrument in the struggle against "imperialism" and a tool in the "planned development" of Ghana's economy. Like Christianity, Marxism must be modified to fit Africa's special needs, Nkrumah believes.

Nkrumah's primary instrument of political power is the CPP. It has gradually grown stronger during its ten years as the government party, so that Ghana has become, for all practical purposes, a one-party state. However, Nkrumah has never espoused the one-party state, unlike his counterpart in Guinea. He has consistently argued that a strong opposition is necessary. Yet his antagonism has been aroused by the opposition, because of what he deems its disloyal tactics. He is convinced of the need for strong leadership. His impatience to press ahead has led him, time and again, to ride roughshod over the opposition; he has deported some of his sharpest critics and imprisoned several political opponents.

The nature of the opposition reveals a good deal about why strong-arm measures were taken. The CPP is a coalition of several tribal groups built around a core of lower-middle-class Africans living in towns and cities. Opposition to the regime has been aroused primarily among the conservatives. St. Clair Drake very ably captures the essential group and class nature of Ghana politics:

> Ghana politics can only be understood in terms of the conflict between one Western-trained elite group (Kwame Nkrumah and his Convention Peoples Party) which represents the interests of the urban masses and the poorer farmers, a section of the ambitious rising business class, the women and the youth, and another group of Western-trained elite who represent the interests of the tradi-

tional rulers—the chiefs, the more well-to-do farmers, the more
"solid" African business and professional men, and perhaps certain
European business interests which fear the possibility of nationalization of their enterprises if the CPP stays in power. The latter
group of political leaders has found its most effective support in an
appeal to Ashanti tribalism and Togoland and Northern Territories regionalism.[7]

Most of Ghana's political difficulties stem from the people's
lack of national consciousness. When independence was gained
in 1957, a small elite of urbanized intellectuals, business and professional people thought in national terms. Most followers of the
CPP and the other parties were, and still are, provincial and
tribal in outlook. Despite its small size, Ghana, like most of the
other new African states, consists of numerous tribal and language groups forcibly unified under colonial rule. This unification must now be accepted, if the nation is to survive. In a country without national consciousness, democracy is made very difficult, for force becomes necessary to achieve national ends.

The Government charged certain members of the opposition
with engaging in a plot against the state, and convinced two of
the three members of the Sharp Commission that the men were
guilty.[8] Certainly a state is justified in protecting itself against
overt attempts to overthrow it by force, but the Ghana Government arrested and imprisoned many persons simply on suspicion.

Ghana has had more than one near-revolution. When the British transferred final authority in 1957, the Ashantis threatened to
rebel unless the British stayed, and some members of the opposition United Party were involved in the rebel movement. At the
same time, considerable unrest was felt among the Ewe tribesmen
in former British Togoland, which was being absorbed into
Ghana.

Nkrumah has been determined to have a united, centralized
government, and has given very few constitutional concessions to
tribalism. The 1960 constitution created several district houses
for chiefs, but these were advisory and honorific. Nkrumah has
eliminated much of the chiefs' powers through new elective local
councils run by the CPP. As a consequence, the chiefs have been
the backbone of the opposition.

The combined opposition of conservative and traditionalist leaders has at times been formidable. Often their tactics have been questionable. But without an effective and free opposition, parliamentary democracy does not exist. How to provide for political opposition which is at the same time effective and responsible is the dilemma of Ghana. Unfortunately, Nkrumah's driving pace does not allow time for such a mature opposition to evolve; it is likely that the CPP will grow in power and the opposition will weaken.

Within the CPP, there has been an ever-growing concentration of power in the executive. Meanwhile, the party has become identified more closely with the government, which has tended increasingly to use the party as an instrument of government propaganda—a trend notably demonstrated by the tactics of the youth corps brigades. Nkrumah assumed direct party leadership in May, 1961. Identification of the party with the government is encouraged by ultra-Africanism, with its goal of central authority.

Economic Planning

Nkrumah's socialism has emphasized welfare and economic growth, but has created little industry. Much of the initiative in fostering new industry must come from the government, because an entrepreneurial class has not yet emerged. Despite considerable talk of African communal enterprise, little progress has been made, outside of a few experiments in cooperative production. Technicians have been imported from Israel to try to accelerate the cooperative movement.

Compared with other West African economies, Ghana is wealthy, having a per capita income of $150 per year. Nevertheless, this is a low figure, and obviously too small to support a very elaborate welfare or educational program. The government's major efforts are directed at enlarging production.

Swift advances were made in education and literacy after the British transfer of power to an African-led Government in 1951. An adult literacy campaign has achieved 35 per cent literacy, and universal primary education has almost been attained. Although the spread of education has lowered its general standards, the

Ghanaians are more interested in educating the masses than in the development of a small elite, British style. Higher education has been extended similarly. Local colleges such as the University of Ghana and the College of Technology in Kumasi have been strengthened and expanded. Hundreds of government bursaries, some provided by Cocoa Marketing Board surpluses, have been granted Ghana students for study in England and America.

Controversial builders' brigades have been created, along the lines of the Civilian Conservation Corps of the United States during the New Deal. The young men get an elementary education and build roads and schools. They are highly militant supporters of the government, and turn out in great numbers at election times to rally the population to the banners of the CPP. The opposition believes the brigades were created for political purposes and fears their paramilitary character. Nevertheless, they enroll numerous young men who would probably otherwise swell the ranks of unemployed, urbanized Africans.

Ghana's major economic need is to broaden the base of her economy. Cocoa is now her major export, but its price fluctuates widely on the world market, and whenever it falls sharply, the government's revenues decline substantially. Through the Cocoa Marketing Board, Ghana attempts to protect the farmers against such fluctuations.

Timber and gold are substantial industries, but both agriculture and industry can be extended. The nation's most famous development plan is the Volta hydroelectric and aluminum program. Already under construction, it will eventually cost some $600 million. The Kaiser Industries Corporation of the United States has assisted Ghana in planning it. Financing for this vast scheme was finally arranged in 1961, when the United States, after much equivocation, agreed to join with the World Bank and Great Britain to provide the long-term loan needed. Private aluminum companies are to produce the aluminum in cooperation with the government of Ghana. The country's first deepwater harbor—at Tema, where for centuries only picturesque surfboats carried out the loading and unloading of ships—has been constructed to service the project. A complex of secondary industries is planned to go up around the aluminum plant. All of these will be supplied with power from the 230-foot dam. The 200-mile-long lake formed by the dam will create a fresh-water-fish industry to add more protein to the starchy cassava diet.

Ghana has failed to attract sufficient private investment for its needs. A great deal of interest has been shown by foreign businessmen—the new hotels are full of them—but, outside of the new aluminum industry, little capital has been invested. The future of private enterprise remains uncertain, despite government assurances that there will be no nationalization. Most of the capital flowing into Ghana is loans or grants from the governments of the United States and the United Kingdom, and from the United Nations. Nkrumah's government has relied extensively on outside technical help, with many British administrative, engineering, and financial personnel remaining after independence.

One goal of Ghana's ultra-Africanist drive is to reduce its economic dependence on the West. Accordingly, it has entered a great variety of agreements with nations of both East and West. Chinese and Russian delegations have arrived in great numbers, and the once-small percentage of Communist-bloc trade and aid is rising. The Russians are assisting in the building of housing developments for 25,000 persons in Accra and 12,000 in the harbor town of Tema. Russian technicians are also advising in the establishment of a string of fishing industries. East European countries are helping to build several secondary industries. And China has granted a $20 million loan in exchange for trade.

Despite Nkrumah's desire to diversify trade, he made it clear that his country would turn to the West first for help. As he wrote in 1958:

> We have to modernize. Either we shall do so with the interest and support of the West or we shall be compelled to turn elsewhere. This is not a warning or a threat, but a straight statement of political reality.[9]

The numerous Western aid programs, including the Volta scheme, indicate that Nkrumah is getting most of what he needs from the West.

The CPP

The rapid extension of social benefits has brought popularity to Nkrumah's government. But the time is rapidly approaching when it will have to deliver more, or opposition will intensify. Reactions in the trade unions to the 1961 austerity budget give an indication of this.

The CPP has enjoyed an amazing unity in its ten-year rule. The inner circle around Nkrumah is made up of nearly the same young Prison Graduates (PG's) who formed the first Government. No serious rival has emerged. "Life chairman" of the CPP, Kwame Nkrumah has no plans for retirement. A cabinet reshuffle and party shakeup in 1961 brought about the "demise" of Kojo Botsio, once a close friend of Nkrumah's, who was forced to resign first from the Ministry of Parliamentary Affairs and then from the Ministry of Agriculture. K. A. Gbedemah, once widely believed to be second in command, was compelled to resign from the Ministry of Finance and other posts. Tawia Adamafio took over the Ministry of State for Presidential Affairs, while Nkrumah assumed the CPP posts of general secretary and chairman of the central committee. These moves weakened potential rivals and gave Nkrumah much tighter control over the party. The purge was also motivated by growing popular resentment against some of the inner circle, who had grown too prosperous in office. Some observers have been alarmed by the rise of the ultra-Africanist "tough guy" of the inner circle, Krobo Edusei, while more moderate leaders waned. Yet Edusei's ascent was counterbalanced by the elevation of moderate, energetic Kofi Baako to the Ministries of Defense and of Parliamentary Affairs.

Pan-Africanism

As a primary architect of pan-Africanism, President Nkrumah believed that Ghana had a special mission in Africa's emancipation from colonialism and its political unification. This has given a major direction to Ghana's foreign policy and made Accra the site of many important international conferences and the source of much controversy.

George Padmore, a West Indian and a close associate of Nkrumah's who contributed extensively to the growth of pan-Africanism, took part in the numerous pan-African conferences beginning in 1919, bringing together Negroes from Africa and the Western hemisphere to seek ways of liberating and uniting Africa. In his book *Pan-Africanism or Communism*, Padmore describes pan-Africanism:

> Pan-Africanism seeks the attainment of the government of Africans by Africans for Africans, with respect for racial and religious minorities who desire to live in Africa on a basis of equality with the black majority. Economically and socially, Pan-Africanism subscribes to the fundamental objectives of Democratic Socialism, with state control of the basic means of production and distribution.[10]

Padmore was Nkrumah's principal adviser on several pan-African conferences. The most important of these was the Accra conference of 1958, which established the All-Africa Peoples Conference. This conference has met annually in various African capitals since that time, its tone gradually becoming more ultra-Africanist. Consequently, many of the Westernized states, such as Nigeria and the French-speaking countries, no longer send delegations.

Nkrumah and Padmore have not realized their early dream of creating unified political units among the newly independent states which would cut across the borders established by the colonial powers. Many of these barriers seem to have grown higher since the territories in question became independent.

Nevertheless, Ghana has established a closer union with Guinea and Mali. These countries have been brought together by their ultra-Africanist world view. Presidents Nkrumah and Touré in 1959 created a Union of Independent African States, whose purpose was "to build a free and prosperous African community in the interests of its peoples and world peace." Their joint statement declared: "The member states or federations will decide in common what portion of sovereignty shall be surrendered to the Union in the full interest of the African Community." After the failure of the Mali Federation, the Mali Republic joined this union, which is really an alliance. These three countries are closely associated with the North African states of Morocco and the U.A.R. in world politics, and the five are known as the Casablanca Group.

These states have a great deal in common with other African states on such broad issues as economic cooperation, boycotting South Africa, and opposing French atomic tests in the Sahara. However, the Casablanca Group subscribes to a militant brand of "neutralism" for Africa.

For many years, Nkrumah has been disturbed by what he sees as an attempt by the colonial powers to hang on to Africa through indirect economic, military, and cultural controls. He describes this as "neocolonialism," "the practice of granting a sort of independence by the metropolitan power, with the concealed intention of making the liberated country a client-state and controlling it effectively by means other than political ones." Many of the West's actions in Africa are viewed in this light by Nkrumah and the Casablanca Group. They cannot believe that the West has accepted neutrality for Africa. Thus, Nkrumah and his associates see the controversies over the Congo, Algeria, and South Africa as fundamentally conflicts between colonial interests and the African liberation movement. However, they do not believe that the Eastern bloc is any more free from self-interest than the West. But when the Communists support the aims of ultra-Africanism in the United Nations and elsewhere, it is not surprising that Nkrumah, Touré, and their associates react with appreciation.

Nkrumah has made it clear from the very beginning of Ghana's entry into world affairs that he believes a "new African personality" is emerging on the world scene, and that it will not be the satellite of either world bloc, but will seek its own destiny and make its own special contribution to world peace. He believes that much of the Balkanization and other troubles of Africa would not have arisen had the rest of the world allowed Africa to sort out her own problems. This view appeals to many Africans and is spreading through Africa as crises continue to develop.

GUINEA: NEW "AFRICAN DEMOCRACY"

This small country has been second only to Ghana as a source of controversy. The first French West African territory to achieve independence, in 1958, it is a neighbor of Liberia and the Ivory Coast.

President Sékou Touré, a colorful, brilliant former trade-union organizer, is one of the most vocal ultra-Africanists. He has the distinction of being the only nationalist leader in French Africa to say "no" to De Gaulle and to France in the 1958 referendum on the Fifth Republic. This resulted in immediate independence for Guinea and the precipitate withdrawal of all French aid and most of its technical personnel. In the ensuing crisis, Touré assumed virtually dictatorial powers.

Disgruntled French quarters have accused Touré of being a Communist. Although he has shown admiration for the Soviet Union and Communist China, and employs strong-arm, one-party tactics, this accusation is inaccurate. President Touré is a Marxist in the French Socialist tradition. He views his country's primary problem as the application of techniques of rapid economic development to the primitive conditions of African communal society. As a correspondent for *West Africa* put it:

> African society, after all, was communal long before Marx and if Sékou Touré and his friends base their work on Marxist principles and methods, it is not because they seek to impose a Communist-inspired dictatorship but because they seek to adapt African society to modern conditions.[11]

The Philosophy of African Democracy

Among the young intellectual leaders of Africa, there is great interest in the "African democracy."

Touré's attempt to adapt Western democratic and socialist ideas to African conditions has already had a wide influence in other parts of Africa. Touré and his followers believe that the communalism of traditional Africa leads naturally to a one-party system, in which opposition, insofar as it exists, occurs within the party. African tribalism operates on the principle of consensus rather than majority–minority rule, and these leaders see in the Marxist concept of democratic centralism a more African political process. Democratic centralism provides for discussion within the party, followed by a decision at the top, and then enforcement by stiff party discipline.

The Parti Démocratique de Guinea (PDG) is organized on the local level into committees of 600, which hold discussions of the government program and propagandize it. Thus the party, rather than the parliament, becomes the decision-making instrument of this "African democracy."

Touré believes that Westerners are narrow in outlook and that a more objective view would see that one-party rule is the natural result of African communalism and existing conditions. He argues that his political philosophy, though Marxist, is not Communist, because it permits religious freedom and the traditional African democratic ideals. Touré studied briefly in Prague and has encouraged the importation of numerous Communist technicians to replace the hastily departed French. This has undoubtedly subjected Guinea to greater Communist influence than other African states. John Marcum quotes Touré:

> A year from now one won't walk into a town and meet a thousand idlers chatting from morning to night . . . If it is necessary to have a scaffold for counterrevolutionaries who still want to hold down this country, France had the guillotine, Guinea shall have the scaffold.[12]

The scaffold has not been erected, but has been a symbolic threat, indicating a willingness to use extreme force, if necessary, to push Guinea ahead.

One of Touré's closest associates, Abdoulaye Diallo, PDG General Secretary, Ambassador to the United Nations and General Secretary of the All-Africa Peoples Conference in 1960, told the delegates at a 1959 Ibadan University conference on representative government and national progress in Africa:

> There is no opposition for opposition's sake and no struggle by individuals to take over power from other individuals in Guinea. Such struggles are a waste of time and energy and therefore inefficient in new countries where social programs are the first consideration.[13]

Here, Diallo points to the heart of the matter: Many African
leaders, whose countries need every ounce of energy for development, feel that they cannot afford the time and energy required
for lengthy debate.

President Touré has said:

> It is not our intention to squander this chance of unity by adopt-
> ing a system which would reduce our political strength . . . A po-
> litical system based on two parties would be a certain check to our
> evolution. The revolutionary dynamism doesn't need any other
> stimulant than our needs, our aspirations, and our hopes.[14]

Several of Touré's lieutenants and associates, such as his
brother, Ismael Touré, and Kieta Fodeba, have had close ties
with the Communist Party in France. Yet Jean Boyer, a French
Marxist ascetic with great influence in Guinea, has shown Touré,
as George Padmore showed Nkrumah, that there are legitimate
directions for revolution other than Communism.

Touré's political philosophy is a pragmatic view of the necessities of survival and progress under Guinea's special conditions,
rather than a doctrinaire Marxism. Touré has said: "It is evident
that certain Marxist concepts suit African conditions, but it is no
less evident that Africa will have to find its own revolutionary
principles. As for the class problems, you will note that there exists in Africa one and the same class, that of the dispossessed."[15]

Economic Independence

When Guinea voted to leave the French Community in 1958,
France immediately cut off all economic assistance and withdrew
most of her technicians. Overnight, Guinea found herself stripped
of financial experts, engineers, even doctors. Bananas piled up
on the docks, since the French refused to take them for export.
After having thus disowned Guinea, France gradually recovered
from her pique and re-established some trade with her, but
Guinea had already begun to look elsewhere.

Guinea has adopted a three-year (1960–62) development plan.
Fifty per cent of the capital is to be spent for production, 30 per
cent for social welfare, and 20 per cent for administration. For a
population of only 2.5 million, this plan has an extraordinarily

large capital expenditure—$120 million. A controversial and un-usual feature is the "human investment" part of the capitalization. Communist China's development programs have employed "voluntary" labor which was actually forced labor. Touré believes that a combination of popular enthusiasm and force can put to work tens of thousands of idle man-hours for the nation's development. In Communist countries, this has worked because of the efficiency of the enforcement system and the effectiveness of the propaganda. It remains to be seen whether this can work in the far more primitive circumstances of Guinea, without the erection of the scaffold Touré spoke of.

Assistance for the struggling economy of Guinea now comes primarily, but not exclusively, from the Communist bloc. This is more the result of skillful maneuvering by the Communist bloc and blundering by the West than of ideological design on the part of the Guinea government. When France suddenly withdrew her support, the United States, out of deference to its ally, failed to respond to Guinea's requests for assistance. The Communist countries, free from any sensitivity to the feelings of France, promptly offered help, which was accepted.

By 1959, 15 per cent of Guinea's trade had shifted to the Communist bloc. The Soviet Union had granted a $35 million loan, much of which was channeled into a polytechnic institute. Czechoslovakia had become the greatest contributor. Several Czech technical advisers were working in the ministries of finance and public works. A Czech became the new harbor-master of Conakry. Communist China had promoted a rice-development project which brought several hundred Chinese technicians to the country. Scores of Guinean students were granted scholarships to universities behind the Iron Curtain. Meanwhile, the United States and the United Nations programs of technical assistance were tied up in red tape. The U.S., in addition to being slow to recognize the new state of Guinea, insisted on certain standard diplomatic privileges for its Point Four personnel, which the Communists had not requested, and which Guinea refused.

Notwithstanding this background, Guinea is eager to receive Western European and American aid for development. Guinean students are being trained in America under the auspices of ICA, and American teachers are helping to staff Guinea's schools. Western capital might be interested in developing the country's substantial mineral wealth, but the danger of expropriation causes much concern, despite international guarantees. An ambitious hydroelectric aluminum project is already under construction on the Konkouré River. Ultimately, an output of 5 billion kilowatt hours of power and 1.5 million tons of aluminum is expected. An international consortium, led by the Olin Mathieson Chemical Corporation, has undertaken this scheme, which will entail an investment of $250 million. However, second thoughts have been developing since the leftward bias of the new government became definite.[16]

Guinea has iron ore deposits under exploitation which may provide up to 3 million tons a year for export. The diamond industry has developed rapidly, climbing from an export value of $64,000 in 1958 to about $10 million in 1959.

Agriculture, which constitutes 90 per cent of Guinea's present production, must be modernized if the peasants' standard of living is to be raised. Areas in both lower and upper Guinea are being developed to grow rice, a valuable supplement to the corn, cassava, and banana crops grown in middle Guinea. For export, the most valuable crops are cocoa, coconut, palm oil, and bananas. In the forest regions, a high-grade coffee industry has been established.

Substantial progress has been made in social welfare and education. Rapid training of Guineans in public administration and technical services has helped restore the vital services of education and medicine, seriously curtailed after the French withdrawal in 1958. An all-out assault has been launched on illiteracy, and, like other newly independent African states, Guinea aspires to have universal education in all but the most primitive areas within a few years.

The average Guinean seems inspired by the new expectation aroused by his own African government. Signs of material progress, of housing and school construction, of factories going up, are all around. Not many seem worried that the police are omnipresent and that only one political party is permitted.

The Government Structure

The principle of the government of Guinea, specified in the constitution, is taken from Lincoln's Gettysburg address: "Government of the people, by the people, and for the people." This is not a calculated deception but a reflection of the country's general admiration for Western democracy.

The government is similar to that of the Fifth French Republic. It has a strong president elected by the people, and he selects his cabinet from a popularly elected single-chamber assembly. The cabinet is responsible to the president, not the assembly. Presumably the only way for popular dissatisfaction to express itself is through the presidential election, held every seven years. Guinea's highly centralized and comprehensive one-party system makes the prospects for any effective opposition very slim. Regional and local administrators are appointed by presidential decree and subject to directives of the minister of the interior. Very little power is left to traditional chiefs and tribal councils. The French colonial administration introduced direct rule, and the new government has made it much more effective through the powerful medium of the PDG.

An independent judiciary is provided under the constitution. Political and religious freedom are specified, and it is declared that "Any act of racial discrimination, as well as all propaganda of a racial or regional character, shall be punishable by law."[17] As in most of the other new African states, the formal guarantees of freedom are explicitly set forth, but the all-important question is how such guarantees are implemented by the government. As Sir Henry Maine observed with regard to the English constitution, "Liberty is secreted in the interstices of procedure." Formal obeisance to the concepts of freedom does not indicate the actual extent of political liberty.

But the spelling out of Western democratic concepts in the Guinea constitution is nevertheless important. The prospect of Guinea's moving toward a truer democracy, as internal conditions improve and it gains experience in world affairs, should not be ruled out. Like Nkrumah, Touré is a passionate advocate of pan-Africanism. He is distrustful of the continuing influence of the Western powers over their one-time colonies. This, plus the long-standing rivalry between Touré and Houphouet-Boigny makes the relationship between Guinea and the Brazzaville Twelve a very strained one. Touré sees Africa's goal as complete independence. Speaking of the designs of "neocolonialists," he has said: "All the plans to restrain this fierce will of Africa for the reconquest of its dignity are being frustrated one after another, and always it is the same burning cry that echoes across our entire continent: Independence."[18]

Guinea's constitution provides for a close association with the other African states. Touré has often stated his desire that Guinea unite with other independent African states, and Guinea, Ghana, and Mali have formed a close bond which began with Ghana's emergency aid to Guinea at the time of Guinea's winning of independence. However, a true, working unification remains for the future.

Left-Wing Neutrality

While leaning to the left, Guinea pursues a policy of non-alignment. Its ultra-Africanists, motivated by the desire to be completely independent, economically and culturally, of former colonial masters, regard the Western European powers as neo-colonial and the United States as a fellow traveler. Guinea's leaders, unable to lift their backward economy by its bootstraps, find it necessary to use Communist aid, since the West has not offered similar help. It is important to realize that Guinea has not gone Communist and that it is not moving inevitably toward Communism. It is an example of the most fully developed form of ultra-Africanism. As has been indicated, certain Marxist concepts lend themselves to the rapid-development programs of the ultra-Africanists. However, those concepts are applied within the context of a nascent African communal culture, giving them a distinctive non-Western character. Like Ghana, Guinea is first and foremost an African nationalist society. Guinea's leaders realize that an excess of Communist ideology would bury the African character, as it was buried by a century of Western paternalism.

Ultra-Africanists will strive to maintain the dignity of their independence as long as they can make progress quickly. They are trying to widen their support throughout Africa by generating enthusiasm for pan-Africanism. As I have indicated, their movement is growing, and considerable evidence exists that the ultra-Africanists may be the wave of the future.

It is therefore especially important that the West support the ultra-Africanists in their desire to be neutral and independent. Yet, certain former colonial powers, particularly France and Belgium, have played bloc politics in Africa by backing the Westernized nationalists and attempting to consolidate them as a barrier to the growth of ultra-Africanism. This is a dangerous and unfortunate game. First, it confirms ultra-Africanist suspicions that the "neocolonial" West wishes to keep its grip on Africa. Second, it saps the independence of the ultra-Africanists. If they are to build a genuine independence, they must have help from the West as well as the East.

United States policy toward Guinea has swung from distrust, when it first gained independence in 1958, to belated and half-hearted support. Uncertainty over Guinea's loyalty and direction put a brake on American action. This diffidence should yield to the recognition that Guinea requires support as much as Nigeria does. No peace and stability can be created in Africa if the U.S. does not extend aid as vigorously and imaginatively to Touré and Nkrumah as it has to other African leaders for fulfilling the hopes of Africa's people.

4.

South Africa:
White Racialism's Last Stand

Freedom and independence have spread southward in Africa like a rising tide, advancing down the continent until coming up against the highlands of white supremacy and empire.

The Portuguese empire, the Republic of South Africa, and Southern Rhodesia have vigorously repressed African nationalism. The Europeans who dominate these areas cling desperately to the nineteenth-century concepts of colonialism—the white man's "civilizing mission," and the inherent "superiority" of the white race. The great majority of settlers ignore completely the scientific and political advances of the last century, and insist on retaining their power and privileges.

The Portuguese profess a belief in racial equality, but practice a policy of "civilizing mission" and suppression of nationalism which amounts to a racialism more despotic than the *apartheid* of the Republic of South Africa. Southern Rhodesia is relatively enlightened.

The emergence of African power in the north makes the white settlers in the south feel increasingly threatened by "black nationalism." A pathological fear seems to grip their governments. More and more isolated from the Western world, they may eventually be overwhelmed by a great black onslaught from the north. Already, Portuguese nationalists in Angola are supplied from the Congo. The new African states are still preoccupied with their own internal problems, but it is conceivable that they

106

will give increasing support to the African nationalists who are suffering brutal suppression under the Portuguese and Afrikaners.

South Africa presents the greatest problems for a peaceful transition. The prospects are that the bloody tyranny of white racialism will some day provoke outside intervention; the critical question is from where such intervention will come—the Africanized states, the Communist bloc, or the United Nations.

PORTUGUESE AFRICA: THE LAST EMPIRE

"To whom shall the people appeal against the silence of the great?" asked the Marquis de Custine in 1839, speaking of the Russian despotism then current.

Until early 1961, the great powers of the world and the United Nations were silent on the plight of the African peoples ruled by the Portuguese.

For 400 years, tiny Portugal has had extensive holdings in Africa. In addition to the two large areas of Mozambique and Angola, she rules Portuguese Guinea, the Cape Verde Islands, São Tomé, and the Fort of San João Baptista de Ajudá. The population of these territories, including Europeans, coloreds, and Africans, exceeds 10 million. Several times the area of Portugal itself, these possessions were, in 1960, the largest and last African empire. New Portuguese settlers have been pouring into Angola and Mozambique, and by 1960 they numbered well over 204,000. Most are poor peasants resettled by the government because of the scarcity of land and employment in Portugal.

With the outbreak of a full-scale uprising in northern Angola and the strong world reaction against Portugal's fierce repression of it, Africa's last empire was crumbling.

Identity

The Portuguese speak of their policy toward their "overseas provinces" as "identity," referring to the single status, under law, for all Portuguese citizens, both in Portugal and overseas. Such a policy is theoretical and not translated into practice. The native African peoples, who outnumber the Portuguese fifty to one, live in a state which has been accurately called "state serfdom." The mass of Africans do not have the civil rights of the Europeans, and they are forced to work for their overlords at one of the lowest wage rates in Africa.

Portugal, under the dictatorship of Premier Antonio de Oliveira Salazar, is a fascist state on the Spanish model. No opportunity exists for real opposition. Those who oppose the regime, like General Delegato, a defeated opposition presidential candidate, and Captain Henrique Galvão, are hounded and even imprisoned as traitors. Only one political party, the National Union, is allowed to function freely. The office of premier is held by Salazar and is not contested. The president is chosen in a national election in which all Europeans and *assimilados* in the overseas provinces are allowed to vote. Opponents of the regime say the results are rigged in favor of the Salazar puppet.

The Catholic Church and the dictatorship rule the overseas provinces, under a concordat whereby church and state jointly carry out their "Christian civilizing mission." The state, recognizing the Catholic Church as an "instrument of civilization and national influence," has given it a controlling position in the state schools for Africans. In return, the church does not interfere in such secular matters as forced labor, and agrees to teach the African the virtues of productive effort.[1]

Since 1951, Portugal has legally recognized its African possessions as overseas provinces. Technically, this means that all residents of these areas are Portuguese citizens. The overseas provinces elect delegates to the Portuguese assembly and vote in presidential elections. Angola and Mozambique each elect three deputies to the 120-member body, and Portuguese Guinea and São Tomé, with Principe, each elect one delegate.[2]

Administration of the overseas provinces is highly centralized. In Lisbon, power is concentrated in the Ministry of Overseas Provinces, and two consultative bodies—the Council of Overseas Provinces and the Conference of Overseas Governors—exercise important influence over the provinces.

The governors-general of Mozambique and Angola are appointed by the ministry in Lisbon and have legislative councils with which they may consult if they so choose.[3] Some of these council members are elected, but the elections are virtually meaningless. The African people are disenfranchised through the *assimilado* system, which gives the vote to only a tiny fraction of them.

The Portuguese have not permitted chiefs to retain important powers. On the lowest level, administration is centralized in the Portuguese administrator, the *chefe de posto*. Not even minor crimes are settled in accordance with native custom; they are taken to the *chefe de posto,* who has judicial as well as executive authority. There are no elections of representatives at any level for the indigenous Africans.[4] This is without doubt the most completely authoritarian rule to be found on the African continent. Even the Republic of South Africa permits limited powers to native authorities in the reserves.

Assimilados

The Portuguese have been in Africa periodically since the fifteenth century. They were the first to establish trading posts through West Africa. Yet, as of 1950, their civilizing mission had produced only 30,039 *assimilados* in Angola and 4,353 in Mozambique—out of nearly 10 million subject Africans! What is an *assimilado?* An African who achieves this status is a Christian and has adopted a European manner of life, forgoing certain native customs, such as polygamy. He has completed military service, speaks Portuguese fluently, reads and writes in Portuguese, and has a trade or profession. His privileges: Social acceptance in the European community, freedom from certain legal requirements for natives (head tax and forms of labor), the right to trial in a court of Portuguese law, and the right to vote.

Until mid-1961, the Portuguese authorities had not encouraged a rapid increase in the number of *assimilados*. Numerous *assimilados* might compete with the Europeans for power. Moreover, the *indigenas,* who have no rights, provide cheap labor. After rebellion had broken out in Angola, the Portuguese announced, in the summer of 1961, their intention of abolishing the legal distinction between the *assimilados* and the "uncivilized." Henceforth all Africans will be citizens of Portugal. However, the right to vote will be limited to the literate and those who can afford to pay $7 per year in taxes. But the centuries-old *assimilado* system will not be changed overnight, any more than the proclamation of legal equality of all citizens in the southern United States has swiftly brought about integration. African nationalist leaders fighting the Portuguese in Angola have called the proposed reforms a fraud, coming much too late to make any difference.

Forced Labor

The *indigenas*—the non-*assimilados*—constitute 99.9 per cent of the African population. They are completely at the mercy of the district administrators, who have vast powers over land disposal, commercial licenses, bank deposits, inheritances, arrest, trial, and imprisonment. Most important, they administer the *shibalo* system, whereby Africans are compelled to work six months of the year, unless they have permits exempting them.[5]

Whereas the assimilated African enjoys a status of equality with the European that is unique in this part of Africa, the *indigenas* are actually serfs of the Portuguese administration and the large plantations. Every male *indigena*, even if he farms a plot of land communally owned by the tribal group, is continuously under the threat of being caught by the labor-recruiting agents of the *shibalo* system. In northern Mozambique, where the *shibalo* system is less important, the Portuguese have introduced the compulsory growth of cotton. Because this has reduced the amount of land under food cultivation, acute food shortages have resulted.[6]

The forced recruitment of workers for private industry is illegal, according to a Portuguese law enacted in 1906. However, numerous reliable reports indicate that *shibalo* continues to flourish on a major scale. One of the earliest exposés of it, *Africa Slave or Free*, was written before World War I by an American, John H. Harris. More recently, the English writer Basil Davidson describes his personal experience with *shibalo* in *The African Awakening* and in several articles in *The New Statesman*. Added material is to be found in the research of Marvin Harris, an anthropologist of Columbia University, and James Duffy of Brandeis University.[7]

Shibalo is the Bantu term for "tributary worker." At the root of the system is the requirement that every African male in Portuguese territory must perform at least six months of productive labor each year. An *indigena* is exempt if he can produce an agriculture certificate, which entitles him to work his own farm, or if he is employed in the urban or mining industries in South Africa. But since only about 5 per cent of the working population in southern Mozambique are legally entitled to remain on their homesteads, and urban jobs are hard to get, the rest either must go to the mines in South Africa or try to elude the *shibalo* hunters.

Legally, those recruited by the district administrators are employed on government projects only. However, a tremendous traffic in labor is conducted by the Portuguese planters, who are pleased to get thousands of Africans to work on their plantations for about 17 cents a day. As a result of bribery or through sympathy with the needs of other Europeans, government officials simply present groups of Africans rounded up by *shibalo* agents with mass contracts. If they refuse to sign, a penalty may fall upon their families, or they may be accused of some crime (for which, according to Marvin Harris, no proof is necessary), convicted, and deported. In Angola, recalcitrant Africans are faced with the grim prospect of deportation to the cocoa plantations on the island of São Tomé. The fate of those sent to this penal island is well known. Many never return. A long sea voyage is the only means of getting to or from the island. Basil Davidson, in *The African Awakening,* reports that a rebellion erupted on São Tomé in 1953, but was fiercely repressed.[8] He concludes that the Africans sent there are actually consigned to slavery:

> They are seized on the mainland. They do not volunteer to go to São Tomé. Once they reach São Tomé they have no remote possibility of leaving without the help of the administration. While there they must work for the employer to whom they are sent . . . The decree of 1946 reasserts an earlier prohibition on their changing from one employer to another. Should difficulties arise in sending them home at the end of their two or four years or longer, then they automatically stay in São Tomé. In none of this do they have a choice, nor any freedom to decide their own fate. Then in what manner do they differ from slaves?[9]

Portuguese local administrative officials have absolute power, because they have both the police force and the law. One method used to instill respect for their civilizing mission is a beating with the *palmatorio,* a wooden paddle the size of a tennis racket, with four or five holes in the center. During a beating, the flesh is sucked up into these holes, creating painful welts. Professor Harris writes:

> Such punishment is usually administered in the presence of other Africans . . . Every administrative post in Mozambique has its *palmatorio,* and recourse to this instrument for the punishment of minor infractions is a thoroughly routine and everyday occurrence.[10]

An important feature of Mozambique's compulsory labor system is the annual export of some 75,000 Africans for twelve to eighteen months of labor in the mines of the Republic of South Africa. By agreement, Mozambique supplies South Africa with a maximum of 100,000 laborers a year to work in the mines. In return, South Africa pays a fee per head and agrees to direct a certain percentage of its shipping through the Port of Lourenço Marques. This system has existed for more than fifty years, and it has become customary for men of the Bathonga tribe to spend a term or more in a South African mine. The amount of coercion employed is difficult to estimate, because work in the mines is well paid and carries considerable prestige. However, Professor Harris concluded that if compulsory labor were not demanded of the Bathonga, the men would be unlikely to leave home for the extremely hazardous underground work. Although working conditions have improved greatly, the death rate from lung disease is still very high among immigrant mine workers.[11]

The Portuguese government has vigorously defended its labor system, and, strictly speaking, it permits no compulsory recruiting for private business. However, the Native Labor Code of 1928, which covers these practices, mentions the "moral obligation" of the natives to procure means of subsistence by labor. This has left the door open to pressures. A U.N. report on "Forced Labor" refers to the recruitment of labor for South Africa and concludes that the measures adopted to enforce fulfillment of a contract "constitute a serious restriction of [the African's] personal liberty."[12]

Color Bar?

The Portuguese claim that there is no color bar in their territories, that their system of civilizing the African is superior to South Africa's. This sentiment is often echoed by poorly informed Westerners. It is quite true that the Portuguese have not brought to Africa the racial-segregation theories of South Africa, but segregated housing, employment, and education have increased as Portuguese settlers have grown in number. The evidence of the *assimilado* and *shibalo* systems demonstrates that there are first- and second-class citizens in Portugal's empire. A more liberal attitude toward interracial marriages and liaisons than the Rhodesias and South Africa manifest does not change the essential master-servant relationship which characterizes race relations in Portuguese territories. Many observers feel there is already a serious growth of racialist theories among the numerous poor settlers pouring in from Portugal. There is real competition between whites and Africans for semi-skilled jobs. The special housing and educational advantages of the Portuguese are threatened by the growing desire of the Africans for these things.

Professor Harris concludes that the Portuguese system is actually worse than South Africa's: "Behind this curtain flourishes an apartheid-like system of separate and unequal treatment more severe in many aspects than that which exists within the Union of South Africa."[13]

Nationalist Revolution

In 1956, I spoke to an African leader of Methodist mission work about the extent of nationalist sentiment among his people. He told me: "Portuguese prisons are not 'hotels' where a budding nationalist can go for a time to rest and await the inevitable surge of nationalism that will set him free. Gandhi and Nkrumah in British colonies faced a more humane opponent. Life-long hard labor and torture are the more likely fate of the African who opposes Portuguese rule."

It turned out that he underestimated the situation. When revolt broke out in 1960, many Africans merely suspected of aiding the nationalists were shot.

For many years, an extensive underground nationalist movement has existed in Portuguese territories. Letters and documents from it have been smuggled out through the Congo. These documents have found their way to the United Nations and other organizations interested in human rights. One such appeal received in 1958 stated:

> Justice is completely unknown . . . Punishments are inhuman and prisoners are neither fed nor clothed . . . Deportation and exile are frequent . . . The whole country lives in terror . . . Men hide night and day . . . to escape military expeditions and forced labor battalions . . . to distant places.

In 1959, the first serious violence broke out when African nationalist guerrillas clashed with Portuguese soldiers in the northern province. The first important nationalist organization was the Union of the Peoples of Northern Angola, secretly formed in 1954 by expatriates in Léopoldville. This movement spread widely underground, and the Union of the Populations of Angola (UPA) came into existence. As revolutionary fervor matured and was countered by more and more arrests, the Front for the National Independence of the Portuguese Colonies became the principal revolutionary center.[14] Nationalist activity in Mozambique lagged behind that in Angola. However, with the establishment of an African Government in Tanganyika, expatriates were able to set up a revolutionary council in Dar es Salaam.

In the past, the Portuguese have been able to control African nationalism by immediate and ruthless arrests, beatings, and exile. São Tomé has been the principal island of exile for political prisoners, most of whom never returned to reveal the horrors they had suffered. But resistance, easily wiped out before, is now possible, because of the base of support in the Congo, where independent African states lend assistance.

The ultimate triumph of African nationalism in the Portuguese holdings is inevitable. But the price will be terrible. The Portuguese have not hesitated to wipe out whole villages with napalm bombs, nor to shoot hundreds of hostages in retaliation for attacks on European farms. Returned American missionaries bring reports of horror. African Protestant ministers have been a special target, because of their sympathy for the nationalist cause. Conservative estimates were that by mid-1961, 1,000 Europeans had been killed and about 50,000 Africans were dead, while another 130,000 Africans had fled to the Congo.[15]

Until 1961, the Western powers supported Portugal in keeping its policies out of international debate at the United Nations. The Portuguese were astounded and embittered when the United States, under the new Kennedy Administration, turned to the U.N. in an effort to force reforms in the Portuguese colonies.

Portugal does not have the resources for a prolonged colonial war and would be vulnerable to an economic squeeze by the United States and European powers who deplore her policies. The prospects of Portuguese settlers' forming a close alliance with South Africa are real enough to be disturbing. Outside of fascist Spain, South Africa is their only ally. During a visit to South Africa in 1959, Portugal's Minister of Overseas Provinces, Vice Admiral Vasco Lopes Alves, said: "We are accomplishing a parallel task in our territories and, if Western civilization is threatened on this continent, South Africa and Portugal now should work together."

SOUTH AFRICA: WHITE DICTATORSHIP

White South Africa is actually a colonial power, holding in subjection millions of Africans who have no more voice in the government than the people of Kenya have in the British Parliament. The only real difference is geography. The South African government is a European enclave in Africa, whereas most colonial powers have been thousands of miles away from their holdings.

These white settlers have no homeland. More than 3 million in number, they are descendants of the Dutch and British colonists who began arriving in South Africa three centuries ago.

The white men who painfully carved out a new nation in the dark continent think of themselves as sons of Africa.

Sickness of Soul

Apartheid, the doctrine of strict racial segregation, means the separation of races into independent groups. This racialism can be viewed as the logical outgrowth of the Afrikaner principle of self-determination. Theoretically, the proponents of *apartheid* believe in giving self-rule to the 9.7 million Africans under their jurisdiction. They intend to accomplish this not by granting equality but by creating separate Bantu states populated by Africans. Their aim is to build a white South Africa and a black South Africa. In theory, they look forward to the day when white South Africa will no longer depend on cheap black labor in the mines and the homes of the whites. Since the white man is inherently superior to and stronger than the black, the "moralists" argue, the temptation to exploit the black man is overpowering. Thus the black man must be placed in reserves to protect him from the rapacious white man.[16] These reserves are now to be called "Bantu states," but they will not be autonomous in any real sense.

This is a preposterous social scheme, yet it represents the thinking of those who hold political power in South Africa. Well-educated men are deliberately constructing higher and higher walls between white men and the various other racial groups, in a desperate attempt to preserve the privileges of the white minority.

The seeds of racialism are already bearing bitter fruit. Among the African nationalists, the moderate, Westernized leaders have lost control over the younger elements, who are strongly attracted to ultra-Africanism and even Communism. They see no hope for peaceful parliamentary change.

Not all South African whites support the government's policies. Many liberals and Christians believe that *apartheid* is morally wrong and politically dangerous, but most of them are silent, because the consequence of public opposition is social ostracism, even persecution. One center of open white opposition is the Liberal Party, headed by Alan Paton, author of *Cry, the Beloved*

Country. Another is the South African Institute of Race Relations, a scholarly research organization of white intellectuals, supported mainly by universities and church groups. Many Christian denominations, particularly mission societies, have denounced the "false doctrine" of *apartheid* and its spurious claims to origins in the scriptures, as stated in the prevailing Dutch Reform Church interpretation.

The United Party is the principal opposition in the South African Parliament. However, it has become increasingly racialist in practice. Although it opposes *apartheid* in theory, most of its supporters offer no clear political alternative.

No country in the world has wider gulfs between its racial and cultural groups than South Africa. The white community, some 3 million strong, is divided into British and Dutch descendants. The isolated Indian community contains about 250,000. The Colored group, of mixed white and African ancestry, numbers about 1.3 million and lives in its own world. The African community of 9.7 million is split into suspicious and hostile tribal groups.

The Conflict of Groups

None of the major peoples of South Africa are indigenous. Only the timid Bushmen, who have now retreated into the inaccessible regions of the Kalahari desert, and the dwindling community of Hottentots have a historic claim to South Africa. And, like the American Indians, they lack the power to assert their claim. The first European settlement began in 1652, when the Dutch established a station on the Cape to supply food and fresh water to ships carrying cloth and beads to the distant East Indies in exchange for spices and gold.

These sturdy Dutch settlers included few women, so that there were numerous marriages and liaisons with the Hottentot women. This was the origin of the colored community, now disowned by the white descendants of those early settlers.

The English, seeking to secure their route to India, seized the Dutch colony a century and a half later, in 1795. Soon British settlers began to arrive and to spread out through what is now

the Cape Province. By this time, the Dutch settlers had developed
their own Afrikaner culture, based on the Bible and the oxcart
and a language derived from the Dutch. Deeply resentful of
British rule, and desirous of keeping their slaves, these rugged
farmers, who lived like the patriarchs of the Bible, packed up
their belongings and trekked north to found the Transvaal and
the Orange Free State. This trek of the Boers, as they were called,
is a sad and often tragic story. Their move into the largely unin-
habited regions of the northeast happened to coincide with a
great Bantu migration southward, led by the fierce Zulu nation.
A series of bloody wars resulted, with many massacres on both
sides. Finally, the Boer rifle prevailed over the Zulu short sword,
and the Bantus were pushed off the best land into tribal reserves.

The Boer War, at the turn of the twentieth century, marks the
eruption of hostilities between the British and the Boers, or
Afrikaners. It took the Afrikaners half a century of bitter struggle to overcome the English. Now that power is in their hands,
they are unrelenting in their efforts to establish Boer superiority
and domination.

Although the British and the Boers were divided over who
should rule South Africa, they were united in their agreement
that it should not be the Africans. After the Hottentots and
Bantus had been pushed into reserves, the new and growing
industries began to demand cheap labor, and millions of Africans
were pulled out of the reserves and into the new urban areas of
Pretoria, Johannesburg, and Cape Town. There, some of the
worst slums of detribalized Africans developed. Although many
Africans rapidly acquired a little education and Westernized
patterns of life, the whites granted them few of the rights of
civilized men. Terrified that they would be overwhelmed by an
African majority, the whites instituted numerous restrictions on
the movement of Africans and the growth of their community.
Among these was the famous pass system, which requires an
African to get a police pass to work or live in a particular area.
If he is caught without any one of up to twelve different passes,
he is either fined or jailed for several months.

Only in the English-dominated Cape Province were Africans
admitted to the common roll of electors. However, this franchise

was withdrawn in 1936, and Africans were placed on a separate roll and allowed to elect only Europeans to represent their interests in the government. These three "native representative" seats were abolished in 1960; most Africans thought they had lost very little.

The smaller but very virile Indian community has been similarly restricted by the dominant whites. The Indians originally came to South Africa as indentured laborers, to supply skilled labor for the plantations and mines. A long series of laws were passed to restrict the Indians, among these the Transvaal Law of 1885 which denied them citizenship and limited them to certain areas of residence.

The Colored community of some 1.3 million has suffered increasing legal restrictions in recent years. Job and housing opportunities are limited. Marriages or liaisons with whites or Africans are prohibited. Recently, they have been removed from the common roll and thus disenfranchised.

Afrikaner Power

As Adlai Stevenson observed during a visit to South Africa in 1956, the country is heading in a direction directly opposite to that of the rest of the world. It is ignoring the warning of South African Edgar H. Brookes: "The day of the white man's overlordship in the world has gone and will never return. The white man's overlordship cannot continue indefinitely in the Union of South Africa, which is inescapably a part of the greater world."[17]

Most of the recent restrictive legislation goes back decades in the thinking and planning of Afrikaner nationalism. Organizations like the Broederbond, the Reddingsdaadbond (RDB), and the South African Bureau for Racial Affairs (SABRA), whose roots extend deep in the cultural and religious ideas of Afrikaner destiny, have developed the idea of *apartheid*. For example, the constitution of the Broederbond states: "The Afrikaner Broederbond is born out of a deep conviction that the Afrikaner nation was put in this land by God and is destined to continue in existence as a nation with its own nature and calling."[18]

The more sophisticated research organization, SABRA, which numbers among its members several leading Afrikaner intellectuals and cabinet ministers, is credited with the first clear development of the idea of *apartheid.*

The racial views of the Dutch Reform Church have been changing. Several of its prominent clergymen, such as B. B. Keet and Benjamin Marias, have attacked the idea that Divine will ordains segregation. Keet has stated: "Everyone, according to the Bible, is my neighbor, of whatever race, people, or nation he may be, and if he is my neighbor I must be able to associate with him."[19]

The Dutch Reform Church is divided over this issue. In the largest synod—Nedevoluits Gereformeered—Professor Keet has some support and considerable opposition. In the other two major synods, there is some soul-searching, but *apartheid* has impassioned support, especially among laymen. *Die Kerkbode,* official organ of the Dutch Reform Church, strongly endorses segregation.

SABRA, the Broederbond, and the Dutch Reform Church have developed the political philosophy of racial separation that the Nationalist Party now in power began to legislate into grim reality.[20] When the Nationalist Party decisively defeated the United Party in 1948, the thorn bush of segregation was already deeply rooted in South Africa. Because they knew precisely what they wanted and had no pangs of conscience about getting it, the Nationalists have added *apartheid* legislation in quantity to protect further the privileges of the European minority.

Legal Barriers

Fear of miscegenation, which often lies at the root of the deepest racial prejudice, resulted in a law forbidding marriages and liaisons between Africans and Europeans, in 1927. The Nationalists extended this bar to relations between Coloreds and whites, by the Mixed Marriages Act of 1949. This law not only prevented any more mixed marriages; it also nullified those already existent, bringing disaster to many families. The difficulty of defining who is Colored added a tragi-comic note to the situation, for many of the oldest Afrikaner families have some African blood in their veins. Heedless of the consequences, the Nationalists pressed on in their determination to preserve the purity of the white stock. They decreed racial registration of all South Africans. This struck certain families like a thunderbolt, revealing to the younger generation that the father or the mother was actually Colored.

Central to *apartheid* is the separation of races into different living areas. Ultimately, the Nationalists want to put all the Africans into their own state, "Bantustan." But as long as South African employers, including housewives, are dependent on cheap non-white labor, this idea will remain a fantasy. In the meantime, segregation of living facilities is being pushed at the local level. Africans, Indians, and Coloreds are not permitted to own land or housing in the more desirable, European sections. Europeans, who account for one-fifth of the rural population, have been given four-fifths of the desirable farm land.

An African must have a permit to live outside a reserve. To leave the reserve for the city, he must obtain a pass from the police, first in the reserve and then in the city. Because the reserves are overcrowded and the cities hold out at least the prospect of a job and perhaps a place to sleep, most young men leave for the cities. There they can live only in the frightful slums and shanty towns that blight every South African metropolis. Under the Group Areas Act of 1950, the government forcibly moved Africans out of these slums and into new locations. Some of these areas, like Sophiatown in Johannesburg, were later transformed into modern housing for Europeans.

The color bar also governs social life and education. It provides separate waiting rooms in railway stations, separate entrances to post offices, and even separate park benches. These separate facilities were the major target of the passive-resistance campaign of the African and Indian national congresses in 1952 and 1953. Africans and Indians began peacefully to use white waiting rooms and white park benches. Soon the jails were filled with these passive resisters, who employed the spirit and tactics of a former South African, Mahatma Gandhi. Finally, the South African government increased the penalties for violating the color bar to up to five years at hard labor and/or lashes. This blunted the edge of the resistance campaign. The Suppression of Communism Act was also used to arrest the leaders of the campaign.[21]

The Bantu Education Act of 1953 aroused more resistance among Africans and white liberals than any other single act of *apartheid*. It dealt a blow to the greatest of all equalizing forces in society—education. Until 1953, most African education was administered by church mission programs. However, for many years, most of the funds came from the government. The Afrikaners decided to take over the schools in order to teach the Bantu his proper place in society. To do this, they simply withdrew financial support from schools remaining under church administration. Many Church of England leaders in South Africa, such as Bishop Emory Reeves of Johannesburg (who was later deported), felt that this was done to redirect African education into technical channels and discourage training in the liberal arts and professions. Present inequalities are very large. Only 4 per cent of the African children go beyond primary grades, as compared to 24 per cent of the Europeans.

More recently, the government has sought to eliminate non-Europeans from white universities. Out of the nine universities and one university college, five have admitted non-European students, but only two have done so on an unsegregated basis. The policy of the Nationalists is to develop separate facilities for higher education for "natives" and to exclude them from white universities. Under this program, they have turned excellent native universities like Fort Hare into virtual vocational centers.

In order to cut out a center of United Party support, the Government took Colored voters off the common roll, arousing furious opposition among both Europeans and non-Europeans. Although this affected only the Cape Province, where Colored voters were on the common roll, it was nevertheless a blow at a principal source of support for the opposition United Party. A political maneuver and an unconstitutional act, the law infuriated the United Party and liberal South Africans. When the courts subsequently threatened to declare the measure unconstitutional, Prime Minister Daniel Malan was so determined to retain the law that he created a new high court to review such political issues. Behind this struggle lay an even deeper one between the Nationalists, who aspired to make South Africa a Republic, and pro-British elements, who wanted to retain existing Commonwealth ties and British constitutional values. This issue was finally settled in 1961, when South Africa became a republic and withdrew from the Commonwealth.

The Opposition to White Supremacy

The majority of South Africans, against whom these racial barriers have been raised, have slowly and painfully built a system of resistance. The opponents of *apartheid*—Africans, Indians, and Coloreds, assisted by a handful of white South Africans—have begun one of the most desperate and hopeless struggles in history. Yet they have preserved a remarkably peaceful and reasonable attitude. The advocate for the accused in the famous Treason Trials, in which many of the leaders of these groups were threatened with execution, summed up their position well when he said, "A battle for ideas has indeed been started in our country; a battle in which on the one side—the accused will allege—are posed those ideas which seek equal opportunities for, and freedom of thought and expression by, all persons of all races and creeds, and, on the other side, those which deny to all but a few the riches of life, both material and spiritual, which the accused aver should be common to all . . ."[22]

The most important non-European nationalist organization was, until the Sharpeville massacre of 1960, the African National Congress (ANC). Its head is Chief Albert Luthuli, a well-educated Christian leader who was deprived of his chieftaincy when he went into politics. In 1961, he was awarded the Nobel Prize for his contributions to world peace. Most ANC leaders have been drawn from the small professional class emerging painfully over many years in the African community. Respectable, moderate citizens, they do not echo the militancy of the nationalist slogans of Ghana and other West African states. At its inception, the ANC was a very moderate organization, as indicated by the aims of its 1921 Constituent Conference:

1) To unite all the various tribes in South Africa.
2) To educate public opinion on the aspirations of the black man of South Africa.
3) To advocate on behalf of the African masses equal rights and justice.
4) To be the mouthpiece of the African people and their chiefs.
5) To represent the people in governments and municipal affairs.
6) To represent them in the Union Parliament, and, generally, to do all such things as are necessary for the progress and welfare of the African people.

Since that time, they had added demands for full citizenship rights, the ballot, and equality before the law. However, it is remarkable that the ANC has never raised the demand that the government be turned over to the majority of its citizens, or that the Europeans return to their ancestral lands. Its leaders, such as Chief Luthuli, Professor Z. K. Matthews, Dr. J. S. Moroka, and Dr. J. Z. L. Njongwe, have advocated peaceful methods of achieving equality. Despite their bitter failure to make progress, especially since the rise to power of the Afrikaners, they have not turned to the advocacy of violent revolution.

The peak of ANC power was achieved during the 1953 passive-resistance campaign against *apartheid* laws. This campaign publicized the plight of Africans and other non-Europeans to the world, even though its domestic effect was to make the government intensify its repressive efforts and to curb the ANC. For years, Prime Minister Malan and his successors used the Suppression of Communism Act to put out of circulation various nationalist leaders. Nearly every important figure in the ANC, at one time or another, has been banned by this act from attending or speaking at political meetings. In 1956, the government arrested a number of ANC leaders, some other non-European leaders, and a few left-wing Europeans, on charges of treason. In all, 156 persons were arrested and tried, and forty-eight organizations were affected. This sensational trial dragged on for three years, until the courts declared the government had no evidence to support its charges of treason or Communist subversion. The Treason Trials are regarded by African groups as a tactic to harass and curb the non-European opposition movement. Although now an illegal organization, the ANC continues to operate underground.

Lack of political cooperation between the ANC and other non-European ethnic groups reflects the jealousies and suspicions which divide them. During the passive-resistance campaign, the ANC cooperated closely with the Indian National Congress, but this was a rare breakthrough between the groups. Other Indian organizations less radical than the Indian Congress will have little to do with the African nationalists, whose program they regard as too revolutionary. Cooperation between the ANC and the Colored political organizations is also poor. Paradoxically, the leading Colored organization, the Non-European Unity Movement, founded to unite opposition among the non-Europeans, is the least cooperative. The influence of Communist, and especially Trotskyite, thought, makes this group doctrinaire and inflexible. The Non-European Unity Movement refused to cooperate with the ANC in the 1953 passive resistance on the ground that this detracted from the development of an attack on the vital center of industry through a general strike and boycott.

The coordination of activities between the liberal Europeans and the ANC has been growing slowly, but it remains weak and formal. Because of its more radical programs, the Congress of Democrats, which is influenced by pro-Communist elements, has found greater favor with the Nationalists than with the Liberal Party. Alan Paton claims that the difference between the Congress of Democrats and his Liberal Party is that the former wants to reconstruct society by rooting out racialism while the Liberal Party wishes to reform existing inequalities.

Paton regrets this painful division among the handful of whites willing to work with the non-Europeans, but he sees signs of closer cooperation, especially since the Treason Trials showed that the Government was incapable of making a clear distinction between the two groups. Leaders in both groups have been hounded by the police and arrested several times. Hundreds of Europeans were jailed along with thousands of Africans, following the Sharpeville massacre in 1960. Paton led the drive in

South Africa, England, and America to collect hundreds of thousands of dollars for the defense of the men and women of all races accused in the Treason Trials.

The Liberal Party seeks support among all racial groups, but has only a handful of African supporters. Its leadership is predominantly European. Patrick Duncan, who participated in the passive resistance in cooperation with the ANC, is the executive secretary. The party's major platform is opposition to *apartheid* and racial domination by any group. It favors the gradual extension to Africans and all other non-Europeans of the ballot and full legal equality. Because the Liberal Party does not advocate immediate universal suffrage, it loses potential African support, and because it proposes immediate steps in this direction, it loses most potential white support. The gulf between European and African political thought is very wide indeed, and the Liberal Party is only a thin thread, stretched to the utmost, connecting them.

Already, the younger intellectuals among the Africans and Coloreds have begun to abandon hope for parliamentary change. They ridicule cooperation with European reformers, and they have developed a militant, ultra-Africanist look. They broke with the ANC over multiracialism and gradualism, arguing that the only just solution is for the African majority to take power and share it only with those who are prepared to be "Africans." Resolutions at a 1959 session of the Pan-Africanist Organization declared: "Multiracialism is pandering to European arrogance . . . We believe that everyone prepared to accept and give loyalty to Africa is an African."[23]

A counterracialist outlook motivates some Africans like Josias Madzunya, who has said "No white man is sincere."

A more rational group, led by Robert Sobukwe, a former lecturer at the University of Witwatersrand and president of the pan-Africanists, talks in terms of majority rule and justifies the exclusion of whites from their party only for the time being. But Sobukwe is in prison, and the more radical group is taking over.

The pan-Africanists accuse the ANC of being Communist-influenced and of selling out the interests of Africans. Walter Sisulu, once secretary-general of the ANC and now under ban, attacks the pan-Africanists: "The so-called 'African nationalism' of the Africanist turns out to be a mere inverted racialism, foreign to the spirit and traditions of the African people."[24]

Some moderate African nationalists feel that the black nationalism of pan-Africanists is as dangerous as Afrikaner white supremacy. Fanaticism breeds fanaticism. These two extremes in South Africa are leading up to a showdown which cannot be very far away.

The protests that led to the Sharpeville massacre of 1960 and the subsequent state of emergency were inspired by the pan-Africanists. Although Sobukwe and many other pan-Africanist leaders were imprisoned and the organization banned, membership has mushroomed, as younger nationalists have joined. Thus, leadership of South Africa's nationalist movement has passed to the ultra-Africanists.

Disaster Course

It is impossible to predict the precise course of events in South Africa. But one fact is certain: The non-Europeans' relatively passive acceptance of white supremacy cannot last. Already, a number of strikes, boycotts, and resistance campaigns have taken place. Most of these have been repressed with fierce brutality by South African police. The bitter struggle will doubtlessly grow in intensity.

Little prospect exists that the non-Europeans can launch a general strike or a campaign of passive resistance more effective than what has gone before, even though the European community is highly dependent on their labor. Neverthelesss, new strikes and boycotts will be staged, and the Afrikaners, having shown their willingness to make the rivers run red with African blood, still have the power to do this in their efforts to hold the country.

Reform groups are at work within the churches and the political parties of white South Africa, but it would be wishful thinking to conclude that these recent currents can reverse the powerful tides of *apartheid* at this late hour.

Many South African liberals believe the only hope lies in positive outside intervention. Bishop Reeves and Paton have often said that they hoped the United Nations and the Western world would take decisive action against South Africa, rather than simply pass resolutions deploring the situation. E. H. Brookes, for years South Africa's leading historian, believed that the United States, because of its experience with its own racial problem, was destined to play a major role in setting a new course for South Africa.

The new African states present a long-term prospect of active support for revolution and possible invasion. All the new African states have imposed a boycott on most South African goods. African political parties encourage their people to refuse to buy South African products or to deal with South African firms. This affects only a small portion of South Africa's trade, but it does hurt certain industries. Following the state of emergency in the spring of 1960, South African firms lost more than a billion dollars in stock valuation. *Apartheid* has proved costly in more than human lives.

Some South Africans have suggested using the Portuguese areas as buffer zones against any potential invasion by the Bantu nations to the north. This might hold off the new African armies for a time. But the question arises: How long can 3 million whites, even strengthened by Southern Rhodesia and the Portuguese territories, hold off 100 million black Africans supporting and supplying the "freedom fighters" in South Africa? And what will be the role of the West should the Communist states intervene? Will it attempt to assure the survival of white supremacy in South Africa? Or will it undertake action, before it is too late, to compel South Africa to alter her disaster course?

SOUTHERN RHODESIA: THE GRAND SETTLER ILLUSION

It is very difficult to leap to safety from a boat about to go over the brink of a vast falls. Such is the tragic plight of the settlers in the Central African Federation. The irresistible current is the force of African nationalism, which has spilled over from the Congo and Tanganyika and is flooding the entire region to the south, sweeping all structures of white supremacy before it.

For more than half a century, the white settlers of the Central African Federation have struggled to build a dominion that would be run by Europeans indefinitely. However, they lacked both the numbers and the ruthlessness of the South Africans, so necessary for success.

The Central African Federation, created in 1953 by Southern Rhodesia, Northern Rhodesia, and Nyasaland, contains 7.3 million Africans and 287,000 Europeans. In Southern Rhodesia, where most of the whites live, they are outnumbered more than 12 to 1 by Africans; yet they have created a system of white supremacy in economic, political, and social life. However, these settlers have not regarded this as a permanent state of inequality but have patronizingly sought to "civilize" the African before granting him his rights. As Cecil Rhodes, the father of Rhodesia, put it, "Equal rights for all civilized men and equal opportunity for all to become civilized." Thus the white supremacy of Rhodesian settlers differs from *apartheid* in theory, but in practice its racial discrimination system has many similarities. There are, however, several factors in the Rhodesian picture which give a faint glimmer of hope that the outcome may be different.

The Dominion Dream

Two men stand out in the history of Southern Rhodesia. They are Cecil Rhodes and David Livingstone—one an empire builder and the other an explorer-missionary. The contrast in their principles symbolizes the dichotomy at the base of the extension of British influence in Africa. Livingstone had a passionate love for the African, and first explored Central Africa with the elimination of the slave trade uppermost in his mind. Rhodes had little feeling for the Africans who occupied the vast regions he exploited; his desire was to accumulate wealth and expand the British Empire. Rhodes dreamed of a new white dominion in Central Africa, modeled on the Union of South Africa; Livingstone dreamed of the expansion of Christendom. To Rhodes, who sincerely believed in the white man's mission to the "uncivilized Africans," the defeat and destruction of the old African kingdoms was the advance of civilization. To Livingstone, friend-

ship, understanding, and honored treaties were the means of
opening up Africa.

Prior to the invasion of the Rhodesias by miners, fortune-
hunters, and settlers in the late nineteenth century, the potentially wealthy and well-watered southern region was occupied
by a powerful tribe, the Matabele, which was an offshoot of the
Zulu nation. The Matabele had a well-organized social unit
and lived primarily off their cattle. They had subjected or driven
out numerous weaker tribes, and were bounded by the Ngoni
to the northeast and the Thonga to the southeast. A leading
authority described the Matabele, Barotse, Bemba, Ngoni, and
Yao—the dominant tribes of the area—as the lions that
"preyed" upon the Mashona, the Thonga, and the Cewa.[25]
Warfare was frequent—but no more so than in Central Europe
during the seventeenth and eighteenth centuries—and covered
an area roughly comparable in size. In centuries long past, a high
level of civilization existed in this area. Many ruins remain, the
most famous of which are at Zimbabwe, as evidence of considerable ability in social organization, if not architecture. Invasions,
wars, and dread diseases had destroyed the vitality of these societies before the European invasion.

At the time of the coming of the white man, the Matabele and
other tribal kingdoms were powerful social units in African
terms, but their primitive weapons and fighting methods were
no match for the invaders. When Rhodes began his penetration of the area through his agents, Rudd and Jameson, the king
of the Matabele was Lobengula, a giant of a man. He knew full
well the meaning of the European encroachment, and used every
device at his command to preserve his land. But he was ultimately outmaneuvered, and driven to flight.

Modern Southern Rhodesian history begins in 1923, when
the private company that had ruled it for thirty-five years, the
British South Africa Company, was faced with bankruptcy and
sold out to the British government.[26] The European settlers
thereupon voted in a referendum to become a self-governing
British colony, and rejected a proposal of association with the
Union of South Africa. This decision, which was arrived at by
a close vote, is often pointed to as proof that Southern Rhodesia

will never link itself with South Africa—a conclusion which does not seem justified by modern developments.

The status which Great Britain granted Southern Rhodesia was unique in the empire. The settlers elected the majority of representatives on the legislative council and established their own government. The United Kingdom retained the power to override legislation in certain areas, such as affairs affecting the interests of Africans. However, that power has never been used. The nature of this government has not been significantly modified.

In a perceptive study, Philip Mason says of the historic orientation of Southern Rhodesia: "This was to be a white man's country and the idea that there should ever be an African majority voting a majority of African members into a Parliament that would rule the country was utterly foreign to the thought of anyone in the colony."[27]

One basic motive dominates all European politics in Southern Rhodesia: Fear of the African majority. African nationalism has grown now to a point where only concession or fierce repression can avoid a bloody showdown.

The European minority of 178,000, against 2.3 million Africans (in 1956), has a tremendous interest in preserving their dominant position. There are virtually no poor whites. The Europeans enjoy one of Africa's highest standards of living, and the per capita income is approximately equal to that of the United States. Yet most of Southern Rhodesia's Africans live under conditions approaching the worst in Africa. Colin Leys, a student of South African politics, in contrasting European and African living standards in Southern Rhodesia, called the one "among the highest in the world" and the other "among the lowest."[28] The greatest number of Africans in major urban centers like Salisbury and Bulawayo are employed in domestic service.

The High Color Bar

Even the settlers agree that their standard of living could not be sustained without the restrictions that bar Africans from numerous vocations and activities. Africans are prohibited from

mining and certain skilled occupations, and even certain types
of farming, such as beef and maize, are restricted. A complicated
system of pricing and taxation makes African maize more expen-
sive; yet the African planter receives less for his maize than the
European. This is justified as a tax to raise money for native-
reserve development. However, the net effect is to decrease the
Africans' ability to support themselves with cash crops, and thus
to drive African labor out of the reserves and into European
farms and mines. The cost of labor is of utmost concern to many
settlers, because their farms and industries could not compete
in the world market without cheap African labor. Much of the
recent opposition to reform in the Rhodesias arises from the
settlers' fear of rising wages. Wages rose one-third between 1953
and 1957. However, African living patterns have changed. Previously, an African father would leave his family in the reserve
while he worked in an industry in Salisbury or Bulawayo, but
now he is likely to bring his family with him, thus making the
average wage of £13, or $36.40, per month far from adequate,
even though it represents a considerable increase over a decade
ago.[29]

At the heart of the economic and political problems of Southern
Rhodesia is land distribution. William Barber believes that even
if the restrictions on African production were removed, the land
situation would prevent any rapid rise in African living standards.
Africans are continuously being moved out of European areas
into crowded native reserves. Already the European settlers hold
half of the land area, including the most fertile and well-watered
regions. Furthermore, only 8 per cent of the Europeans are
farmers, while the great majority of Africans depend on farming for their livelihood. In 1957, a government select committee
reported that out of the 31.7 million acres of European farm
holdings, only from 3 to 4 per cent were under cultivation.[30]
Thus, the system of land apportionment, besides creating tremendous unrest among Africans, exerts a powerful brake on
agricultural production.

Southern Rhodesia's system of land distribution can be understood only in terms of the settlers' goal of a rapid increase in the
white population through immigration. The influx of white set-

tlers, mostly from South Africa and the United Kingdom, has enabled the white population to grow at the high annual rate of 10 per cent, so that a goal of .5 million or more in the two Rhodesias by 1970 does not seem unattainable, leaving aside the doubtful prospect of political stability. White immigration is often justified as a source of much-needed skilled labor. However, each immigration costs the government £2,500, and critics argue that many more Africans could be trained in the same skills for the amounts being expended on white newcomers.

Educational opportunities are similarly unequal for black and white children. For Europeans, education is compulsory until age fifteen. For Africans, even a primary education is unsure, and high school is very improbable indeed.[31] In 1960, only two African secondary schools could provide the Cambridge senior certificate necessary for entrance into the University College of the Rhodesias at Salisbury. Because the British Government's grant to this college specified that the student body be inter-racial, this is the first educational institution in Southern Rhodesia to adopt integration in the classroom. By the middle of 1959, thirty-six Africans, one Indian, and one Colored student were enrolled, along with 130 Europeans.

Government spokesmen have attached great significance to certain breakthroughs in racial barriers, but although it is true that a well-dressed African can now enter certain hotels and restaurants in Salisbury and not be thrown out or insulted, and official segregation on the railways and in post offices has been abandoned, the fundamental areas of segregation—land distribution, job opportunities, and advanced education—remain untouched.

Any government which has attempted to initiate significant reforms on behalf of the African population has found its position gradually undermined. Colin Leys, in a careful study, concludes: "Nothing is more striking in Rhodesian politics than the way in which under different party labels the opposition has consistently based its electoral appeal on the doctrine of European Supremacy."[32] This happened in 1958 to the Garfield Todd government of the United Rhodesia Party, which sought reforms in the wages and franchise of Africans. Settler opposition, both

inside and outside the government, replaced Todd with Sir
Edgar Whitehead, and the 1958 elections saw the outright segre-
gationist Dominion Party emerge as a powerful opposition, only
two seats short of a majority. Immigrant Afrikaners from South
Africa have swelled the ranks of the Dominion Party to the point
where it threatens to take over. Now the Whitehead government,
pressured by London, is seeking reforms, and faces powerful
resistance.

The Party System

Prime Minister Whitehead professes a policy of "partnership"
under which the African is to be raised gradually to the level
of the European and slowly admitted to full citizenship. The
Dominion Party is far more racialist and believes in separate
development of the races. It would like to sever all British control immediately. Most of its leaders deny that they support
apartheid, but a Dominion government would pursue racial
policies very similar to those of South Africa, and this would
probably lead to a close association of the two countries.

A small, liberal, interracialist party, led by Garfield Todd, has
won little support for its program of more rapid integration of
the African into political and economic life. It has allied itself
with liberals in Northern Rhodesia to create the Central African
Party. Each political party in Southern Rhodesia has formed a
federation party for the federal elections. The United Rhodesian
Party has a federal counterpart called the United Federal Party,
and the Dominion Party's federal group retains the same name.

Outside Rhodesia's parliamentary system exists the growing
African nationalist movement, which is becoming increasingly
impatient with the "partnership" policy proclaimed by the settler government. Most Africans view "partnership" as a fraud
which deceives no one except naïve outsiders in England and
the United States.

The leading nationalist organization in 1961 was the National
Democratic Party (NDP) led by Joshua Nkomo, a moderate nationalist educated at Adams College in South Africa. Fortunately
for Nkomo, he was out of the country during the 1959 emergency,

when the government cracked down on the growing power of
the nationalists and banned the Southern Rhodesia National
Congress (SRNC), imprisoning numerous leaders. At the middle
of 1961, several of these leaders were still in prison. The previous
head of SRNC, Micael Mawema, was sentenced, under the Un-
lawful Organization Act, to four years at hard labor. (The NDP
was banned in December, 1961, and its assets seized. Shortly thereafter, the Zimbabwe African Peoples Union was formed by
Nkomo.)

Stirred by the advances of Africans in the north, the Southern
Rhodesians have begun to organize and demonstrate *en masse.*
When Nkomo returned home on November 20, 1960, to take over
leadership of the NDP, he was welcomed at the airport and
along the route to Salisbury by 10,000 followers shouting "Freedom!" Nkomo began as a moderate nationalist, but the increasingly radical demands of his followers have forced him to call
for more sweeping reforms.

Until mid-1961, no provision existed for African representation in the legislature of Southern Rhodesia. Qualified Africans
were admitted to the common roll, but the requirements as to
education, income, and employment were so high that only a few
thousand Africans could meet them, and these voters were too
scattered to exert a measurable effect on any election. The 1957
government white paper on the African franchise limited the
number of Africans who could qualify for the common roll to
no more than 20 per cent of the electorate, thus assuring that,
even if the Africans made rapid progress, their vote would continue to be severely limited. A special election roll exists for
Africans, and periodically its requirements are raised. The settlers defend this practice on the grounds that Africans are not
entitled to vote until they have acquired "civilization."

Early in 1961, a government white paper announced projected
reforms in the rights and representation of Africans. It called for
a declaration of rights to be drafted which would protect Africans
against further discriminatory legislation. From their special roll,
Africans would begin to elect fifteen members in the sixty-five-
seat legislature. Requirements for the special roll would be lowered to permit some 50,000 Africans to vote. However, the Do-

minion Party rejected these recommendations, which had been worked out under pressure from the British government. The proposals were put to a referendum and adopted by a substantial majority. The African nationalists opposed these proposals as too limited. They conducted their own referendum, and according to NDP officials, 372,546 Africans voted against the proposals, and 471 in favor. The liberal settlers, led by Garfield Todd, are only slightly encouraged by the limited steps achieved in behalf of African political rights.

The settlers of Southern Rhodesia are increasingly concerned over events in the Central African Federation of the Rhodesians and Nyasaland. They are fearful that the federation will soon be dominated by Africans, since they gained control of Nyasaland in 1960 and the pressure is mounting for an African government in Northern Rhodesia. Meanwhile, the agitation for withdrawal from the federation heightens in Southern Rhodesia. Thus the federation is being pulled apart by two irreconcilable forces.

The Character of Central African Federation

The primary impetus for creation of the Central African Federation in 1953 was the settlers' desire to combine the large white population of Southern Rhodesia with the wealth in copper of Northern Rhodesia. United, the settlers hoped to be strong enough to hold off the pressures from the black north for African equality.

Much favorable interest was generated in England for the federation, because it would create a larger, more viable productive unit in Central Africa. One of the strongest arguments used by many pro-federation liberals was that the federation would keep the Southern Rhodesians from drifting into a close union with South Africa.

Despite virtually unanimous opposition by the Africans in the two northern territories and some resistance among those in Southern Rhodesia, federation was pushed through. The Africans, fully aware of the settlers' motivations, had an exaggerated fear that federation might mean the loss of their tribal lands in the northern territories. Considering the history of land distribution in Southern Rhodesia, this fear was understandable. A campaign of passive resistance to federation was launched in Nyasaland, which had the most to lose and the least to gain. This campaign was quickly broken by the government. Nevertheless, the African nationalist movement in Nyasaland has consistently urged a boycott of elections of representatives to the federation.

From the very beginning, the Central African Federation has produced sharp party differences in England. A Labour government initiated talks on forming the federation, but backed away from the idea when the opposition of the Africans became apparent. After the Conservative government was formed in 1951, it soon reached agreement on a federation constitution. Because Great Britain retains the power to decide the future of the federation, even though it has let a great deal of this power slip away, the federation presents a very grave issue for the British people.

The constitution distributes the powers of government so as to preserve some control over vital African affairs in the hands of the territorial governments. The following areas of jurisdiction were reserved to the territories:

1) Changes in their own territorial constitutions;
2) Local government;
3) African native authorities and the development of native law;
4) African agriculture and land;
5) African education through the secondary schools;
6) Trade unions and industrial disputes;
7) Public order and police;
8) Mining.[33]

A great deal of publicity was given to the establishment of an African Affairs Board, which could hold up, and appeal to the British Government from, any legislation which it deemed discriminatory against the African. One such appeal was made in 1957 against new federal legislation on the franchise. The appeal was rejected. When the board later passed into the hands of the United Federal Party, Sir John Moffat, former chairman of the African Affairs Board and leader of the Northern Rhodesia Liberal Party, asserted that the board could not longer be considered "an impartial or independent body."

The federation franchise system is similar to that of Southern Rhodesia, with a common roll and a special roll for Africans. Property and education requirements for the special roll are high, limiting the number of African voters. The representation system is highly complex, and has the effect of placing the fifty-nine assembly seats in the firm control of the Europeans. Twelve seats are reserved for Africans, but Europeans control the vote for eight of these.

Despite such provisions, Sir Roy Welensky, Prime Minister of the federation and head of the United Federal Party, is convinced that federation can be made to work as a proper vehicle of partnership, provided assimilation is not too rapid. In his view, "All too often in recent years the emergent peoples of the Continent have been offered gifts of democracy and 'freedom' without the precaution being taken of ensuring that they are able to make that use of them expected by the donors." While he admits that the federation makes no pretence at being a democracy now, Sir Roy believes that it is moving in that direction.

However, Sir Roy is faced with a powerful African demand for equality now, and a growing group of settlers, centered in the Dominion Party, who will leave the federation before accepting anything approaching equality for Africans.

The prospect is dim indeed that the federation can reconcile the opposite interests of the settlers and the Africans. Nevertheless, some well-tempered observers in England and Africa believe that the federation has justified its creation. They point to the outstanding economic progress made between 1953 and 1960, and the rise in the Africans' productivity and wages. Lowering of the color bar in the copper belt, and especially in Southern Rhodesia, is attributed to the influence of the federation. Most important of all is the crack in the wall against African representation in Southern Rhodesia.

Critics of the federation argue that much of the economic progress was in the copper belt and probably would have taken place without federation. They claim that the lowering of the color bar in Southern Rhodesia involved those areas where it has the least significance—restaurants and post offices—and left the basic areas of land distribution, skilled occupations, and elective representation fundamentally unchanged.

However, these questions are likely to become academic before long, for it does not seem possible to reconcile the interests of white supremacists and black nationalists within the federation constitution's "partnership."

There seems to be a law of equal and opposite reactions in African politics. The extreme of white supremacy breeds the opposite extreme of ultra-Africanism. Not even the highly oppressive regime in South Africa can wipe out African resistance.

Some British liberals who have devoted much attention to this problem, such as Philip Mason, believe the federation might be preserved if the powers of the federal government were diminished and the two northern territories were given greater autonomy, with African majorities in the legislature.[34] Colin Leys believes that the federation can survive only if African predominance is accepted without delay in the two northern territories and introduced quickly in Southern Rhodesia; he favors the use of force to achieve this end, if necessary.[35]

The African nationalist viewpoint appears more realistic: The federation is dead, and unless the settlers show some common sense, the devil will have his due.

TWO | # The Challenge
to
Policy

5.

The Growth of
Communist Influence

Communism has been attracting great interest among all African nationalists since World War II, particularly among ultra-Africanists. Although the number of African converts is not great, the ideas of Communism are growing in influence. The prospect of Communist seizure of an African state is remote. The more real threat to Western interests is the gradual growth in Communist-bloc influence over Africa.

Communism in Africa, as in most of the underdeveloped world, moves along two paths: First, it offers the example of what the Soviet Union has done in little more than forty years in transforming one of the world's most backward societies into the second-ranking industrial power; second, its continuous ideological attacks on the vestiges of Western imperialism and white supremacy persuade many Africans that they have a champion in the Communist bloc. Some have come to the conclusion that Lenin's interpretation of imperialism contains a large element of truth. The new form of imperialism developed by the Soviet Union means little to most Africans, particularly those who still live under colonialism or have only recently emerged from it.

Most of the leaders of African nationalism, both Westernized and ultra-Africanist, are fully aware of the subversive aims of Communism, and take steps to counteract its influence among their followers. But at the same time, they try to use the influence of the U.S.S.R. as a lever against the "colonial powers." They

know that if they fail to obtain independence and a rising standard of living for their people, they will soon be replaced by more
militant leaders, some of whom may be attracted to Communism.
Communism has been most successful in areas like Indochina,
where nationalism has been frustrated in its fulfillment by Western powers. The advocates of hate seize the newborn child of
nationalism and make it their own when it has been disowned
by the West.

In the West we often find hysteria on the subject of advancing
Communist influence. There is a dangerous tendency to associate
all that is anti-Western with Communism, when a great deal of
such sentiment is simply an expression of the desire to be free
from Western control. Smear tactics are employed too often in an
effort to stem the rising revolutionary tide. (Most Frenchmen in
Algeria were convinced, during the height of the conflict, that
the FLN had gone over to the Communists.) On the other hand,
many well-meaning liberals often overlook the real nature of
Communist strength in order to minimize alarms raised by conservative special interests. The West must be extremely wary of
this emotional oversimplification of issues, and gauge accurately
the true extent of Communist strength.

Although Soviet trade with all of Africa does not amount to
very much, compared with that of the Western countries, it is
several times greater now than it was before World War II. In
1956, U.S.S.R. exports to Egypt amounted to $22.6 million, and
its imports from Egypt amounted to $16 million. The next-
largest African exporter to the U.S.S.R. in 1956 was South Africa
($2.1 million), which imported only $498,000 of goods from the
U.S.S.R.

Total Communist-bloc exports to Africa in 1956 amounted to
$146.5 million, and its imports were $173 million. A high percentage of this trade was with Egypt, as a result of the arms agreement, and Czechoslovakia led the bloc in exports to Africa.
Guinea has become a trading center for Communist China,
which is seeking to penetrate the continent far more extensively.

Compared with the Western powers, the Communist bloc has
a negligible volume of trade with Africa. However, most of it is
with the newly independent countries, not the colonies, and it

has just begun. It is likely to grow rapidly in importance. The Russians have pushed hard by sending trade missions to the newly independent governments of Ghana, Guinea, Morocco, and the Sudan, and these countries in turn are, for the first time, sending trade missions to Moscow. Already the Russians are offering favorable terms, as in Egypt, in order to get a foot in the door. At first, most of the new African countries are cautious about entering into broad agreements with the Communist bloc, but as they gain self-confidence, they start to play the game which several Asian countries have found so profitable—inviting competitive offers of trade and aid from the West and the Soviet bloc.

Technical and Economic Aid

Russian programs of technical assistance are under way in Egypt, the Sudan, Morocco, Guinea, Ghana, and Ethiopia, and several other African states are negotiating such agreements. Several hundred Communist technicians are believed to be working in Egypt and the Sudan, engaged in the Aswan High Dam program and various other agricultural, irrigation, and industrial projects. The Russian hospital at Addis Ababa is a great success with the Ethiopians.

From 1955 to 1959, the Communist nations gave about $2 billion of economic and military aid to underdeveloped areas in Asia and Africa. Now an increasing proportion of such aid is finding its way into Africa (about $197 million in loans from 1959 to mid-1961).

Because they realize that African countries are sensitive about any possible political strings attached to economic assistance, the Russians try to persuade the Africans that Western imperialists grant assistance for a political price, while the Communists extend help purely in the interests of African advancement. Armenian Arzamunian of the University of Moscow, director of the Institute of World Economy and International Relations, stated this clearly at the Afro-Asian Peoples Conference in Cairo, in 1957:

We the Soviet Union can build factories and a transport system and also a research center or a university, as well as a hospital or a cultural institute ... Do what you think best in your own interest. Tell us your needs and we are able to render you whatever assistance or anything else. In return for our help we ask no direct advantage, no privileges, no participation in the administration, no concessions, no raw materials, no accession to a strategic or diplomatic system, neither alteration in your system of government, nor changes in your domestic or foreign policy.[1]

The Russians have developed information programs through their newly opened diplomatic posts. The one in Accra, for example, has a staff of more than seventy persons. The attractive displays and well-stocked library shelves offer many Africans their first view of how the Communists develop the "workers' state." It is impossible to gauge the impact of this on formative African minds. But since most of this material was censored or prohibited by the colonial government until only a short time ago, its appearance gives Africans a window on a part of the world about which they had known almost nothing. It is not surprising that many should be attracted by it.

Travel and study programs in Soviet countries are now widely available to Africans. Colonial governments were wont to restrict travel behind the Iron Curtain, often refusing to issue travel papers to students invited to youth festivals or educational institutions. With the withdrawal of Western control from British and French West African territories, such restrictions ended. No accurate figures exist on the number of African students traveling or studying in the Soviet Union and other Communist countries, but all reliable estimates indicate it is in the thousands. By 1960, Guinea alone had 186 students in the U.S.S.R., 56 in East Germany, and 36 in Czechoslovakia.[2] A great attraction to students and their governments is the Communist offering of opportunities in science. Late in 1960, Nkrumah announced that several hundred Ghanaians would go to the Soviet Union and other Communist countries to study science.[3] He noted that this was an experiment and that it would not succeed if the students were subjected to too much ideological indoctrination. Free transportation and tuition are offered Africans by the newly established Afro-Asian Friendship University in Moscow.[4]

Ideology and Reality

The Russians' understanding of events in Africa is grossly distorted by their Marxist interpretation. They tend to view each situation in the context of the people's struggle against imperialism. When the nationalist movement in Ghana (the CPP) denounced Communism, Moscow reacted by calling such nationalist parties "imperialist stooges" and declared they were not truly revolutionary. At one stage, the Communists backed the reactionary traditionalist parties, such as the National Liberation Movement centered in Ashanti, describing them as the true representatives of African nationalism.[5] This, however, soon proved to be clearly false, and the Communists had to adopt new tactics.

One new approach is to encourage academic research and analysis of Africa. The Institute of Ethnography of the U.S.S.R. Academy of Sciences in Moscow convened a meeting in 1956 to "establish agreement for the plan of scientific research work on Africa in the Institutes of the Soviet Academy of Sciences." The conference outlined a course of Soviet studies on Africa through 1960. Seven major fields of study were selected, with various subjects scheduled for publication in each area. Some of the more significant studies:

Under Section 1, "History of Africa"—"History of the Culture of the Peoples of Western Sudan and Arabian Colonization of East Africa."

Under Section 2, "The Imperialist Partition and Repartition of Africa"—"Anglo-German Rivalry in East Africa During the Second Half of the 19th Century" and "The Struggle of the Mashona and the Matabele Against the Colonization of Rhodesia."

Under Section 4, "The Economic Situation and the National-Liberation Movements in Africa after World War II"—"Economic Development and the Struggle of the Peoples of Nigeria Against Imperialist Enslavement after World War II" and "Liberia under the Oppression of American Monopolies."

Other sections included political studies, African philology, and geography.[6]

Despite their obvious ideological bias, these Soviet studies rep-

resent a new, massive-research approach to Africa that will undoubtedly influence the shaping of Soviet activities in Africa. In
1959, an African Institute was formed in Moscow under the direction of I. Potekhin.

Increasing numbers of Soviet scholars are visiting Africa. Professor Potekhin, then director of the Institute of Ethnography,
did a three-month study in Ghana.[7] He later returned with a
number of his colleagues to the All-Africa Peoples Conference in
Accra. To some observers, this was a massive Soviet invasion of
Africa, but Professor Potekhin seems to feel that an American
invasion preceded him.[8]

Strategic Interests

The Soviet Union is keenly interested in Africa's vast natural
resources, which are probably of more value to the less endowed
Communist-bloc countries. The Soviets' major strategic interest
in Africa should be viewed within the context of the over-all cold
war struggle: The Communists would greatly weaken Western
Europe if they could secure a strong grip on parts or all of
Africa.

The prospect of a direct Communist frontal assault anywhere
in Africa is practically nonexistent. There is no Communist state
bordering Africa. The Soviet Union would present a direct military threat to Africa only in the event of a war in the Middle
East. Recent events in the Middle East show that even ultra-
Africanism poses a major obstacle to the advance of Communism.
The principal dynamic of the United Arab Republic is pan-
Arab nationalism, which leaps over the artificial barriers created
between Arab peoples by European powers. It is important to
realize that this is not a Communist force—and is not necessarily
even an ally of Communism, but could be its strongest opponent
in the Middle East.

Although the U.S.S.R. has no interest in direct military expansion in Africa, it does seek ideological penetration and the
shrewed manipulation of nationalist parties, so as to weaken the
position of the Western powers and advance the day, which it
is confident will come, of "the peoples' revolution" in various

parts of Africa. The Communists have not yet penetrated very deeply into Africa, but this is no cause for complacency. The struggle of ideas will not be settled in the near future, but will continue for the next several decades. And the Russians can afford to wait, if the gradual deterioration of relations between the West and the Africans continues.

Communist Ideas and Parties

Arab nationalists in North Africa are the most politically conscious and often the most frustrated Africans. Egypt, Algeria, and Tunisia suffer chronic overpopulation problems. A growing gap separates the middle class from the mass of peasants and workers. As a consequence, an increasingly pro-Communist wing is developing within the trade unions of Morocco and Tunisia. In Egypt, where trade unions are more tightly controlled, this group has been driven underground. Meanwhile, because of various political reasons, there is little Western help in these areas.

The Algerian war has contributed most to the growth of Communist influence in North Africa. Alienated by the West's continuing support of France, the Algerian nationalists have drifted eastward in their search for arms and financial help. All the other North African countries have helped, but the U.A.R. has been the most consistent ally. Morocco and Tunisia have been restrained by their dependence upon France and the West for financing of their own development programs. Communist influence was not an important factor at the start of the Algerian war, but it has grown steadily during the years of conflict. The Algerians have received the blessings of the Soviet bloc and have had to resort to the threat of openly accepting Communist assistance. This development led President Bourguiba to remark to an American correspondent: "Stick with France and you will not only lose the Algerians, you will also lose all of North Africa to the Communists and eventually all of the African continent as an inevitable consequence."[9]

The Communists are exploiting skillfully their opportunities to pose as champions of colonial independence movements through the various forces, such as pan-Islam and the pan-

African–Cairo axis. Moslems throughout Africa are naturally attracted to the anticolonialism of the U.A.R. The religious bond plays an even more significant role in African politics than in U.S. politics. Moslem influence in sub-Sahara Africa has been much greater in history than is commonly recognized in the West; it exerts even greater influence now. In the French Sudan, Senegal, Niger, and Nigeria, Moslems form the majority, and in all West and East African areas, Moslems are a strong, fast-growing minority.

At the Cairo Conference of 1957, which founded the Afro-Asian Peoples Solidarity Council, the Soviet Union and the Asian Communists quietly played a skillful game. While the Soviet Union was officially represented in the conference, they and other Communist delegates were content to operate in the background. It is never clear whether Nasser is using the Communists in the Afro-Asian Peoples Solidarity Council or they are using him. However, it is certain that the Communists have a foot in the door of this anticolonial, anti-Western movement.

Communist influence in nationalist movements south of the Sahara is often exaggerated by former colonial powers seeking U.S. aid for their programs. No major nationalist movement in Africa is Communist-dominated. A distinction must be made between a hard-core ideological Communist who has read Marx and Lenin and accepts the latest doctrine propounded by Khrushchev and an African who admires the Soviet Union and is prone to accept Communist propaganda because it is anti-colonial. The hard-core Communists are only a handful, but the pro-Soviet group is sizable and growing.

A few hard-core Communists can be found in the French-influenced areas of Africa. Here the trade unions and student associations have offered fertile ground for Communist ideology. The French Communist-led General Council of Workers (CGT) was the most active of French trade unions in developing affiliated unions in former French colonies. It persuaded the African affiliates to join the Communist World Federation of Trade Unions (WFTU), and this provided a continuing point of contact for certain African unions in the former French Cameroun and Upper Volta. The Christian trade unions, which are anti-Communist, are growing, but they suffer from their identification with French colonial interests.

Some Communist influence developed in the trade union movement of Ghana, but this seems to have been effectively counteracted by vigorous action on the part of Nkrumah. He forced disciplinary action against the former chairman, Antony Woode, and E. C. Turkson Ocran, both prominent members of the CPP.

In the past several years, the International Confederation of Free Trade Unions (ICFTU) has been doing vigorous organizational work in Africa, with regional offices in Ghana and Kenya. It has wooed several fledgling trade unions away from the WFTU and established affiliates in East Africa, the Federation of Rhodesia and Nyasaland, Southern Cameroons, Gambia, Malagasy, Nigeria, Sierra Leone, Somalia, Morocco, Tunisia, and Algeria. However, several African leaders from Guinea, Morocco, Ghana, and Tunisia have decided to take African trade unions out of the cold war by forming the All-African Trade Union Federation (AATUF), whose aim is to represent "independent organizations rejecting all foreign interference in African trade union affairs."

Perhaps the strongest pro-Communist trade union and peasant organization exists in the Sudan, where the present federation, centered in the Gezira scheme, is thought by some observers to be Communist-led.[10] Even under the new dictatorship, Communists are permitted to operate much more freely in the Sudan than in her powerful neighbor to the north.

The Union des Populations du Cameroun (UPC) has often been described by the French and Western press as Communist-led. This is a gross exaggeration of the extent of Communist influence. Although Marxist in part, the main ideological content of the UPC stems from the Presbyterian training of most of its leadership and the tribal groups of the Sanaga-Maritime and Bameléké regions. The principal leader, Dr. Félix-Roland Moumié, who died of poisoning in Geneva in 1960, was said to have accepted Communist aid. He certainly participated actively in the Afro-Asian Peoples Solidarity Council, but he was no more a Communist than Touré of Guinea. As much, if not more, Communist influence once existed in the now conservative, pro-French

RDA in the Ivory Coast. Moumié and his associate Um Nyobe were the victims of an international conspiracy to discredit their revolutionary movement.

Considering the strength of the French Communist Party and the great freedom it has enjoyed in the colonial areas, it is remarkable that its influence has been so slight. However, the Communists appear to have the upper hand in the African student organizations in Paris, and many of the leaders are taken on guided tours of Eastern Europe and to youth conferences there. This same radical tendency is seen in African student groups in Great Britain. It should be kept in mind, however, that such student organizations have been far to the left in political orientation for many years, and that doctrinaire views of students change very rapidly when they return to the more conservative political climates of home.[11]

It is not surprising that the largest Communist organization in Africa is found in South Africa. Here, the racialist policies of the dominant white minority have provided perfect conditions for the development of political extremism. It is impossible to establish the number of Communists because the party is now illegal and underground. The hard core does not number more than a few hundred, but its influence is swelled by numerous fellow-traveler groups.

Originally, most of the Communists in South Africa were white immigrants from England who brought their Marxism from the slums of London and Birmingham to the shanty towns of Johannesburg and the mining areas. W. H. Andrews is regarded as the father of South African Communism. He immigrated in 1893 and became active in the South African Labour Party, from which he split during World War I, taking with him his International Socialist League, which was a predominantly white organization.

Later the Communist Party drew non-whites into its program and by the time it was outlawed in 1950, it had become a primarily non-white organization, although several important leaders were European. Since the party was banned, the Communists have worked through various front organizations, among them the Congress of Democrats, formed in 1952, which pulled to-

gether a number of progressive organizations, many of whose
members were not Communists.

The Communists have infiltrated the non-white nationalist
and trade union movements in South Africa, but it is difficult to
establish how much influence they exert over these organizations.
The Afrikaner press is convinced that all non-white political
movements are Communist-directed. Even more detached observers have mistakenly accused the African National Congress of
being Communist-led. But although some Communists and fellow travelers have from time to time held influential positions
within the ANC, it is not Communist-dominated, and such
accusations have done much harm. The struggle for control goes
on internally. Many African leaders such as Chief Albert Luthuli
and Z. K. Matthews are determined to keep the Communists from
taking control.[12] Their task is made immensely difficult, because
the government's severe oppression tends to draw all persecuted
elements together. As we have noted, Communists now consider
the Pan-Africanist Congress an important group to penetrate.
The racial feeling in this organization is so strong that European
Communists are not trusted, and therefore the African converts
are depended on to influence this powerful African movement.

In 1955, the Communist fronts and the non-Communists joined
in drafting the now famous Freedom Charter, which won world-
wide support for its ringing plea for full human rights in South
Africa.

Because of increasing repression by the government, which does
not distinguish between Communists and non-Communists but
views all opponents of *apartheid* as subversives, the non-Communists appear to be losing their struggle against Communist
penetration. Hard-pressed South Africans fighting *apartheid* find
it increasingly difficult to reject assistance from the Communists.

The non-European trade union movement, which established
the South African Congress of Trade Unions (SACTU) in 1955,
is heavily infiltrated with pro-Communists. Although willing to
work with the ICFTU, the Congress has also sought help from
the WFTU, and now attempts to draw support from both camps.
The ICFTU continues to try to work with SACTU because of the
difficult situation in South Africa. Its oppressive laws restrict

union leadership to whites, and Africans are expected to join white trade unions.

– White supremacy is Communism's greatest ally in Africa. There exists the very grave prospect that the Communists will gain control of the major nonwhite political organizations as a result of the revolutionary spirit engendered by racial oppression. This can happen not only in South Africa but also in Southern Rhodesia and the Portuguese territories. The only real alternatives having an appeal to a great mass of people were the nonviolent resistance campaign launched in 1952 by the ANC and the revolutionary uprising in Northern Angola.

The Congo Republic, under the strange and erratic leadership of Patrice Lumumba, provided one of the latest examples of Communist influence. Lumumba was not a Communist, and the Communist group in the Congolese nationalist movement has always been small. However, they briefly achieved key points of influence in Lumumba's government. The Belgian Communist Party gave Lumumba substantial help, as did the Soviet Union and Czechoslovakia, and a few leading Belgian Communists acted as advisers to him. Evidently the Communists planned to occupy a key role in the new Republic of the Congo, but they overplayed their hand. One of the earliest centers of activity was the Czechoslovakian Consulate General in Léopoldville. Several Congolese leaders, including Antoine Gizenga, vice premier under Lumumba and president of the fellow-traveling African Solidarity Party, visited Prague and Moscow in 1959 and 1960. Alphonse Ngurubu, president of the Peoples' Party in the Léopoldville area and Minister of State under Lumumba, visited the Thirteenth Congress of the Belgian Communist Party in Liège. Such associations are not necessarily evidence of Communist allegiance. Leaders of the National Congolese Movement (MNC) in the Stanleyville area have, as demonstrated by the Gizenga government, a pro-Soviet orientation. Communist influence existed in pockets of this organization, as the Centre de Regroupement Africain (CEREA) in the Kivu province.

The Soviets' sudden intervention in Congo affairs in August and September, 1960, when they bypassed U.N. administrators to send in arms, trucks, and technical personnel, produced a reaction of alarm. This helped bring about Colonel Joseph Mobutu's coup and the ousting of the U.S.S.R. embassy and personnel from the Congo.[13] President Kasavubu's government subsequently took a strong anti-Communist position. Although Communist influence persists in the Stanleyville Province through the MNC and certain members of the African government, the Adoula Government has succeeded in establishing a firm neutral policy, thus limiting Communist influence in this now familiar African way.

Communism has not developed a mass following in the Congo, and the few intellectuals who sought to move the Congo into the Soviet orbit blundered badly. Clearly, the vast body of Congolese nationalists is not Communist.[14] Indeed, most leaders would prefer to adopt the neutral position of other African states, but with the U.N.'s intervention they are subject to all the pressures of the world ideological struggle.

Communist prospects outside the white-settled regions of sub-Sahara Africa and certain parts of North Africa are very dim at present. First, the reactionary, land-owning aristocracies—so successfully exploited as targets in Asia—exist in only a few areas of Africa. The chieftain system is rapidly yielding to more representative political systems, and land redistribution is replacing the old communal divisions. Further, the pressure of population on the land has not seriously affected political attitudes, in most sections of Africa.

The second factor that weakens Communist appeal is the rapid change that has taken place in postwar colonial policies, particularly within the last several years. The old Communist shibboleths regarding colonialism are scarcely relevant in former British and French West Africa, where great strides have been made in creating economically strong and politically self-governing African states. The intelligent African views the dogmatic and often inaccurate Communist assertions with suspicion and scorn.

The final and most significant reason is the political astuteness and positive leadership of many African nationalists. Although anti-imperialist, they have not been taken in by Communist tactics.[15] They mean to chart their own policies, independent of the pressures of both East and West. As long as such leaders can show significant progress, Africa will not go Communist.

6.

Africa at the United Nations

Almost overnight, the focus of United Nations debate has shifted from the Middle East to Africa. Africa is moving into the mainstream of world affairs. The tremendous problems of transition in this complex continent have become matters of world concern. By the end of 1960—called the "African year" at the United Nations—twenty-two African states had become members. This brought U.N. membership to ninety-nine and gave the forty-six-member Afro-Asian bloc a near-majority. Although by no means a solid front, these countries possess a common viewpoint on such subjects as condemnation of colonialism and racialism.

The Congo crisis plunged the United Nations into the heart of Africa, involving it more comprehensively than any event since the Korean war. When the Belgians decided, in 1959, to give the Congo its independence within a year, most nations applauded the move, not realizing how inadequately the Belgians had prepared the Congolese to govern themselves. (One diplomat summed up the situation as follows: "The Belgians did not leave too soon, they left too suddenly.") There were only a handful of trained Congolese administrators when independence came, and not a single Congolese officer in the army. The Congolese troops, refusing to take orders from their Belgian officers, mutinied, and a nightmare of rioting and pillaging followed. In this chaotic aftermath, opportunistic African leaders in Katanga Province, steered by Belgian mining interests, announced its secession from

the new Republic of the Congo. Unable to cope with these disastrous events and unwilling to destroy his country's "neutralism"
by seeking the intervention of one of the big powers, Premier
Lumumba turned to the U.N. Secretary-General Dag Hammarskjöld wisely selected troops from neutral nations, primarily
African and Asian, to constitute the intervening force. At the
same time, he established a fifteen-member advisory committee
on the Congo. A team of U.N. administrators, headed by a U.N.
commissioner who was Hammarskjöld's personal representative,
was flown to the Congo to keep essential welfare and government
services going.

Although unity and complete order were not achieved overnight, the U.N. kept the conflicting parties from tearing each
other to pieces and averted widespread starvation and the complete breakdown of health facilities. Despite big-power efforts to
exploit the U.N. action for cold war gains, the U.N. has succeeded in bringing contending Congolese factions together to
discuss closer union.

The U.N. will probably remain in the Congo for some time to
come, trying to put together the pieces of an extremely complex
puzzle. Its major function is to prevent a complete breakdown
while more permanent solutions are sought.

Many observers believe that such intervention and conciliation
will be major functions of the U.N. in Africa during the years
ahead. Such difficult problems as South African racialism, the
future of South West Africa, and the break-up of the Central
African Federation are looming ominously close on the horizon.
This prospect will be examined in more detail in the final chapter, but let us look at the background of African and colonial
issues before the United Nations.

Africans, both as official representatives and as nationalist
leaders, have continually sought out the United Nations to focus
world concern on their struggles for justice and freedom. Often
their expectations of U.N. action have been excessive, and at
times their tactics have been questionable, but in the main they
have found the U.N. a very important means of awakening the
conscience of the world to the responsibilities assumed a decade
and a half ago at the San Francisco Conference.

The Great Debate

The United Nations has often been slightingly referred to as that "great debating society." Indeed, it *is* a debating society, and one that can focus the eyes of the world upon the contending parties.

The function of debate is absolutely vital. Even though decisive action seldom results from the U.N. debates, tangible results are in the making. A full debate clarifies the opposing positions and enables representatives to devise compromises and then put pressure on their own governments to accept them. Public opinion is often aroused, and this in turn creates pressures which, over the years, can change a government's hardened position. The nations, particularly the big powers, are increasingly desirous of winning and retaining the good opinion and support of other governments.[1] In the United Nations, the Afro-Asian bloc of "neutral" nations come into their own by exercising independent judgment. Neither the United States nor the Soviet Union can afford over a long period to pursue policies which would alienate a large segment of this group. Occasionally, policies will run counter to the opinions of this group, as in bomb tests or colonial issues. But a constant pressure, over the years, upon the major powers to be conciliatory in debate and flexible in policy brings about new positions and negotiations.

On the vital issues of colonialism, race relations, economic development—those immense problems associated with the emergence of the new areas of Africa, Asia, and the Middle East—the United Nations has exerted particularly important influence.

The great powers' responsibility for the welfare and advancement of the peoples of the underdeveloped areas has been constantly proclaimed on the floor of the United Nations. The technical-assistance programs and the Development Fund of the U.N., weak and inadequate though they are, have initiated many reforms and offer the prospect of ever-growing assistance to the poverty-stricken areas of the world. The Soviet Union originally described these programs as "capitalist ventures" intended to perpetuate colonialism, but they had to abandon this position or risk losing the respect of the "neutral" nations, who were among the strongest proponents of these programs.

Africa and the General Assembly

The Afro-Asian bloc has raised most of the African issues in the U.N. They have been vigorously opposed by the European colonial powers, who have usually argued that colonial issues were matters of "domestic jurisdiction" and did not belong in an international forum. It takes only a simple majority vote to place an issue on the agenda of the General Assembly, and this has been achieved with growing frequency because of the mounting number of Afro-Asian countries in the U.N. More and more, the colonial powers have been forced to debate these issues in the committees of the General Assembly and before the Assembly itself.

The Security Council has been playing a reduced role in this area, in part because of the West's refusal to permit discussion of disputes over colonial policies of permanent members. Conducting such debates in the General Assembly limits the possibilities of action but permits much freer exchanges.

A resolution of substance by the General Assembly requires a two-thirds majority, so the Afro-Asian bloc has not always succeeded in pushing through vigorous resolutions in support of its views.[2] It has usually had to accept a compromise put forward by the Western Hemisphere nations, including the United States and its noncolonial allies.

The Assembly is split into four major blocs—Western Hemisphere, Western European, Eastern European, and Afro-Asian. The Western Hemisphere bloc has been able to prevent the Afro-Asian bloc from gaining complete control of the General Assembly, but it has succeeded in this only by putting pressure on the colonial powers (1) to debate issues with the anticolonial faction, and (2) to consider more liberal policies.

North Africa

Beginning in 1952, the questions of Morocco and Tunisia were placed on the agenda of the General Assembly. France vigorously resisted this move, claiming that the subjects fell under the "domestic jurisdiction" clause—Article Two, Section Seven of the U.N. Charter. Moreover, France argued, the General Assembly had no right to discuss treaty arrangements between France and these North African protectorates. However, the thirteen Afro-Asian nations who brought the complaint declared that France was violating her treaty and the principles of human rights while denying self-determination.

For the first two years, France refused to take part in the debates of the General Assembly over her North African policies. Other Western powers tended to sympathize with her, but the United States favored airing the issues in order to ease the tension, and then carefully abstained in the critical votes. Strong resolutions calling upon France to recognize "full sovereignty and independence" for these protectorates were defeated, and milder resolutions were adopted, expressing a hope that negotiations for a settlement would continue.[3]

While some French political leaders steadfastly maintained that France would continue to ignore the intervention of the United Nations in Morocco and Tunisia, the more liberal leaders felt pressured to work out solutions with the nationalist representatives of these two countries. In 1954, the Mendes-France government began negotiations for an agreement with the Tunisians for internal autonomy, which was completed by the Edgar Fauré government in 1955. In the same year, the French brought Sultan Mohammed of Morocco back from exile and granted him virtual independence. Thus, in less than three years, the issues relating to Morocco and Tunisia were resolved. It would be too much to claim that the United Nations brought this about by its intervention. The nationalist rebellions in each country were decisive forces. But a combination of rebellion and international pressure convinced the liberal and central leaders in France that they must come to terms with the nationalists. At that time, they were strong enough to resist the demands of the *colons* and of the militarists and crypto-fascist elements in France that France maintain her presence in North Africa.

The Algerian question, although containing many of the same elements as the Moroccan and Tunisian issues, falls into a different category. In the Thirteenth Session of the General Assembly, a strong resolution calling for acceptance of self-determination for Algeria passed the First Committee, but by one vote failed of adoption in the plenary session of the General Assembly. The United States abstained rather than oppose this resolution, a move that was regarded as highly significant. In the Fifteenth Assembly, the Algerian FLN gained more votes, with the addition of new African nations, and secured passage of a resolution calling upon the U.N. to intercede in the French–Algerian conflict on behalf of Algerian independence. A resolution calling for a U.N.-supervised referendum failed by a tie vote in committee. However, for the first time, despite a French boycott and Western-bloc opposition, the U.N. went on record as favoring overwhelmingly (63 to 8, with 27 abstentions) independence for Algeria.[4]

The new African states of the French Community, led by the Ivory Coast and Senegal, attempted to conciliate between France and the Algerians. They urged the Assembly to request negotiations between the two, rather than a referendum supervised by the U.N.

South Africa

One of the longest-standing General Assembly debates has been over South Africa's violation of human rights in her policy of *apartheid*, and her failure to adhere to mandate obligations to South West Africa, assumed under the League of Nations.

South Africa has never recognized the right of the United Nations to take up these matters, maintaining that they are entirely domestic. Because the General Assembly insisted on debating these issues, South Africa not only refused to participate but practically withdrew from the U.N. for a period. In the Thirteenth Assembly, South Africa returned to take part in some issues affecting it, and is now participating in virtually all matters.

World concern over the racialist *apartheid* system in South Africa led to the establishment, in December, 1952, of a three-member Commission on the Racial Situation in the Union of

South Africa. The commission's task was to investigate the extent of South Africa's violation of the concepts of human rights inherent in the principles of the U.N. Charter, which it had accepted. The Western powers, including the United States, supported South Africa's contention that this was a purely domestic matter. But the General Assembly, dominated by a strong Afro-Asian viewpoint, saw in South Africa's increasing discrimination a threat to the equalitarian ideals at the core of the U.N. concept. Comparisons were drawn, not without justification, between *apartheid* and Hitler's racialism, with its ultimate threat to world peace.

South Africa absolutely refused any cooperation with the commission, and even failed to permit its members to enter her borders. However, a great deal of valuable material was placed in the public record by the commission's examination of the effect of the new *apartheid* laws on the social fabric of South Africa.[5] Year after year, the commission came to the same conclusion about the laws of South Africa. As stated in the 1954 report: "Laws and regulations enacted since [1953] are as incompatible with the obligations assumed by the Union of South Africa under the provisions of the Charter relating to human rights, as were the measures previously adopted."[6]

United States representatives, keenly aware of strong U.S. opposition to a system of racial discrimination in Africa, spoke against racialism while at the same time deploring this particular intervention in South Africa's domestic affairs, but the U.S. abstained from voting on the resolutions. When the question of continuing the life of the commission came up, the United States voted against it. Renewal of the commission fell short of the required two-thirds majority, and it died in the Tenth Assembly, in 1955.

However, the U.N.'s annual reviews of South African racial policies did not end. Every succeeding Assembly has passed a resolution condemning policies of governments that persecute and discriminate against racial and religious groups in violation of their pledges to the United Nations. Security Council resolutions condemned the actions of the South African government during the Sharpeville massacre of March, 1960, with firm support from the United States. Since 1959, the United States has openly sided against South African *apartheid* in the U.N. debates. Other Western powers, however, take the view that racial policies are an internal matter and not a proper subject for international resolution. This view is diametrically opposed to the African states' mounting desire for international action against South Africa.

The mandate territory of South West Africa is another matter of long-standing dispute between South Africa and the United Nations. South Africa refused to recognize any obligation to place South West Africa under the trusteeship system of the United Nations, even though all the other nations followed this course with their former League of Nations mandates. The objective of South African policy, particularly under the Nationalists, has been to incorporate South West Africa. They have, to date, been blocked by the intervention of the United Nations and the lack of enthusiasm shown by the small white community in South West Africa.

United Nations interest in the problem was awakened by the protests of various tribal groups, such as the Hereros, against absorption by South Africa. The Reverend Michael Scott, an Anglican clergyman and former missionary in South Africa, persuaded the United Nations to establish a special committee for the South West African question in 1953.[7] For years, he has been the chief spokesman for some 600,000 African and Colored people of the territory. South Africa forbids leaders of the indigenous peoples of South West Africa to travel abroad, although several, such as Mburumba Kerina and Fanuel Jariretundu Kozonguizi, leader of the South West Africa National Union, have escaped and given testimony at the U.N.

The General Assembly has passed numerous resolutions calling upon South Africa to make reports on her administration of South West Africa. The International Court of Justice ruled that South Africa had no obligation to place the territory under the trusteeship system, but that it had the responsibility of continuing to make reports and allowing petitions to be submitted to the United Nations.[8]

South Africa rejected this ruling and opposed all attempts by the South West Africa Committee to implement supervision. Finally, however, it agreed to discussions with a special commission acting for the committee, consisting of Great Britain, the United States, and Brazil. The commission suggested a partition of South West Africa—the rich southern section to go to South Africa and the barren northern region to become a trust territory. But this solution was rejected by the Africans and overwhelmingly voted down in the Fourth Committee of the General Assembly.

In 1960, Liberia and Ethiopia took legal action against South Africa in the International Court of Justice. They charged that South Africa had violated the mandate she assumed in 1920 by practicing *apartheid* and suppressing civil rights. Under Article Seven of the original mandate, South Africa had agreed to submit to the League of Nations' international tribunal any dispute with "another member relating to the interpretation or the application of the provisions of the mandate."

The Fifteenth General Assembly passed, by a vote of 78 to 0, a sharp resolution calling on South Africa to end all racial discrimination in South West Africa. It also established a commission to investigate conditions there. Previous U.N. attempts to send an investigating committee had failed because South Africa denied them permission to enter the area. The United States and Great Britain were not happy with the resolution, and subsequently abstained. In the debate, they tried vainly to moderate the mounting African fury against the Union, and a wide and dangerous rift opened between the United States and the African states.

If the United Nations had not exerted international pressure on South Africa, South West Africa would long ago have been swallowed up by the hungry Afrikaners, who are particularly desirous of its mineral wealth. Thus, the last hope of the indigenous peoples of South West Africa is the United Nations.

Trusteeship

When the United Nations trusteeship system was drafted, an attempt was made by anticolonial countries to strengthen the structure of international supervision. This was vigorously resisted by the European colonial powers, and the final compromise satisfied no one. A Trusteeship Council was formed, with a seat for each administering power plus each big power. An equal number of rotating, nonadministering powers were appointed. Time and again, this balanced representation has led to a deadlock.

The trusteeship system has proved far more effective in influencing the development of trust territories than the League's mandates did. While its function has been essentially supervisory and not directly administrative, it has spiritedly debated important issues affecting the lives and welfare of peoples under its jurisdiction, and has decisively influenced the policy of certain administering powers.

These African territories were placed under trusteeship: Cameroons (British), Cameroun (French), Ruanda-Urundi (Belgian), Somaliland (Italy), Tanganyika (British), Togoland (British), and Togoland (French). South West Africa was given a different status at the insistence of the General Assembly that the U.N. possessed important responsibility to the League of Nations. By the end of 1961, the only trust territory that was not either independent or on the threshold of independence was South West Africa. The relinquishment of these trust territories was achieved far more rapidly than many African leaders had dared hope.

The disposition of former Italian colonies was the first difficult trust-territory issue. Because Italy was a defeated power and not then a member of the U.N., the status of Libya and Italian Somaliland remained uncertain for a time. Finally, the General Assembly agreed on a formula for their independence within a limited time. Britain, France, and Russia each tried at some point to gain the Assembly's consent to its administration of Libya, a barren land but strategically situated on the Mediterranean. The Western countries reluctantly agreed, in 1949, that Libya should be granted independence within two years.[9]

Italy was again appointed to administer Italian Somaliland, but only for ten years. By 1960, Somaliland was to become independent. The General Assembly and the Trusteeship Council undertook the close supervision of the transition period of both territories.[10]

French and British Togoland have made peaceful transitions to self-government, avoiding disastrous pitfalls, under the auspices of the Trusteeship Council. The U.N.-supervised plebiscite in British Togoland in 1957 made it possible to integrate it peacefully into the new state of Ghana. Considerable opposition to this merger had been voiced by the Ewe tribe, so the referendum served to register the general will. Even more fundamental was the U.N.'s supervision of the 1958 elections in French Togoland, which brought the genuine nationalist force to power. For years previously, elections in the French territory had been rigged.

Independence for the two Cameroon trust territories was voted at the special session of the General Assembly early in 1959, as the result of some very complicated efforts by the Trusteeship Council to deal with the riot-ridden French Cameroun. The U.N. decision to hold plebiscites to determine the particular form of independence poured oil on the troubled waters. However, the Western powers, by opposing any new elections in the French Cameroun prior to independence, maneuvered to keep in power the pro-French Ahidjo government. This was strongly opposed by all African states in the U.N. In early 1961, the British Cameroons was given the choice of unification with Nigeria or with independent Cameroun. The northern section chose to join Nigeria, and the southern section Cameroun.

In other African trust territories, the influence of the Trusteeship Council has been less pronounced. But the reports of visiting missions have been of great importance. Every three years, these missions toured each territory and reported their findings to the Trusteeship Council, which then discussed them with the administering power. Although the administering authorities usually managed to conduct the visiting missions on an official tour, the missions have frequently produced stimulating contact with unofficial representatives of nationalist movements. The growth of the Tanganyika African National Union has been encouraged by such contacts. A 1953 move by the Afro-Asian nations to establish permanent observation posts in the trust territories, strongly opposed by the administering powers, was defeated by one vote in the General Assembly.

The petition system has been an important method of conveying nationalist views to the Trusteeship Council, which has received a vast amount of information and representatives of numerous African groups. Some of these, like Sylvanius Olympio of Togoland and Julius Nyerere of Tanganyika, have been extremely effective. For South West Africa, the petition hearings were instrumental in precipitating U.N. action.

Trusteeship Council deadlocks between the colonial and anti-colonial powers have often been resolved by reference of the issue to the General Assembly. Here the Afro-Asian bloc has prevailed increasingly, in recent years. Their major war cry has been a demand for "target dates" for independence. This has now become a thing of the past, since the U.N. will soon complete its trust obligations in Africa. Only the thorny South West Africa issue remains.[11]

The trusteeship system provides for the transfer of any non-self-governing territory to U.N. trusteeship, but no colonial powers have taken advantage of this. They prefer to retain direct control. However, every administering power has a certain international responsibility arising from its non-trust territories. This is specifically recognized in the U.N. Charter in the "Declaration Regarding Non-Self-Governing Territories." In Article 73, the administering powers of the U.N. pledge themselves to promote the well-being of dependent peoples and "to develop self-government" and "free political institutions."

To implement this pledge, a Committee on Information from Non-Self-Governing Territories was created in 1949. Its purpose was to collect information on social and economic matters only. The administering powers have for the most part refused to supply political information to the committee, on the ground that this is outside its province.

It was the Afro-Asian bloc that pushed through creation of the Committee on Information from Non-Self-Governing Territories, over the opposition of all the colonial powers (except New Zealand), who objected that this was an invasion of domestic jurisdiction.[12] The British and French have cooperated with the committee by supplying information and discussing questions, but the Belgians have blown hot and cold. At one point, they withdrew completely because they believed the committee was exceeding its authority.

The most difficulty has been created by Portugal, which refuses to acknowledge that it has any responsibility to the committee. Portugal argues that its colonies are mere overseas extensions of its European territory. Thus, it contends, it is not obligated to make reports on these areas to the committee. This attitude has drawn fiery protests from the Afro-Asian bloc and pre-cipitated a tense series of discussions by the Fourth Committee of the General Assembly on what constitutes a non-self-governing territory. In the main, opinion has been divided along familiar lines—the Western administering powers siding with Portugal against the criticizing Afro-Asian nations. Portugal is also sup-ported by certain Latin American powers because of their close cultural, religious, and historical ties.

The United States backed Portugal through a long series of maneuvers in the General Assembly. Then, in 1961, the U.S. re-versed this policy. African pressure was great enough to achieve passage of a motion of censure of Portugal in the Fifteenth As-sembly. Since then, in both the Security Council and the General Assembly, Portugal has had few friends.

Almost from the beginning of the Committee on Information, a running debate has surrounded the submission of political data. The European administering powers have insisted that this obli-gation cannot be construed from the wording of Article 73, whereas the nonadministering powers, indirectly supported by the United States, have contended that political information is necessarily a part of adequate economic and social information. When the General Assembly sought to press this point upon the colonial powers by resolution in 1952, Belgium withdrew from the committee in protest. As there is no way of forcing such in-formation from the administering powers, the deadlock has per-sisted. Only the United States voluntarily supplied the desired political information, concerning Puerto Rico.[13]

In summary, the Committee on Information from Non-Self-Governing Territories has gathered an imposing amount of infor-

mation, but its work has been of limited value, mainly because
several of the administering powers have refused to cooperate.

Technical Assistance

The Economic Commission for Africa, with headquarters in
Addis Ababa, illustrates the great change in U.N. activities in
Africa over the past decade. Its success offers a marked contrast
to the meager achievements of the Committee on Information
on Non-Self-Governing Territories.

The Economic Commission was created in 1958 because of
the strongly expressed wishes of the newly independent nations
of Africa. The colonial powers were not enthusiastic about its
creation, but only Belgium abstained. Its task is to make surveys
and studies in cooperation with African states and to recommend joint utilization of resources and techniques of economic
development. It also serves as a central planning agency for the
developing U.N. Technical Assistance Program in Africa. All independent and some colonial nations are represented on this
commission. Britain, France, and Belgium are members; the
U.S. and the U.S.S.R. are observers.

With the growth of the new African states, the activity of the
U.N.'s functional agencies there has expanded far more rapidly
than anticipated. The Congo emergency action has taxed the
resources of the U.N. to the limit: The FAO has supplied surplus foods; the WHO, medical services; and the various economic
boards, numerous staff members to keep the government agencies running. The World Bank and other U.N. agencies have
undertaken extensive loan programs—including a loan to Nigeria
to expand its railroads and the promise of a loan to Ghana for
her Volta scheme. UNESCO has helped a number of countries
in basic education and cultural-exchange programs, and the
U.N. has had a scholarship program for trust-territory students.

For many years, the U.N. was excluded from numerous areas
in Africa because the colonial powers preferred to administer
and finance their own programs. They regarded the U.N. as a
dangerous symbol of independence. But now that most of Africa
is independent, the demand for international programs is un-

limited. Most of the new states would rather receive assistance from the U.N. than from the big powers. They believe that they can retain their neutrality this way, and satisfy their real needs rather than provide propaganda showpieces.

The Afro-Asian nations have long sought the creation of a U.N. capital fund to supplement the Technical Assistance Program. The latter has been able to provide only technical assistance and not capital aid. The great powers originally opposed this, arguing that they could not afford it and wanted control over the expenditure of their funds. However, Afro-Asian pressure created the International Development Agency, the United Nations Special Fund, and, in the Fifteenth Assembly (1960), the Capital Development Fund. Thus, the Afro-Asian group have realized at least part of their goal. Great hope was aroused in the African nations when President Eisenhower, in his address to the Fifteenth General Assembly, called for creation of a $100 million Special Fund for Africa. The Kennedy Administration adopted a similar proposal.

Africa has indeed come of age, and the United Nations has become the primary arena in which the new relationships between the Western powers and independent Africa will be evolved.

7.

Origins of
American Policy

The changes in American policy toward Africa effected by the
Kennedy Administration—particularly those at the United Nations—have created considerable surprise and speculation. These
changes do not indicate fundamental reversals of policy but arise
out of a new balance that is being struck among the several interests, principles, and approaches that have long governed
America's relations with Africa.

This policy has stirred increasing controversy in recent years.
Some critics have declared that America had no policy on Africa.
Among these was Chester Bowles—recently Under Secretary of
State and now special adviser to the President and roving
Ambassador to Africa, Latin America, and Asia—who in 1956
outlined a new approach in a series of lectures at the University
of California (later published under the title *Africa's Challenge
to America*). The formative Herskovits Report for the U.S. Sen-
ate Foreign Relations Committee, published in 1959, begins:
"The United States has never had a positive, dynamic policy for
Africa,"[1] and condemns America's "negative ad hoc approach"
to Africa.[2]

Foreign critics have ranged from the Communists, who see
American policy as capitalist imperialism, to a significant group
of West Europeans who accuse the United States of siding with
African nationalism. The Afro-Asian world has often received
from the United States a general impression of uncertainty, tim-

idity, and equivocation on issues involving colonialism, race
relations, and Africa's economic development.

American policy, it should be realized, is torn by a basic conflict. The traditional American support for the rights of man
and liberation from colonialism is frequently countermanded by
the strategic necessities of contemporary foreign policy. A perceptive analysis of this dilemma has been made by C. W. De
Kiewiet: "The political and historical ideal of independence
for subject peoples and the strategic need for dependable bases
and safe lines of communication dwell together in American
foreign policy."[3]

Foreign observers are quick to see this. During a discussion
with the author, a leader of the Algerian FLN remarked, "The
Americans sympathize with us, but their support is for France."

The ideal of self-determination is a strong motivating force
in American policy toward Africa. A nation that began its history in subjection to a colonial power is naturally sympathetic
to the cause of people who are still ruled by unrelieved tyranny.
This deep commitment to liberty manifested itself after World
War I, when Woodrow Wilson insisted that the colonies taken
from the Central Powers must not be divided up as spoils that
belonged to the victors but should become mandate territories
under the League of Nations. During the last years of World
War II, Secretary of State Cordell Hull piloted the creation
of the U.N. Trusteeship Council. And in 1956, American opposition to the invasion of Egypt by Great Britain, France, and
Israel affirmed its basic sympathy with the colonial peoples.

But these outstanding instances of humanitarian concern have
been overshadowed by a primary dedication to strategic considerations. In its quest for military bases and raw materials from
Africa, especially strategic minerals, the United States has been
extremely careful not to irritate its European allies, who formerly dominated most of the African continent. Thus, U.S. policy
toward Africa has been primarily influenced by America's interests in Europe. Another major factor, of course, has been the cold
war. Only secondary consideration was given to the rights and
well-being of Africans. This in large part explains the strange
and often awkward attitude of the U.S. delegation to the United

Nations during the past decade on issues involving South Africa, North Africa, and many of the trust and colonial territories.

Many foreign-policy analysts endorse such a policy on the ground that the world's security is threatened continuously by Communist aggression. They argue that a big power's obligation is to chart its course by national interest and to reject the sentimental attraction of moral law and the needs of the world community. However, all too often these self-styled "realists" have overlooked the truth that all the military might the West can muster cannot match the strength of the respect of men who form a majority of the human race. Hans Morgenthau, although a prominent "realist" in foreign policy, wrote in 1953:

> The United States has tended to opt in virtually all respects for the policies of the metropolitan powers, however modified and qualified in detail, and it has subordinated its long-range interest in the autonomous development of the native population to short-range considerations of strategy and expediency.[4]

Many indications suggest that the Kennedy Administration is giving higher priority to the principles of our democratic heritage in its policy toward Africa.

One clue is found in a concluding statement made by Bowles in his University of California lectures on Africa:

> Here we must express the fervent hope that we shall soon come to view the Soviet challenge not negatively as a mortal danger, but positively as an opportunity for which the continuing political, social and industrial revolution of Jefferson, Lincoln, and Henry Ford has equipped us as no other people on earth.
>
> In that direction alone can we rediscover our own traditional sense of national purpose and thus rededicate our energies to the only objective which will give us common cause with a majority of mankind—the pursuit of freedom, opportunity, dignity, and peace for all men everywhere.[5]

The new American policy toward Africa can best be explained by an analysis of the various interest groups in America which are concerned with Africa. American policymakers like to say that American policy is determined by the "national interest." But it must be realized that there are numerous groups, often

with conflicting interests, which make up the "national interest."
They range from those who view their own and the national interest in terms of narrow profitmaking to those who see America's
well-being within the context of rising levels of life in Africa.
The final decision is a compromise or balance between the com-
peting points of view.

There are three major categories of interest groups affecting
American policy toward Africa—humanitarian, economic, and
strategic. These have several subgroups and are often interrelated.

Humanitarian Involvement

A wide range of humanitarian groups interested in Africa have
matured within the past decade. Large foundations, such as the
Rockefeller Foundation and the Ford Foundation, have financed
health and education programs directed at improving the living
standards of Africans and American understanding of Africa.
However, by far the largest humanitarian investment of Americans in Africa has been and continues to be the Christian missions.

The work of Christian missions is properly described as humanitarian because it has helped create educational and social institutions for the improvement of African welfare. American
missionaries, both Protestant and Catholic, have built schools
and hospitals the length and breadth of the continent. In 1955,
there were 2,659 Protestant American missionaries in sub-Sahara
Africa, and in 1959, there were 785 American Catholic missionaries. In the days before the colonial governments became wel-
fare-conscious, the missions carried the brunt of the struggle
against disease and illiteracy. Often the missionaries introduced
new crops and agricultural technology to Africans—in Uganda,
for example, the missionaries began the now-flourishing cotton
industry.

The missions today are being rapidly transformed into national churches, owned and run by Africans, with missionaries
as fellow workers, rather than bosses. Their leaders are Africans
educated and trained in the mission school system. Most of
Africa's new political elite began their education in mission-

operated schools, and some, like Kwame Nkrumah and Julius Nyerere, were for a time teachers in the mission system.

The Jan B. Smuts School of Social Work in Johannesburg was one of the most outstanding contributions of American mission work in Africa. Established by Dr. Ray Phillips more than thirty years ago, it gave South Africans fundamental training in the techniques of community self-help and in the adjustment to industrial life. Since they were taught equality and human dignity at the same time, it is not surprising that this worthy enterprise was closed by the government's *apartheid* program.

The necessity of giving financial support to these Christian endeavors abroad has brought many Americans in touch with Africans and their problems. Mission boards have carried on a wide program of education about the poverty and backwardness in Africa. Some returned missionaries have spoken out against all systems of racial discrimination in Africa. African Christians and students have come to America to lecture and study.

Dr. Emory Ross, one of America's leading Africanists and a well-known missionary, has for years sought to direct American policy toward Africa along humanitarian lines. In Dr. Ross's view, "There are already footpaths of American philanthropy in Africa." He calls for a much greater program of mutual support and aid with Africa:

> That real and heavy task, essential for Africa, for us, and for the world, is the creating of Christian Community in and with Africa— that Christian Community which is open not only to all peoples but which has concern for all of the life of all of the people. In such a Christian Community what has come to be called "Point Four" is a basic and historically accepted major element—the aiding of all the life of all the people. Land, food, clothing, shelter, health, religion, literacy, literature, education, communications, recreation, economics, family, community, government—all of these things are or should be, the Christian concern of Christians everywhere, for everybody.[6]

American mission influence on policymaking has been directed at greater economic support for improved living conditions. It sees Point Four as an extension of the original mission educational, medical, and agricultural programs. At times, the missions have appeared to be almost the tools of colonial powers, but at other times, they have vigorously defended the rights of Africans, as when the Anglican Bishop of the Church Missionary Society in Uganda urged the return of the exiled Kabaka of Buganda, in 1954.

A powerful humanitarian link with Africa, especially south of the Sahara, is the kinship between the American Negro and the African. Until very recently, American Negroes generally preferred to forget their "primitive" origins and concentrate on demonstrating that they were really no different from white Americans. However, a number of prominent American Negroes, such as Marcus Garvey and W. E. B. DuBois, and, more recently, Horace Mann Bond and Langston Hughes, have opposed this trend and striven to make the Negro proud of his African heritage. Except for the short-lived Garvey movement, which helped develop Liberia, these Africanists won few followers. But the past decade has witnessed an amazing renaissance of Africanism among American Negroes. Negro scholars, churchmen, and political leaders have begun to include Africa and Africans in their conception of the role of the Negro in the modern world.

A high point was reached in this African renaissance in America with the birth of modern Ghana in 1957. Here, for the first time, the American Negro could point with great pride to an accomplishment of his people in Africa. Dr. Kwame Nkrumah, a product of one of the finest Negro colleges in the U.S., Lincoln University, established the first all-African democratic government. Moreover, the birth of modern Ghana brought to world attention the greatness of the ancient civilizations of Africa. The Ghana Kingdom of the thirteenth century rivaled in splendor and power the contemporary societies of Western Europe. Two centuries ago, the black man's civilizations were destroyed by the white man and the Arab, and the conquered peoples were sold into slavery. But today, Ghana has thrown off the imperial yoke, regained its sovereignty, and emerged as an important member of the world community.

The American Negroes' concern for Africa lay dormant for more than a century after the founding of Liberia. The struggling little community which had landed at Providence on the shores of Africa was practically forgotten. Then Marcus Garvey roared up from Jamaica in the 1920's, shouting "Back to Africa" and "Think Black." Before he was finally exposed as a fraud, Garvey had enrolled millions of American Negroes in his cause of sending Negroes to Liberia to escape discrimination in the U.S., thus arousing a great deal of interest in Liberia, and in Africa in general. Nkrumah has stated that a book about Garvey, *The Philosophy and Opinions of Marcus Garvey,* played a large role in shaping his nationalism.

This set the stage for the rise of pan-Africanism among American Negroes. Pan-Africanism has been a movement between the new African intelligentsia and the Negro intellectuals of the United States and the West Indies. Its primary impact in the 1930's was on young rising African nationalists like Nkrumah in Ghana and Azikiwe in Nigeria, who received great inspiration from the writings and comradeship of George Padmore and W. E. B. DuBois.

American Negroes have also given much impetus to the study of Negro art and literature as a culture in its own right, on a par with other great streams of thought in Europe and Asia. One group particularly identified with this renaissance is the American Society of African Culture, in New York.[7] An increasing flow of educators, students, writers, and artists, both to and from Africa, indicates the rising influence of Negritude.

A number of Negroes are assisting in Africa's emergence through their own work in U.S. government agencies. Perhaps the most prominent of these is Dr. Ralph Bunche, already a hero to schoolboys in remote villages of Africa. Negro voters, a sizable political force in American politics, are increasingly concerned over the white-supremacist governments of Africa, and have a basic sympathy for African nationalism. The National Association for the Advancement of Colored People is very influential in domestic U.S. policy, and its influence on the country's foreign policy where Africa is concerned is growing. It clearly favors basing U.S. policy toward Africa on human rights rather than on security considerations.

Foundations and educational groups have advanced amazingly during the past decade in their programs to exchange students and scholars and to increase American support of African education.

The Carnegie Corporation has supported research programs in Africa for many years, among them the Institute of Social Research at Makerere University College in Uganda. Both the Rockefeller Foundation and the Ford Foundation have assisted scientific and educational programs and have given funds to hundreds of scholars to enable them to do research in Africa. The African-American Institute has sponsored a program of support for scholarships for African students in America. Between 1927 and 1960, the Carnegie Corporation spent more than $5.5 million on African activities, and between 1952 and 1960, the Ford Foundation spent more than $2.5 million on its sub-Sahara programs. Northwestern University and Boston University pioneered programs of study in the African area, which have since spread across the country.[8] A three-way arrangement by Michigan State University, the University of London, and the government of Nigeria created the University of Nigeria. Now that the colonial powers have been removed and their jealousy is no longer an obstacle, assistance to African education will unquestionably be accelerated.

Economic Interests

Our economic interest in Africa is growing with increasing momentum. The reason is a historic coincidence of great significance: When the African colonies, a prime source of raw materials, achieved their independence from the European political and economic complex, the United States ceased being a raw-material-exporting country and became a raw-material-importing country.

In some ways, the interests of American private capital are similar to those of British and French capital in the late nineteenth century. But there are also many new aspects. American capital ventures are subject to many controls—trade unionism, the strong respect for human rights in American liberalism, the Christian missions, and the American Negro communities. But probably most important of all, African nationalism is strong and militant in most areas where private American capital is being invested.

The greatest American economic interest in Africa is already of a public character, directed toward welfare and development rather than profit. American capital invested in Africa is about equally divided between public and private funds. Private-capital investment will continue to grow, but it is rapidly becoming secondary to government programs of economic aid.

By 1960, American private investment in Africa totaled more than $1 billion, which amounted to only 4 per cent of U.S. overseas investments. Between 1955 and 1957, this increased 55 per cent.

American firms are most interested in Africa's enormous mineral wealth. Liberia has some of the richest iron ore deposits in the world, and the known American reserves are beginning to thin out. Thus, the Liberian American Mining Company (LAMCO) and Republic Steel have begun the exploitation of rich iron ore deposits in Liberia. It should be added that the Liberian government has increased its share in these economic concessions and is currently contracting for 50 per cent of the profits, as in the agreement with the Liberian American Swedish Minerals Company and LAMCO.[9]

In 1953, the U.S. imported 9 per cent of its steel-making ore, and this rose to 25 per cent in 1956. In that year, the U.S. imported 1 million tons of iron ore from Liberia, and this soon rose to 3 million. Algeria, Morocco, and Tunisia are also sources of iron ore.[10]

Keen interest has developed in Northern Rhodesian copper, where the American Metal Company has extensive shares in mineral extraction. Some $50 million of private American capital is invested in Northern Rhodesia, virtually all of it in copper, chrome, manganese, and lithium mines. Also, Canadian-American capital has been developing the copper deposits in Uganda, a project made possible by a new rail link and power supply from hydroelectric facilities on the source of the Nile at Jinja.

By 1960, about $500 million of private American capital was invested in the Union of South Africa, making it the greatest African center of American investment.[11] Most of this was in mining such minerals as gold and uranium, and sizable amounts were in petroleum and manufacturing. It is significant that, during the late 1950's, U.S. investment slackened in the Union of South Africa and interest shifted to the Rhodesias. This has been attributed in part to the political difficulties and uncertainties created by the racial policy of the South African government.

A decade ago, America was exporting oil: today it is rapidly increasing the amount it imports. Thus, with the discovery of huge reserves in Libya and Algeria, and the uncertainty of Middle East supplies, American interest in African oil deposits has reached an all-time high. Several American oil companies have secured large concessions for exploration of African territory. In Libya, Standard Oil of New Jersey holds rights over 18.8 million acres where giant deposits have been found. In Algeria, Standard Oil and Gulf Oil are collaborating with French companies in the development of the Sahara field, estimated to contain 1 billion tons of oil. Other areas of intensive exploration by American-owned or -controlled companies are Ethiopia and Somaliland in East Africa, and Nigeria and Angola in West Africa. Promising strikes have already been made by Standard Oil of New Jersey near Luanda. Socony Vacuum obtained concessions in Northern Nigeria in 1955, and Gulf Oil was granted exploration rights in Ghana in 1956.

Uranium, the most strategic of all minerals, is found extensively in the Congo, especially in Katanga Province, and the Republic of South Africa. Until considerable deposits were found in North America, the U.S. imported most of its needs from Africa. However, since the North American deposits are not expected to last more than a decade or two, it is highly important to ensure that the African uranium supply remains available to the West.

In 1960, the United States received 3.4 per cent of its total imports from Africa, and sent 3.2 per cent of its exports to Africa. In the past, a major limitation on trade with the United States was the dollar problem. European governments, hard-pressed for dollars, were reluctant to allow their African colonies to indulge in extensive dollar purchases from the U.S. The independent countries of Africa are less restrained, but limits are set by their exports to the U.S. With the easing of the dollar shortage, trade possibilities have improved. However, U.S. trade with Africa is not growing as rapidly as with other parts of the world. Liberia is the only country in Africa that does the majority of its trading with the United States. More than 80 per cent of its exports go to the U.S., and more than 60 per cent of its imports come from the U.S.

American companies with interests in Africa tend to support the policies of the existing regime. In colonial territories, they usually pursue a "don't rock the boat" line. They generally accept existing wage patterns and labor policies—even racial discrimination, as witnessed in Northern Rhodesia and South Africa. However, they have occasionally resisted such policies— as when the American Metal Company exerted pressure on white trade unions in Northern Rhodesia to reform their racial practices. American companies are, of course, anxious to have their government protect their interests against seizure or any form of discrimination.

Africa is at the bottom of the list of all major areas receiving American aid. In part, this is a reflection of the secondary place accorded to Africa by American strategy in world politics. This in turn is because, until recently, most of Africa was under colonial control. Colonial governments have frankly preferred to be the principal benefactors of native populations, and to some extent they intend to continue their dominant roles even after their colonies have attained independence. The French have not encouraged American aid in their former territories. Neither the Portuguese nor the Belgians have been particularly eager to receive American aid for their colonies and spheres of influence. And, although the British have been most open to assistance in colonial areas, they have been very wary of American supervisory teams.

American aid has tended to enter those independent areas where it has strategic interests or developing commercial relations. Thus, Libya, with its air bases, has been favored. Central Africa, with its American mining investment, has benefited from considerable U.S. government and World Bank support to expand its railways and develop the Kariba Dam hydroelectric scheme. But this tendency is giving way to more general support.

Prior to World War II, U.S. public financing in Africa was nothing.[12] In 1960, the United States was providing economic assistance of one type or another to some twenty-six African countries. With the subsequent rapid increase in the number of independent countries, this aid has been extended. U. S. aid went from $4 million in 1952 to $214.4 million in 1960.[13] This excludes military programs, which amounted to only $10.2 million in 1960. Surplus foods formed an important part of the program, while only $20 million was budgeted for technical cooperation programs.[14] Additional funds in the form of a Special Program for Tropical Africa (SPTA) were requested by the Administration, but not adopted by Congress.

The Development Loan Fund has become an important agency for Africa. In 1960, Liberia, Tanganyika, Tunisia, Libya, and Ethiopia all received small loans from this fund. Also, international agencies have assisted in many African countries. The International Bank of Reconstruction and Development, 40 per cent of whose capital comes from U.S. sources, had lent more than $400 million to African areas by 1960.

The U.N. Emergency Force in the Congo called for sudden expenditures of U.S. funds to help meet the cost of the U.N. action. Because the Congo operation will probably be necessary for several years, an increasing amount of American financing for Africa through the U.N. is needed.

Although annual American economic aid to Africa has grown rapidly, it has not yet equaled the $600 million a year provided by European countries with present or former territories.

Prospects are bright for swift expansion of American assistance programs in Africa. The Administration and Congress are increasingly aware that African areas are critically in need of development. Moreover, concern is rising for the stability of newly independent states which are at times cut off from the direct capital support of their former colonial patrons.

Hydroelectric development is perhaps the most promising area for large sums of U.S. government aid. Inga, on the Congo River, has been studied because it has the largest hydroelectric-power potential in the world, with its 150 miles of rapids and an annual flow several times that of the Mississippi at its mouth. Significant bauxite sites which, if electric power is available, can produce huge quantities of aluminum, are under active development in the Cameroons, Ghana, and Guinea.

Many valuable mineral deposits cannot be adequately developed until transportation facilities are expanded. Africa's railway system is the most underdeveloped of any major continent in the world: Most areas have only two or three major lines extending a short distance inland from the coast. The harbors are most inadequate for the mushrooming demands of world trade. Accra, a thriving commercial center, does not have an adequate port, and many ships are forced to load and unload by means of hazardous surfboats. Roads in all areas are completely inadequate for commercial development.[15] The World Bank has loaned sizable sums to Nigeria, South Africa, and Central Africa to expand their railway systems. But the United States has done little in this field except to develop the harbor facilities at Freetown in Liberia; also, in late 1961, it provided support for the Volta scheme.

Opportunities for sound, productive U.S. economic-aid programs exist in numerous parts of Africa. The Kennedy Administration is examining them with the intention of giving Africa much higher priority in American aid. If Congressional and public approval is gained for a major economic-development effort in Africa, U.S. policy will have achieved a far more effective balance of major instruments.

Strategic Interests

America's military security has been the major factor determining its policy toward Africa. And since the bulwark of its military preparedness has been the NATO alliance, the interests of its members have had a profound effect on U.S. actions vis-à-vis Africa. This has created tension between African nationalist movements and American policy. It continues to be a source of bad feeling, because military policy has not kept pace with the past decade's transition from colonialism to nationhood.

A number of considerations entered into the numerous decisions of the United States to support the colonial policies of its allies in Africa. The first was the grave concern that loss of their African possessions might deprive the European powers of vital sources of economic strength and so weaken their capacity to resist Communism in Europe. A second was the concern that, if America should oppose their colonial policies, dissent might arise within NATO. A third reason, less widely held by respected authorities, was the fear that the Soviet Union might attempt a direct invasion of the African continent, possibly through the Middle East. A fourth reason was America's increasing dependence on Africa for strategic minerals—uranium, columbite, diamonds, copper, iron ore, and oil.

North Africa has been the scene of primary American military interest in Africa. Some strategists look upon Africa, and especially North Africa, as a second line of defense against a Russian attack on NATO. They point out that it was from North Africa that the Allies launched their offensive against the Nazis. Thus, positions of strength, both naval and air bases, in the Mediterranean are considered of great importance by NATO planners in the Pentagon.[16] During and after World War II, a string of American bases was established across North Africa, from Libya to Morocco. The Libyan bases were originally established by Allied forces and later expanded in agreement with the new Libyan government which came into existence in 1951. Naval and air bases were created in Morocco by agreement with France. When the new government came to power in Morocco, these agreements were not recognized, and increasing pressure was exerted on the United States to withdraw from them. The U.S. agreed to do so on a gradual time schedule that many Moroccans consider too slow.

American arms aid for the independent states of North Africa has increased significantly. In 1960, Morocco received approximately $40 million in military support. Earlier, Tunisia had received small-arms shipments over the protests of France, which claimed they would be used by Algerians and not Tunisians. Although the United States is reluctant to engage in arms competition with the Communist bloc, pressures are being put on her to supply greater amounts of military equipment to these North African states because of increasing Communist aid to these areas.

American involvement in the Algerian war is the classic example of how strategic planning affects African policy. Although the U.S. has very explicitly given its support to the principle of self-determination in Algeria, American arms transferred from the NATO theatre in Europe have been used extensively by the French in the long and bloody conflict. In 1956, this writer saw French troops riding off to battle in American jeeps, equipped with American rifles and ammunition. It is beyond dispute that American military supplies sent to France for use in the defense of NATO have been applied against Algeria. France was, legally speaking, within her rights, since the NATO theater extends to the Tropic of Cancer.

American policy on this heated issue has never been clear. Public statements have been made by U.S. officials regretting the use of American equipment, but no serious attempt has ever been made to prevent the misuse of American arms, despite the presence in Paris of the NATO high command under the direction of an American commander-in-chief. Internal French politics has been made highly unstable by the Algerian crisis, and some argue that suspension of arms aid to France for NATO would bring about even greater instability, perhaps revolution, within France. Yet this does not detract from the historical fact that American policy in Algeria for many years allowed strategic considerations to exclude any other—particularly that of the well-being and self-determination of the majority of the Algerian population.

In sub-Sahara Africa, there have been fewer direct American military agreements. Friendly links have been maintained with South Africa, which has, until very recently, been treated as an ally. American naval vessels from time to time have made friendly calls at Cape Town and Port Elizabeth, despite the fact that American Negro personnel were given less hospitality than the white Americans. South Africa, although it has withdrawn from the Commonwealth, retains defensive links with the United Kingdom. Thus, strategically, there is a closer tie to South Africa than most American policymakers have been prepared to admit publicly.

Ethiopia has received a substantial amount of American mili-

tary aid, primarily for an air force. In 1959, a mutual-assistance
pact was signed by the U.S. and Liberia. Liberia has extended
a small amount of police-arms aid, and the United States agreed
to consult Liberia in the event of aggression.[17]

NATO military agreements with Portugal have greatly influenced America's policy toward Africa. The primary motive was
to maintain bases in the Azores. Until the Kennedy Administration changed the policy, the U.S. consistently opposed Afro-Asian
attempts to compel Portugal to cooperate with the United Nations and introduce measures to advance the indigenous peoples
toward self-rule. Few other aspects of American colonial policy
brought more criticism, from both internal and external sources.
The 1959 Herskovits Report to the Senate especially criticized
Portugal's "nineteenth century colonial policy" and America's
acquiescence to it.

It is most unlikely that any of the new African states, whether
they are traditionalist, Westernized, or ultra-Africanist, will seek
mutual-assistance pacts with the United States. Only the older
African states, Liberia and Ethiopia, have close military ties
with the United States. A few have such agreements with the
former mother power, as do the African members of the French
Community, and Nigeria with Great Britain. Some African states
have purchased arms from the United States. A few of these
same states, like Morocco, Ghana, and Guinea, make it a policy
of their positive neutrality to purchase arms and seek military
aid from the Communist bloc as well.

The overriding problem for American strategy is to adjust
to the positive neutralism of the new African states. Africa can
no longer be treated as an extension of Europe in terms of military security, any more than she can in terms of political developments. This is a difficult adjustment for American policy, because
it goes against the pattern of policy developed over the past
decade. It requires the acceptance of "nonalignment" as a political fact of life in Africa.

Even if it wished to, America could not change Africa's new
neutralism. Any U.S. effort to build a series of military agreements with several of the Westernized nationalist states, like
Tanganyika, Nigeria, and the French-speaking areas, would be

disastrous—even worse than the procolonial policy has been. As has been brought out in this study, the increasingly powerful ultra-Africanist political groups all over Africa would react with great emotion, sweeping public opinion with them, against such commitments by their governments.

The Old and the New Policy

Although American policy toward Africa until recently was determined primarily by strategic factors, since the emergence of independent and "neutral" Africa, economic and humanitarian considerations have exerted mounting influence. The extreme security-consciousness and European orientation of 1945–60 appear to be yielding to a more pro-African outlook on the part of the Kennedy Administration.

Neither Truman nor Eisenhower was able to fulfill the expectations which Franklin D. Roosevelt aroused for American postwar support of African nationalism at the 1943 Casablanca meeting of the Big Three and in the Atlantic Charter. Time and again, when the United States was forced to choose between the interests of its NATO allies and the aspiration of African nationalists, the decision went to the colonial powers.[18] In the United Nations, this policy was apparent when the United States acquiesced in the destruction of the Commission on the Racial Situation in the Union of South Africa; supported the South Africans in their contention that *apartheid* was a matter of "domestic jurisdiction"; defended the Portuguese against Afro-Asian attacks; helped exclude from the Security Council debates on French policy in Morocco, Tunisia, and Algeria; voted against target dates for independence for trust territories, despite the pleas for such a program made by the American representative himself. In the most tragic demonstration of the American dilemma, the U.S. voted in the Fifteenth General Assembly with the colonial powers against an Afro-Asian resolution urging a speedy preparation for the end to colonialism. American opposition was voted against the best judgment of its U.N. mission, on direct instruction from President Eisenhower. One member of the U.S. delegation even rose and applauded the adoption of the resolution.

Not all United States votes were procolonial during the Truman–Eisenhower years. On numerous occasions it abstained. In a
few instances it supported the African nationalists, the most striking example being the Suez crisis in 1956. During the last two
years of the Eisenhower Administration, a change set in, primarily because of the increasing number of African states in the
United Nations. In 1958, the United States supported a condemnation of *apartheid* by the General Assembly.[19] After the
Sharpeville massacre in 1960, Ambassador Henry Cabot Lodge
introduced a resolution of censure of South Africa in the Security
Council. However, these acts were offset in the fall of 1960,
when the U.S. opposed the African choice of Liberia for a seat
on the Security Council by supporting—of all powers—Portugal.

The creation, in 1958, of a separate Bureau of African Affairs
under an Assistant Secretary of State for Africa signified American
recognition, very belatedly, of Africa's importance. New em-
bassies and consulates were opened in Africa, and American influence was exerted directly in these areas for the first time. But
this did not solve the need for a new direction in policy.

One of the first acts of the new President-elect in 1960 was to
designate an important liberal political figure—former Governor
G. Mennen Williams of Michigan—as Assistant Secretary of
State for African Affairs. This gave a "new look" to the Kennedy
African policy, which was given impetus by the role of the American delegation at the United Nations under the leadership of
Adlai Stevenson. In addition to increasing the pressure on the
South Africans, the United States surprised the world by supporting a resolution for the investigation of Portugal's colonial
policies.[20] And Assistant Secretary Williams, on his first tour
of Africa, stated that the U.S. upheld the idea of "Africa for the
Africans" without regard to color, thereby touching off a furor
of white-settler and colonial protest.

Despite these statements of encouragement for African nationalism and a clear indication that a new era of relationships
with Africa was under way, tangible evidence that America had
finally broken through the deadening dilemma in her African
policy had not become evident by mid-1961. American sympathy
for the aspirations of the African revolution had been voiced,

but it remained to be demonstrated how the United States would use its great wealth, skills, and power to support these struggling new nations. The challenge before America was well expressed by a South African writer:

> The dilemma is absolute: if the United States is to make her presence felt in Africa, she is going to have to collide with some of her staunchest strategic allies; if she persists in sacrificing the doctrine of self-government to power politics, she is going to breed a bitterness against the West in Africa that will poison the peace of the world for decades to come. Fundamentally, of course, her choice is not between Africa and Europe; it is between the two sides of herself. As the United States will help to decide the future of Africa, so inevitably in the process she will be deciding her own.[21]

This sharp criticism has the cutting edge of truth. A really new approach to Africa is impossible unless the United States rededicates itself to the ideas of human dignity that shaped its very beginning.

8.

New Policy Approaches

There is no other part of the world where the United States has such a great opportunity, and where it has done so little, as in Africa.

We have seen how Africa is moving swiftly out of the period of colonialism into the new age of independence. African nationalism is not completely embittered against the West and the United States. Many leading Africans, including ultra-Africanists as well as Westernized nationalists, are continually turning to the West for advice and assistance. The economies and political systems of all these emerging African states are in a precarious condition of underdevelopment. The United States has the political influence and the economic power to initiate dynamic new programs of social growth across Africa. Yet, it has been hesitating, straddling the fence on most major issues, thus confusing our allies and alienating the new African states. Like Hamlet, it has been perplexed with doubts and paralyzed by a lack of nerve. Meanwhile, the Communist bloc has stepped up its propaganda offensive directed at the emergent nations.

Unfortunately, history is not going to wait very long for Americans to make up their minds as to what they intend to do in Africa. We have seen nationalism in Asia frustrated and then completely soured against us, particularly in Communist China. Africans are not going to wait much longer for the United States to decide whether it is really interested in advancing and enhancing human dignity, or merely concerned with preserving its own immediate security.

Many intelligent interpreters and policymakers are too easily convinced that we are involved in an unresolvable dilemma. Unfortunately, the issue is usually settled with a meek acceptance of the status quo. In actuality, we do neither our allies nor ourselves a service by yielding to this defensive, unimaginative course. Close cooperation between Europe and Africa is desirable for the future. Yet this can grow only out of a completely voluntary acceptance of such cooperation by the new African states who recognize that they have as much to gain from as to give to this association. We do ourselves and our European friends great harm, if we support them in the continuation of any kind of colonial or neocolonial relationship in Africa. Such a course only invites crisis after crisis and ultimately leads to disaster. As W. W. Rostow puts it:

> If the Free World is to survive, it cannot afford to have its foundations periodically shaken by costly and disruptive crises like those in Indo-China, Cyprus, Algiers, and Suez. The American posture of standing back in public dissociation from these affairs—while its day-to-day actions connive in policies that help yield desperate crises—will not do.[1]

It should be clear by this time that we may all be sucked into the maelstrom created by the collapse of colonialism, unless we strike out bravely on a new course.

We shall have to carry our European friends with us. But this is not as difficult as some people would have us believe. As has been noted, the colonial and African policies of the metropolitan powers are made up of a number of conflicting interests and goals. They manifest growing tendencies in the direction of welfare and humanitarianism, supported by major political forces at home. It is politically feasible for progressive policies to find strong political support in all these countries, with the probable exceptions of Portugal and Spain. In discussions of the classic Allied rift, the Suez crisis, it is often forgotten that U.S. policies at that time were supported enthusiastically by the British Labour Party. In short, there are wide boundaries within which European policies can be shifted by forceful and inspiring leadership on the part of the United States.

We should keep in mind that there are many areas of agreement with our European friends. These must be emphasized. We are mutually interested in affirming the dignity of man in Africa. Together, we can share in a new humanitarian approach to Africa's future.

Perhaps most important of all, we need to change our Western colonial perspective on Africa. There are scarcely any colonies left. Our relations with Africa are carried out directly with independent African states. Already, metropolitan powers are a fading influence. The decisive force has passed to the African states. America must therefore build her policies in terms of the needs and aspirations of the "new African personality."

U.S. policy needs to be reconstructed now on a foundation of strength rather than weakness, by emphasizing our vast humanitarian interest in the new, independent Africa. This does not mean the abandonment of strategic considerations, but simply the realistic appraisal of what our true strategy should be—namely, a properly balanced program in which America's primary interest is seen as the advancement of the dignity and well-being of the African people. This goal should be accepted as a moral responsibility by a people willing to share with others the technology that has made possible for all the access to a richer life. Moreover, no inherent contradiction exists between this goal and the welfare and happiness of the American people, for every true national interest (as distinct from a group self-interest) intersects the interest of other nations at a higher level—a plane of mutual interest.

To do this, we will have to get over our paralyzing cold-war mentality, which regards every major issue of our foreign policy as another battle with Communism. There are much greater causes to serve than making sure that Africa does not go Communist. Communism touches only on the fringes of Africa today. At the heart of Africa is a vast sea of poverty and suffering. We of the West have the means to abolish most of this unnecessary misery. To use our economic and scientific skills toward this end should be the predominant aim of American policy.[2] If we do this, we need have little fear that Communism can gain the revolutionary initiative in Africa.

Many unflattering things will have to be accepted. Our egos will be badly hurt when the Africans reject our pet democratic theories and insist that they have a better—African—way to organize their society. If they refuse to join us in a holy war against Communism, some people will be tempted to think them naïve and foolish. Neutral independence is difficult for the American cold-war mentality to accept. We like to think in terms of black and white, of right and wrong. Yet we have seen how the new African personality has already set its face against active involvement in the power struggle between East and West.

Of course, African neutrality is divided between Westernized and ultra-Africanist nations. We will need to find ways of working with the various forms of nonalignment, rather than embracing one and rejecting the other. This will be difficult to do, because of the power-struggle temptation to build alliances and play one group off against the other.

In the long run, a primarily humanitarian policy will help stabilize the world balance of power. Actually, humanitarianism and realism are not as far apart as they seem. It is extremely important that Africa not shift to one side or the other in the balance of power. Should large sections of the world shift their weight, the precarious balance could be tipped enough to bring the whole system down in total war. In the context of the nuclear stalemate between the two major camps, factors of population and resources become all the more important. Should the open door to Africa be closed to the West by internal revolutionary developments, the war machines might very well be set into high gear, with the Western powers taking precipitous action, as in Suez, to protect their interests.

There is an "operative" side to policy that is in many ways more important than the "declarative" side. This operative policy may actually be in conflict with the declarative. To a great extent, this has been true with respect to Africa. We have not lacked for high-sounding declarations of principles on many occasions, but the operative policy which would fulfill the high principle has often been absent.

The following policy approaches are suggested to make operative a more balanced humanitarian policy.

Viable Independent States

The numerous new African states, large and small, weak and strong, must be given full respect and recognition by the United States. They are all becoming members of the United Nations, and as equals in the international community they deserve our respect and support. Although the United States can recognize that the metropolitan powers who gave these countries their independence have a special concern in their economic and political advancement, we should not give silent support to a policy of special spheres of influence or neocolonialism in any form. Of course, voluntary arrangements such as the British Commonwealth of Nations and the French Community should be accorded full respect.

As long as the avowed policies of the new nations are "nonalignment" or "positive neutralism," such expressions of sovereign will should be respected by the United States. As we have noted, this policy embraces a number of actual positions, ranging from leaning toward the West, as in the case of Nigeria, to leaning toward the Communist bloc, as in the case of Guinea. Respect for nonalignment does not mean that the United States must itself take a neutralist position. There is no reason why we should not attempt actively to win as many friends as possible among the new nations. What is all-decisive is the manner in which we go about it.

We must avoid those past tendencies of American policy to condemn morally a nation which avows neutrality. Unfortunately, this is linked with our habit of rewarding our friends and denying our enemies—which too often have included the "neutralists" in the eyes of such policymakers as the late Secretary of State John Foster Dulles. The lion's share of economic and technical assistance has been awarded to nations who have entered into close alliances with America. The African nations having the closest military agreements with us—Libya, Morocco, Liberia, and Ethiopia—have received the most from us. The Central African Federation has received special treatment for economic reasons, as well as security interests.

Maximum economic viability for all the new nations, regardless of whether they lean to the right of the left of neutralism, should be a cardinal objective of American policy. Ultra-Africanist governments especially must not be spurned and thus pushed into the arms of the Communists. The growth and stability of Ghana, Guinea, and the U.A.R. are of the greatest importance.

Formation of broader political and economic units among the many small new African states is a legitimate objective. In fact, most African leaders recognize that economic viability cannot be achieved if each country continues to build its own trade, industrial, and communications systems. However, America will for some time have to accept the great limitations that nationalism and tribalism place upon the realization of sound, rational objectives. At the same time, we can be helpful in bringing about integration in Africa as we did, under the Marshall Plan, in Europe.

Representative and Responsible Government

American policy should take into account the trend toward authoritarian government in Africa. Under the impact of ultranationalism, executive authority is maximized and legislative authority minimized. Opposition parties, if they exist, are often hounded, if not actually outlawed. And African leaders propound theories of the "African democracy" which, in our view, distort the fundamental basis of government rooted in the consent of the governed.

It is hard to find in Africa the combination of balanced forces from which to create a democratic system. However, it is conceivable that a threshold of democracy can be reached once an adequate educational, economic, and cultural base is built. With the growth of a sense of national unity and the development of numerous national groups, the conditions for democracy become more fertile.

American policy should have as a central objective the transformation of authoritarian patterns of government into true democracy, but with a great deal of tolerance. We should exercise infinite patience in the achievement of this end. Progress will

inevitably be slow, under the difficult conditions presented by
Africa. Assistance should not be withheld for such purely political reasons as our dislike for the form of government adopted
by Guinea or the U.A.R. or any other African state. Judgments
would be better made on the basis of the responsible use of power
by the governing group. Helen Kitchen expressed this well: "The
U.S. should not close the door to assistance for any regime which
clearly represents the popular will, even when it seems tem-
porarily to favor ties with the USSR or China."[3] Even a dictatorship can be highly popular, and many in Africa are. Some
authoritarian governments, like those in Guinea and Tunisia,
do use resources for the expansion of public welfare and economic progress. If such governments show signs of enlightenment,
there is as much, if not more, justification in assisting them as in
assisting Iran, Pakistan, and Vietnam—nations with unpopular
governments into which billions of dollars of American aid have
been poured.[4]

We of the West need above all to appreciate that it is entirely
possible for new democratic forms of government to evolve under
African conditions and traditions. Tribal forms of agreement
through unanimity rather than majority rule and talking out of
issues are deeply ingrained in Africa's past. Under monolithic
nationalist movements which lump many tribal and class interests together, such as TANU in Tanganyika, the democratic
struggle between group interests can take place within a single
party. However, we need to be on our guard against sanctioning
new systems which actually distort and destroy the true values
of the free society. This is a complex and delicate matter of interpretation which will require great patience and understanding.
Finally, all Westerners working in Africa should keep in mind
that paternalism is passé. All we can do is influence indirectly
the judgments of Africa's new political leaders. They are the
ones who will now determine the destiny of the African states.

An Arms-Free Africa

American policy should place less emphasis on the purely military considerations of alliances and bases that have dominated so

much of our policy toward Africa in the past. Our major strategic aim should be to assure the genuine independence and neutrality of those African states that choose to pursue this policy.

Strong neutral government can be one of the staunchest bulwarks erected against the spread of Communism. Corrupt and reactionary governments shored up by American military support in parts of Asia and the Middle East have often proved disastrously susceptible to the gradual subterranean penetration of revolutionary Communist forces. One of the greatest dangers of military support is that irresponsible governments will misuse it to build up and maintain their own power, as in South Korea. In Africa, far removed from any actual threat of Communist invasion, such support is particularly unnecessary. American assistance should be directed primarily toward creating the sound economic advances that are the best guarantees against extremism and Communism. A country like Ethiopia would create much greater security for itself and the United States if, instead of spending the money it receives on an air force, it developed and expanded a more productive agricultural system. To seek arms agreements with Westernized countries like Nigeria is to invite political instability.

The major dilemma is the arms race. Once one side in the cold war begins an arms build-up in Morocco, Guinea, or Ethiopia, the other side believes it cannot be left behind and proceeds to make more attractive offers. In addition, neighboring states become frightened and place requests for military assistance with the big powers.

The U.S., Great Britain, France, and the U.S.S.R. should reach an agreement with the African states through the United Nations to limit the supply of arms going to the African continent. This proposal has already been put forward by Prime Minister Harold Macmillan of Great Britain and has been given favorable consideration by American officials. The agreement should specify the types and amounts of weapons to be supplied by the great powers. An agreement to declare Africa a nuclear-free zone would be an excellent first step. An inspection system would, no doubt, be necessary to assure compliance. The utmost speed is necessary on such an agreement before the pattern of arms build-ups among the new African states gets beyond the point of control.[5]

The question of American and Western bases in Africa is very difficult. In the interests of greater security and stability within the continent, I believe more would be gained by a gradual Western withdrawal, as a control system went into effect, than could be achieved by attempting to keep bases that are politically insecure and increasingly outmoded by long-range rockets.

Rapid Economic and Social Modernization

Unquestionably the keystone of American policy toward the independent states of Africa must be the economic and technical assistance offered. A crash program of economic development should be launched, increasing many times past expenditures for Africa. The U.S. effort ought to be equal to that of the metropolitan European powers, which approximates $600 million per year. All of the African states need extensive aid to create basic public services such as power and transportation, and to render basic social services, such as health and education. Most African economies are weak, being based almost entirely on mineral extraction or agriculture. Nearly all have plans for developing some industry and expanding social services to their rapidly growing urban communities.

Certain countries, such as Ghana and Tunisia, have political and economic structures mature enough to absorb extensive economic aid. Others are more backward and can absorb little capital, but need technical assistance and education. Through the careful tutelage of the British, Ghana has developed a highly skilled and responsible civil service and middle class. We might well select Ghana as an exemplary area for rapid social development. Many economists have suggested that the Volta scheme be developed by the United States, not because it is the safest investment for American capital but because it is a social risk worth taking to demonstrate what American assistance can do for an African state with strong democratic tendencies. Africa needs a series of Volta schemes to develop her industries and give her people a better life.

American surplus food provides a principal source of assistance for Africa, as yet not largely utilized on that continent. Food can be capital, as well as supply immediate relief and improved living standards. In several countries, food surpluses have been used as wages for workers on government projects.

Two of the largest American surpluses, stored at great expense in U.S. government facilities, are corn and wheat. Corn is a staple of Africa (where it is called maize). Wheat is used less commonly, but demand for it is increasing. Protein foods such as dried milk are desperately needed. A protein-deficiency disease called *kwashiorkor* kills hundreds of thousands of babies each year.

A priority food program should be launched for Africa. The North African countries, particularly Egypt, have received most of the food supplies, but much more can be done for most African states. Such aid has the added advantage of enabling the recipient countries to divert scarce land and resources from food production to cash crops and other industries. By joint agreement, some counterpart funds from the sale of U.S. surplus food are utilized for education, welfare, and communications development.

Technical assistance, a more complex undertaking, needs careful study and expansion. There are four major problem areas: balanced economies, land and credit, education and research, and social welfare.

Balanced Economies

U.S. economic and technical assistance should aim primarily at developing well-rounded African economies. Their one-sided character is a carryover from the colonial pattern of the past, which stressed raw materials for export to the mother country. Ghana and Guinea are virtually one-crop economies; should the bottom fall out of the world market for cocoa or coffee, either could be ruined.

Although the existing pattern of primary production will no doubt have to be continued for some years, greater diversification of production must be encouraged. Some new industries, such

as oil refining and the manufacture of textiles, cement, and glass-
ware, may be uneconomic at the outset and even detrimental
to Western industrial interests. Yet they will have to be protected
and helped in the initial phases, if long-term progress is to be
made. This does not mean that all national desires for the creation of steelworks or aircraft industries ought to be encouraged.
There are difficult choices to be made in planned production. It
will be most important to encourage the growth of regional
economic patterns within the new federations, wherever feasible.[6]

An experimental approach to African production is required.
New forms of public and cooperative production are both possible and desirable. Public development has proved more effective
than private enterprise. This has been demonstrated in certain
basic industries such as housing, electricity, cement, and raw-
material processing. Joint state and private enterprises in the
Congo have shown remarkable vitality. Cooperatives, especially in
the processing of such crops as cocoa, coffee, and cotton, are
especially suitable to African development. With financial and
technical assistance, the new states can take giant strides, as
already shown in Ghana and Nigeria.

Land and Credit

Improved agricultural production is the key to rapid and far-
reaching increases in living standards. Agriculture in the new
African states is extremely primitive. It has sprung up within
the last few decades without adequate scientific direction. Unlike
Asian farmers, Africans have not had centuries of population
pressures to teach them, by famine, productive farming. Much
of the European initiative has been directed at plantation agriculture, and in some areas it has even been hostile to peasant
cultivation of cash crops which would cut into labor and land
resources.

Possibly the greatest handicap of all is the landownership system. Much careful direction needs to be given African states in
the transformation of their communal land systems into modern
private ownership or cooperative development farms. If the
farmers do not own the land they till, it is tremendously difficult

to devise an effective credit system. Since credit is indispensable to efficient, mechanized farm production, this problem must be solved. Cooperatives are workable in some parts of Africa, but they will take a long time to develop properly, because they require a well-informed and responsible membership to operate effectively.

Under colonial governments, it was very difficult to alter the land tenure system because Africans believed any such reform was aimed at depriving them of their traditional land rights. Such experiments in Kenya and other parts of white-settled Africa, where the government had given large tracts of land to Europeans, served only to intensify these feelings. However, in most of the independent states, programs for radical reform of the land and credit systems are under way. The United States could do much to forward this basic change. In Egypt and other North African countries, feudal land systems under which both European and native minorities own large tracts of the most fertile land need to be further broken up for peasant production. Where large units of production are desirable, the proceeds must be more equitably distributed by progressive taxation. How undeveloped tracts of land can be brought under African production without driving out productive European farmers is a major problem in East and Central Africa, where white minorities have a monopoly of rich, undeveloped land. In most of black Africa, tribal communalism stifles individual initiative and land development. New laws and incentive systems, supported by credit and agriculture extension services, are badly needed.

Because there usually is a vested interest in the existing system, the easiest course is to leave the system alone. But the United States will have to come to grips with this vast problem, if the condition of the noncolonial African peasant farmer is to be improved to any significant degree.

Education and Research

Much progress has been made in recent years in education and research, but the starting point has been so low that an immense task lies ahead.

There are so many gaps in the educational systems that it is difficult to know how to attack them. If possible, an overall system should be worked out with each country, rather than piecemeal efforts. There is a desperate need for schools, most especially at the primary and secondary levels, and a shortage of teachers. A partial and temporary solution would be to import teaching staffs from Western and Asian countries, whose young college graduates would in great numbers welcome the chance to spend a few years teaching in Africa. Certainly their knowledge of language and the liberal arts could be used, but even more welcome would be rudimentary knowledge of accounting, agriculture, carpentry, mechanics, child welfare, and sanitation and dietetics, to implement the proliferating programs of community development throughout Africa. Private groups in America, such as the American Friends Service Committee and Operation Crossroads Africa which have begun such programs, should be encouraged. But the major task is government aid, carried out through programs like the Peace Corps. Africa has a greater need for semiskilled personnel than any other part of the world, and the Peace Corps, if properly directed, could have enormous impact in this area. But simultaneously many African teachers must be trained, so that they can go out and start schools in the bush. Since universal primary education is the goal of every independent African state, some U.S. assistance should be directed here.

Higher education in Africa presents America with a tremendous opportunity—to expand national education programs and to multiply scholarships. Some 1,200 African students are studying in America, a number that should be increased tenfold if we take our opportunity seriously. This can be done only through increased scholarship aid by the U.S. government. Many universities and colleges are already cooperating in such a program and are anxious to expand it.

Higher-education programs and traditional secondary education should be supported in every one of the new states. Many have no institutions of higher learning. Former British areas are the most advanced, but even their facilities are woefully inadequate. Professional schools are particularly deficient.

Through its AID programs the United States could sponsor

development of a network of university programs across Africa, modeled on the East African university program, under which several specialized colleges in several countries are to be linked in a joint administrative unit, the University of East Africa. These include a medical and agricultural college at Makerere in Uganda, the Royal Technical College in Kenya for engineering, and the projected Tanganyika University College for law and the social sciences. American land-grant universities are especially suited to assist in developing such a program, in cooperation with European institutions. The new University of Nigeria is an example of such cooperative development of higher education. The American university pattern of a liberal-arts foundation plus technical training in agriculture or science has greatly impressed many African leaders, and they are eager for assistance.

Education in Africa must move forward quickly at all levels. Technical skills and primary education are the most immediate needs, but higher levels cannot be neglected, if qualified leadership in depth is to be developed. The Belgian Congo experience clearly demonstrates the perils of inadequate training for leadership at the highest levels of the society. If the United States does no more than help create the basis of the new educational structure of Africa, it will have greatly influenced the course of history there. There is a passionate thirst for knowledge among the peoples of Africa. We cannot afford to let this opportunity slip by.

Social Welfare

Rapid economic development always gives rise to a legion of social evils because of the dislocation of traditional ways of life. Most of the new states do not have the resources or personnel to create social-welfare institutions.

All the new states have chronic unemployment or underemployment. In North Africa, unemployment is at its worst, with 25 per cent or more of the working population in Tunisia idle. Even in prosperous Ghana, underemployment creates much hardship; women stand around in the market places all day under the hot sun in order to sell a pair of shoelaces.

Unemployment insurance is virtually nonexistent in these low-wage areas. Yet suffering and a sense of futility are just as acute for these peoples as for those in a developed country. The effects can be dangerous on the political mentality of people who have seen the vision of a new world but find their homeland's political system without hope for them. Unemployment benefits, slum clearance, recreation facilities, clinics, and adult education are all areas for intensive study and expansion in the new African states.

A strong democratic labor movement is a necessity for balanced economic growth. In most of these areas, labor has been instrumental in the nationalist movements. However, trade unions are centered only in the main cities and operate in only a few industries. Their organizations are weak and their leaders poorly trained. Migratory workers are the most pitifully exploited groups in the new states, especially in black Africa. They are completely unorganized.

In the British colonies, official assistance for trade-union organization did much to improve the lot of labor. Now that these are independent states, the trade unions still need technical assistance on organization tactics, government legislation, and welfare programs. A strong, responsible labor movement is one of the most stabilizing factors in an underdeveloped area. The United States will gain much and contribute, as well, to human welfare in Africa if she engages in an extensive program of trade-union development. A labor mission should be attached to every ICA program in Africa. Already, U.S. trade unions have shown concern over this need and are participating in the ICFTU training programs in Africa.

Full Racial Equality

The African areas with a sizable permanent European and Asian minority pose the most difficult dilemmas for the United States and Western Europe. The close racial and cultural ties between the mother country and the white minority create an emotional sympathy from which it is difficult for any Westerner to separate himself.

First of all, American policy should make it absolutely clear to Africa and the world that we have no more sympathy with the programs of white supremacy in certain African territories than we do with those in parts of the United States. Speedier integration in our own country is the first step to take. Only after that can we act with moral authority in Africa.

Failure to give concrete evidence of our dedication to full racial equality has been the weakest point in our entire approach to Africa. The African people are more sensitive to this shortcoming than to any other. The world does not know precisely where the United States stands in relation to the growing structure of white supremacy in South Africa. We have deplored racialism in general but never directly supported programs to alleviate it. We practice segregation in our own embassy in South Africa and at diplomatic functions there. During the course of the tragic Mau Mau uprising in Kenya, where tens of thousands of Africans lost their lives, American statesmen never once publicly stated their abhorrence of the system of white supremacy established by Kenya settlers, although this system was a major factor in bringing about the rebellion.

Our guiding principle should be full equality for all in Africa. This means that ultimately the African people will be the controlling voice in every African government from Cairo to Cape Town. A European minority cannot expect to continue indefinitely its subjection of the African minority anywhere on the continent, including South Africa. Therefore, American policy should be clearly directed toward bringing about as rapid and peaceful a transition as possible to a state of equality in which no group is the victim of those who possess political power.

The rate at which transition to such a more equitable society can take place will vary according to the realities of each area in Africa. American influence should everywhere be on the side of those forces favoring the elimination of racial barriers in employment, social life, and politics.

In Kenya and East Africa, there have been many improvements, and the prospects are for the eventual emergence of fairly stable communities, dominated by the African majority and based on nonracialism. American programs can assist, especially by broadening the economic base and educational opportunity. Interracial educational programs offer special prospects of success.

The Central African Federation is clearly unworkable. African nationalist parties in Northern Rhodesia and Nyasaland have bitterly fought the federation, and will withdraw from it the moment they gain political power. Since Great Britain has declared her intention to hand over power shortly to the African majority, the white groups have no alternative but to accept the inevitable. Any alternative that permitted the white minorities to continue their political discrimination against the Africans could not have American support, under the democratic principles we have laid down. Once Nyasaland and Northern Rhodesia gain their independence, they could continue close economic cooperation with each other. New communication links could be built with Tanganyika and the projected East African Federation of African States.

Southern Rhodesia will have to be dealt with differently. Here, white supremacy is in power and will not, in all probability, yield willingly or peaceably to the African majority. Great Britain, having long since lost control over events in Southern Rhodesia, is most reluctant to attempt to compel it to grant equality to Africans. Time, turmoil, and growing realism may bring a solution to this unhappy land. Because Africans of neighboring states are not likely to stand by while their brothers are suppressed in Southern Rhodesia, some U.N. intervention may become necessary.

A clear American responsibility is to assure Central Africa that all the economic and technical-assistance programs are free from racialist taint. In the past, education and public services, particularly in Southern Rhodesia, have been demarcated sharply on racial lines. No American assistance should be used to maintain discriminatory facilities. American diplomatic personnel should be instructed to avoid segregated social activities and to maintain at all times a policy of full equality, even at the risk of controversy.

South Africa presents the most explosive problem of all. For years, the United States has evaded responsibility on the issue, but can do so no longer. Because this has become an international issue and is handled in various ways by U.N. members, consideration of our alternatives is taken up in the discussion of the United Nations, which follows. It should be clear that the United States cannot avoid taking a forthright stand. Our influence should be exerted constantly on the side of those South African groups who wish to move toward greater equality and justice for the oppressed races.

Much good is being done in South Africa by nongovernmental agencies such as missions and foundations. These groups are in touch with the progressive, hopeful forces of the country, and often they provide an important link to the African nationalist, as through the African Legal Aid and Defense Fund of the American Committee on Africa. The exchange-of-persons program has also been an important medium of injecting equalitarian values into South Africa.

The United States must now reassert the principles on which it was founded by removing any direct or indirect sanction of discrimination in South Africa. It must sponsor only nonsegregated programs and refuse support to any activities which involve segregation, whether social or economic.

If we have the courage to implement our convictions, we can gain considerable initiative throughout the awakening continent.

Using the United Nations

The United Nations had been on the fringes of the major conflicts on the African continent, but the Congo crisis plunged it right into the middle of things. The neutral character of the U.N. makes it the logical mediator in the struggle among the great powers for leadership of the "revolution of rising expectations."

Thus, the United States should place much greater emphasis on the U.N. in its African policy. The particular African issues at the U.N.—apart from such major crises as trusteeship and South African *apartheid*—may not be important in themselves, but they are significant as part of the great ideological battle for the respect of emergent peoples. The peoples of Africa watch our actions at the U.N. closely, and they evaluate the sincerity of our

professed devotion to justice and human welfare by our positions
there.

Obviously, the United States cannot compete with the Soviet
Union as a champion of the anticolonial viewpoint. We are a
part of the West, and certain of our interests put us in conflict
with other parts of the world. Furthermore, the Afro-Asian interests are not always identical with those of the rest of the
world. Every nation and area is guilty in some measure of pre-
senting its particular interest as the universal one. However, the
United States can try to pursue a policy as close to the universal
in viewpoint as possible.

Today the United Nations fulfills two roles of major, universal
interest in Africa. First, it assists in the birth of new independent
states. Second, it helps these states develop strong economies and
democratic institutions. In what concrete situations might the
United States support these two U.N. functions?

The U.N. Charter provides, in Article Ten, for a free and full
discussion by the General Assembly of issues that have bearing on
world peace. Colonial issues have been raised with increasing
frequency by the Afro-Asian states. The metropolitan powers,
however, have consistently maintained that these are questions of
domestic jurisdiction, under Article Eleven, Section Seven of the
Charter, and therefore not proper subjects for U.N. consideration. Because only a simple majority can place an issue on the
General Assembly agenda, the increasing numbers and influence
of the Afro-Asian states have brought such debates on with increasing frequency.

The Western European argument is neither legally right nor
politically sound. The United States should endorse a broad view
of U.N. authority to debate issues concerning world peace. If a
significant group of nations fears that a colonial revolution
threatens to create international tension, this should be adequate
ground for U.N. debate, in either the Security Council or the
General Assembly. Of course, this principle cannot be extended
to permit debate of every instance of colonial dissatisfaction with
the administering power. The Charter cannot be stretched beyond reasonable interpretation to attempt virtual internationali-
zation of all colonial territories. But clearly, revolutions like those

in Algeria and Angola have international repercussions that make them legitimate subjects for consideration by the world's principal peacemaking body. Serious rebellions may well break out in other parts of sub-Sahara Africa, and in a world dominated by the cold war, almost every colonial revolution involves the rival blocs. It is far better to call upon the United Nations, as in the Congo, than to allow a great-power struggle for control to take place, without regard for the interests of the African nations themselves.

The subject of U.N. intervention in African conflicts is much more complicated. Active measures like the call for a cease-fire or the dispatch of an international observation team or police force, are not always helpful. Yet in certain cases—and we are likely to see a growing number in Africa—the U.N. provides the only alternative to chaos. U.N. intervention in the Congo in 1960 was the only way to save the new republic from a self-destructive conflict that might well have involved the great powers. Africans and their leaders have a special respect for the U.N. In their eyes, it is a neutral agency and therefore acceptable as an authority. When African troops and personnel from other African countries comprise most of the mediating force, it is particularly effective.

The U.N. should be prepared for a long period of responsibility for maintaining order and administrative functions in the Congo, as well as in other parts of Africa. But with similar crises likely to arise in Central and South Africa, the U.N.'s administrative and budgetary machinery have already been strained nearly to the breaking point. It is poorly prepared to meet new responsibilities as a mediator. American leaders should prepare our country for a long-term program of supporting the U.N.'s Congo operation, and seek backing in the United Nations for a special emergency branch of the U.N. Secretariat to handle interventionary actions. A genuine international police force, made up of contingents earmarked for it by member nations, should be created on a permanent, rather than emergency, basis. Special African troops should be selected and trained for this type of service.

Race relations in Africa are an international issue. There is no escaping the fact that slavery and colonialism have left bitter feelings in many parts of Africa.

Certain U.N. functions, such as investigation of the violations of human rights, can be clearly construed from the Charter. But the world needs to know more about the precise results of *apartheid* in South Africa, the direction of political forces in Central Africa, and the meaning of the *assimilado* and forced labor systems in the Portuguese territories. Adequate information on such issues will help equip the United Nations to take steps to ease the sources of tension and conflict in Africa.

When the United States helped bring to an end the Commission on the Racial Situation in the Union of South Africa, it earned a great deal of antipathy among the African and Asian states, many of whom saw in this a reflection of the internal racial difficulties of the United States. Fortunately, there has been, in recent years, a shift in U.S. views. We have supported forthright resolutions criticizing racialist practices in South Africa. But we must go further.

The only areas in the world where race relations are not improving are Central and South Africa. Whites and other minorities are beginning to face counterracialism in some of the new states. This may well become a serious problem. A constructive approach under the Charter would be the creation of a commission on the racial tensions in Africa to study and report upon the current trends of public opinion and policies there.

Such reports could be utilized by member nations in adopting programs to ease the developing racial passions.

There would be much merit in drafting a special racial equality covenant for adoption by member nations, as a means of urging enlightened reform, not only in Africa, but in other parts of the world as well.

In short, a variety of approaches are within the scope of the Charter and the practical possibilities of the United Nations. They only await the initiative of some big power, preferably the United States.

The refusal of South Africa to cooperate with the United Nations in her mandate administration of South West Africa has already been noted. Like the French in Algeria, the South Africans claim the U.N. has no proper jurisdiction. However, the legal case for intervention is accepted by most nations, who hold that South Africa accepted certain international obligations under the League of Nations that she cannot renounce without the consent of the U.N. as legal successor to the League. To cope with this situation, several positive steps could be taken at the U.N., which would be greatly strengthened if the United States assumed leadership.

The U.N. Committee on South West Africa could not only investigate the plight of Africans living in South West Africa but also recommend improvements in the country's economic and racial laws. Although South Africa would, in all probability, ignore such recommendations, they would strengthen the case of Liberia and Ethiopia, who are proceeding against South Africa in the International Court of Justice.

Should the court hold that South Africa has violated her mandate, the U.N. can move to divest her of South West Africa and transfer that territory to another power or to the U.N. Trusteeship Council, under which Italian Somaliland was administered for ten years. With the development of U.N. emergency administrative machinery, this prospect takes on reality.

The United Nations may well have to take firm action against South Africa. This might result from a combination of events, such as the continuation of cruel *apartheid* policies and fierce repression of any non-European organized protest, together with South African refusal to recognize her international obligations under the South West African mandate. The U.S. should push ahead in its efforts to persuade South Africa to meet its obligations. Failing this, the next step would be coercive action—perhaps economic boycott or actual armed intervention. By not ruling out the possibility of such stern measures, the United States will alert South Africa to the fact that these issues have reached a most critical phase and that we stand with the overwhelming majority of the world in believing that some solution must be reached. The apparent alternative is that the majority of Afro-Asian states will press hard for stern measures, but that the South Africans will ignore them as long as the Western powers do not oppose her. Our readiness to move toward enforcement measures as a final step may convince South Africa before it is too late.

The United Nations Trusteeship Council will shortly have put itself out of business in Africa. Where there were nine trust territories, only one remains. (Tanganyika became independent in December, 1961.) Ruanda-Urundi will be the last to gain independence. The U.S. can assist Tanganyika's transition by pressing for maximum international capital and technical assistance to support that country's educational and productive plans. Now that nationalist ministers have taken over the direction of development, prospects for full utilization of such aid are much greater. In Ruanda-Urundi, the major problem is to create a stable, representative government, between the warring Bahutu and Watutsi tribesmen, who are historic foes. The former are agriculturists, who, in pre-German times, were serfs of the Watutsi cattle-owning overlords. Since the Bahutu are far more numerous, the Watutsi are fearful of unfair treatment under a democratic government. The question of the ultimate destiny of Ruanda-Urundi is a serious one. Obviously it would be better off if it merged with a stable, productive country.

A special and continuing interest in the development of former trust territories should be a U.N. policy. All these countries depend on outside assistance. U.N. resources for technical assistance are more limited than those of the major powers, and member nations should assume an obligation to these states, as they are offspring of the U.N. The U.S. should take the lead by agreeing to aid U.N. programs for new African nations that will continue beyond independence. Such assistance might be channeled through the Special U.N. Fund for Africa.

The United States might also accomplish much in the United Nations with regard to non-self-governing territories. We have already noted that, although the U.S. has supported the work of the Committee on Information from such territories, it has held aloof from many of the critical debates within that committee, and sometimes has taken a position difficult to reconcile with humanitarian ideals and the best interests of dependent peoples.

The colonial powers have tried to draw an arbitrary distinction between social and political information. The fact is, all information related to the progress and welfare of dependent peoples is a legitimate concern of this committee. A vigorous effort should be made to obtain such information from the Portuguese. Should Portugal resist such persuasion, U.N. members should apply economic sanctions.

The Economic Commission for Africa, established in 1958, provides a bridge for continued economic collaboration between the newly independent states of Africa and the Western powers. Also, it can be used to coordinate planning for the new states. As the U.S. favors achieving maximum economic and political integration among the numerous new states, we would do well to become a member of this commission, along with the European metropolitan powers. The African states would welcome this indication of concern. The argument that we should not join the commission because Russia would then join too is unrealistic, since the Russians have direct contacts in Africa by other means.

Some of the newly independent peoples distrust the motives of any Western power offering economic assistance. However, many of their leaders believe that if they could obtain such assistance though U.N. agencies, they could overcome their peoples' fear that their newly won political independence was being surrendered in exchange for such assistance. Although neither the U.S. nor any other major power would agree to channel all of its aid to Africa though the U.N., a much greater portion of such help could be handled this way.

The U.N. technical-assistance program is starved for funds. Before the Congo crisis, less of this limited aid had gone to Africa than to any other major underdeveloped region. Now Africa has acquired a priority. It is to be hoped that the U.S. will back fully the creation of a special African fund with sufficient means to help underwrite not only expanded technical assistance but development programs. The fund should have pledges of at least $250 million per year. By leading the move to set up such a program, the United States could do more to advance the general prosperity of Africa than by any other single step. Such an effort would also be a clear indication that the

United States is determined to make a fresh and hopeful approach to Africa.

Another extremely constructive move would be to lead a Western campaign for massive economic development through all the U.N. agencies. Many channels for this aid exist (such as the U.N. Special Fund), but they lack the substantial capital necessary for serious development. To implement U.N. programs that hold any hope for closing the "poverty gap" in Africa, a much higher priority will have to be given them, in U.S. policy and budgeting.

By focusing on the U.N. and giving emphasis to its agencies, the U.S. can capture the imagination of the emergent millions of Africans. To them, the U.N. is a compelling symbol of the new world. We could release tremendous energies for progressive, peaceful development by so placing ourselves in the forefront of humanity as it struggles to build a greater common dignity and prospect for peace.

However, in our search to discover what we can do in Africa, we must not overlook the fact that what Africans themselves decide to do is far more important. Africa's destiny now rests in the hands of Africans. This may disturb those Westerners who cannot shake off paternal fears developed through past centuries. But Africa's leaders are as wise and as capable, as foolish and inept, as any group of leaders on any major continent. The difference is that they lack experience and must struggle under very difficult circumstances. Their people are for the most part uneducated; they demand immediate material progress, despite limited resources and unbalanced economies. Tribalism, anti-Western and counterracial feelings are widespread. Yet, over most of Africa, astounding progress is being made. An Indian social scientist summarizes the new nations' prospects as follows:

Difficulties exist to be surmounted by the will, persistence, and energy of man. In varying degrees all these countries are facing up to these problems. To what extent they will succeed depends on many factors, not the least of which are the vision of their leaders, the response of the general public, the new dynamism which political independence has given to the people, and the assistance and sympathy of more advanced nations.[7]

The energetic self-confidence of nineteenth-century America characterizes the African nationalists in their approach to the task of building new nations. If they succeed, all humanity will move forward with them. If they fail, all humanity will share their loss. Certainly we cannot assure their success by our sympathetic support and assistance, but we can be of enormous help. This we should do, not as a people frightened that the dominance of Western civilization is coming to an end, but as fellow human beings who can see beyond the fallibilities in human nature to the great contribution which these emerging African peoples can make to the enrichment of common humanity and the fulfillment of Divine purpose through all races and nations.

Notes

INTRODUCTION

1. Coleman, *Nigeria: Background to Nationalism* (Berkeley, Calif.: University of California Press, 1958), p. 425.
2. Ward, *The Interplay of East and West* (New York: W. W. Norton and Co., 1957), p. 56.
3. Emerson, *From Empire to Nation,* (Cambridge, Mass.: Harvard University Press, 1960), p. 11.

Chapter 1

VANISHING PATTERNS OF TRADITIONAL NATIONALISM

1. See Charles F. Gallagher, "Observations on Moroccan Political and Economic Problems," *American Universities Field Staff Reports,* V, No. 1 (July 30, 1959), 4.
2. See Rom Landau, *The Moroccan Drama* (San Francisco: American Academy of Asian Studies, 1955), p. 323.
3. Gallagher comments: "In terms of international politics neo-Istiqlal attitudes betray an even firmer orientation toward the doctrine of 'nondependence' and an increased trend away from lingering vestiges of French and Occidental protectivism." Gallagher, *op. cit.,* p. 6.
4. Douglas E. Ashford, "Elections in Morocco: Progress or Confusion," *The Middle East Journal,* V, No. 1 (Winter, 1961), 1.
5. Benjamin Rivlin gives an account of the constitutional reforms in "Towards Political Maturity in Morocco," *Current History,* July, 1959, pp. 23–24.

6. See Gallagher, "Morocco Goes Back to School," *American Universities Field Staff Reports* (letter, September 15, 1958).
7. See M. Tahis, *"La Libération Economique,"* *Al Istiqlal*, January 1, 1960, pp. 8–9.
8. In March, 1960, the United States announced that Morocco would receive $40 million in aid, of which $23 million would be Development Loan Fund capital.
9. Population estimates vary. Ethiopians claim a population of more than 19 million, but Western sources place it much lower.
10. See W. E. H. Howard, *Public Administration in Ethiopia* (Groningen: Wolters, 1956), p. 171.
11. Ernest W. Luther, *Ethiopia Today* (Stanford, Calif.: Stanford University Press, 1958), p. 43.
12. See Howard, *op. cit.*, pp. 74–85.
13. See *Ethiopian Commercial, Industrial, and Agricultural Journal,* May, 1949, p. 17.
14. See Luther, *op. cit.*, pp. 77–78.
15. *Ibid.*, p. 121.
16. See Czeslaw Jesman, *The Russians in Ethiopia* (London: Chatto and Windus, 1958).

Chapter 2

Westernized Nationalist Patterns in Transition

1. For an excellent description of traditional feudal power in the Northern Province, see Coleman, *op. cit.*, pp. 353–57.
2. See A. Williams Babatunde, "Where Does Nigeria Go from Here?", *Africa Report,* October, 1960, p. 4.
3. Chike Obi, *I Speak for the People* (Ibadan: Dynamic Party, 1960), p. 4.
4. See John Hatch, *Africa Today—And Tomorrow* (rev. ed.; New York: Frederick A. Praeger, 1962), pp. 31–50, for a full description of these conferences.
5. For a brief survey of Nigeria's capital needs in her seven-year development plan, see *Economic Survey of Nigeria, 1959* (Lagos: Federal Government Printer), pp. 87–90.
6. John Hatch, Foreword to Arthur Skeffington, *Tanganyika in Transition* (London: Fabian Commonwealth Bureau, 1960), p. 5.
7. *Tanganyika Report to the General Assembly of the United Nations* (New York: United Nations, 1958), Part II, p. 4.
8. Julius Nyerere, "Will Democracy Work in Africa?", *Africa Special Report,* February, 1960, p. 4.
9. Kawawa, "Africanisation," *Africa South in Exile,* V, No. 1 (October–December, 1960), 97.

10. Quoted from editorial, "East African Federation Is Tanganyika's Goal," *Africa Report*, October, 1960, p. 2.

11. See Skeffington, *op. cit.*, p. 22.

12. In 1958, there were 546 societies and 319,000 members in Tanganyika, marketing more than £11 million worth of produce. *Ibid.*, p. 19.

13. *Ibid.*, p. 16.

14. *Tanganyika Trade Bulletin* (Department of Commerce and Industry, 1958), pp. 23–30.

15. See *Tanganyika Report to the General Assembly* (1958), p. 50.

16. *Tanganyika African Standard*, March 7, 1961.

17. Quoted in *Africa Report*, October, 1960, p. 1.

18. See Thomas Hodgkins and Ruth Schachter, "French-Speaking West Africa in Transition," *International Conciliation*, No. 528 (May, 1960), p. 412.

19. See Richard Adloff and Virginia Thompson, *French West Africa* (Stanford, Calif.: Stanford University Press, 1958), p. 117.

20. *Ibid.*, pp. 126–28.

21. Gwendolen Carter points out that seven Europeans won seats in the 1957 elections, with RDA backing. *Independence for Africa* (New York: Frederick A. Praeger, 1960), p. 110.

22. Berg, "The Economic Basis of Political Choice in French West Africa," *American Political Science Review*, June, 1960, p. 403.

23. See *The Republic of the Ivory Coast* (New York: French Information Service, 1960), p. 4.

24. *Ibid.*, p. 11.

25. A good description is found in George H. T. Kimble, *Tropical Africa* (New York: Twentieth Century Fund, 1960), II, 411–12.

26. *The Republic of the Ivory Coast*, p. 32.

27. "Basic Data of the Economy of Liberia," *United States Chamber of Commerce Economic Reports*, 1960, Part I, pp. 57–59.

28. Many authorities have referred to this problem. One of the most recent was Thomas R. Adam in his *Government and Politics in Africa South of the Sahara* (New York: Random House, 1959), p. 112.

29. Quoted by Thomas P. Melady in *Profiles of African Leaders* (New York: The Macmillan Co., 1961), pp. 105–6.

30. See *Case Study of the Firestone Operations in Liberia* (National Planning Association, 1956), pp. 24–25.

31. See R. Earle Anderson, *Liberia: America's African Friend* (Chapel Hill, N. C.: University of North Carolina Press, 1952), p. 109.

32. "Basic Data of the Economy of Liberia," p. 16.

Chapter 3

THE RISE OF ULTRA-AFRICANISM

1. Mabogunje, "Nigeria and Tomorrow's Africa," *Africa South in Exile*," V, No. 1 (October-December, 1960), 101.
2. *Ibid.*, pp. 101–2.
3. Source unknown.
4. Reprinted in *Africa Today*, IV, No. 2 (March–April, 1957), 4.
5. Robert Lystad made a socio-political study of these people in *The Ashanti; A Proud People* (New Brunswick, N. J.: Rutgers University Press, 1958).
6. Bankole, *Kwame Nkrumah* (London: Allen and Unwin, 1955), p. 32.
7. Drake, "Independence and Crisis," *Africa Today*, IV, No. 2 (March–April, 1957), 11.
8. See *Enquiry into Matters Disclosed at the Trial of Captain Benjamin Awhaitey Held on the 20th and 21st January, 1959, Before a Court-Martial Convened at Gifford Camp, Accra, and the Surrounding Circumstances* (Accra: Government Printer).
9. Nkrumah, "African Prospects," *Foreign Affairs*, October, 1958, p. 53.
10. Padmore, *Pan-Africanism or Communism?* (New York: Roy Publishers, 1956), pp. 21–22.
11. *West Africa*, March 14, 1959, p. 247. These conclusions are supported by Robert Good in "Tyranny or Puritanism in Sékou Touré's Guinea," *Africa Report*, October, 1960, pp. 5–7. He points out that although Guinea has swung far to the left, it is not Communist.
12. Marcum, "Report from Guinea," *The New Leader*, December 1, 1958, p. 5.
13. Quoted from Melady, *op. cit.* I am indebted to Dr. Melady for his insights into Touré's political philosophy. He believes that Touré is not a Communist but a practical African nationalist.
14. *Ibid.*, p. 91.
15. For a detailed outline of the philosophy of Sékou Touré and the program of the PDG, see the reports of annual party conferences published by the Republic of Guinea—especially the Fifth Congress, *L'Action Politique du P.D.G.*
16. Professor H. R. Rudin refers to this reaction of the consortium in "Guinea Outside the French Community," *Current History*, July, 1959, p. 16.
17. For the text of Guinea's Constitution, see *Giant Stride Forward: Republic of Guinea First Year of Freedom* (Washington, D.C.: In-

formation Service of the Embassy of Guinea to the United States, 1960), pp. 10–12.

18. Touré, "Africa's Destiny," in James Duffy and Robert Manners (ed.), *Africa Speaks* (New York: D. Van Nostrand Co., 1961), p. 36.

Chapter 4

SOUTH AFRICA: WHITE RACIALISM'S LAST STAND

1. See Lord Hailey, *African Survey* (New York: Oxford University Press, 1956), p. 231. He writes that the Concordat of 1941 in Article 68 gave the Church responsibility for "moral uplift . . . it being understood that by moral uplift is meant the abandonment of indolence and the preparation of future rural and industrial workers who produce enough to meet their own necessities and fulfill their social obligations."
2. *Ibid.,* p. 230.
3. *Ibid.,* pp. 354–55.
4. Gwendolen Carter, *op. cit.,* pp. 98–99, discusses the administration of Angola during her visit there in 1959.
5. See Marvin Harris, *Portugal's African Wards* (New York: American Committee on Africa, 1958), p. 9.
6. *Ibid.,* pp. 30–33.
7. Duffy, *Portuguese Africa* (Cambridge, Mass.: Harvard University Press, 1959), p. 131. He writes, "The reality is pretty much the same today as it has been for four hundred years: the indiscriminate use of the African for Portuguese profit."
8. Davidson, *The African Awakening* (London: Jonathan Cape, 1955), p. 229.
9. *Ibid.,* p. 228.
10. Harris, *op. cit.,* p. 11.
11. Marvin Harris has an excellent study on this system: "Labour Emigration Among the Mozambique Bathonga: Cultural and Political Factors," *Africa,* XXIX, No. 1 (January, 1959).
12. *Report of the Ad Hoc Committee on Forced Labor, United Nations E/2431* (Geneva: International Labour Organization, 1953), p. 77.
13. Harris, *Portugal's African Wards,* p. 6.
14. These nationalist groups are described by Homer Jack in his pamphlet *Angola: Repression and Revolt in Portuguese Africa* (New York: American Committee on Africa, 1960), pp. 19–21.
15. Malcolm McVeigh, "Angola: Labor in Chains," *Africa Today,* VIII, No. 8 (October, 1961), 9. See also Franklin Schaefer, "In Angola Racial Civil War," *Africa Today,* VIII, No. 4 (April, 1961).
16. C. W. De Kiewiet points out this "higher purpose" of the doctrine of *apartheid* in *The Anatomy of South African Misery* (London:

Oxford University Press, 1956), p. 48. He says: "Such generosity is illusion, and such liberality is fantasy. It is a vision of a false and unattainable Utopia imposed upon a native population that does not aspire to it."

17. Brookes, *South Africa in a Changing World* (Cape Town: Oxford University Press, 1953), p. 50.

18. Quoted in Carter, *The Politics of Inequality* (New York: Frederick A. Praeger, 1958), p. 252.

19. Keet, *Whither South Africa?* (Grahamstown: University Publishers, 1956), p. 3.

20. See Carter, *Politics of Inequality,* for an outline of the work of SABRA.

21. See Leo Kuper, *Passive Resistance in South Africa* (New Haven, Conn.: Yale University Press, 1960), for an excellent survey.

22. Quoted in *Africa South,* I, No. 3 (April–June, 1957), 11.

23. Peter Rodda, "The Africanists Cut Loose," *Africa South,* III, No. 4 (July–September, 1959), 25.

24. Sisulu, "Congress and the Africanists," *Africa South,* III, No. 4 (July–September, 1959), p. 31. Also see "Congress and the Africanists," *Africa South,* IV, No. 3 (April–June, 1960), 24–33, for the pan-Africanist reply.

25. Philip Mason, *The Birth of a Dilemma: The Conquest and Settlement of Rhodesia* (New York: Oxford University Press, 1958), p. 39.

26. The years of the company's rule and its gradual bankruptcy are well described in Colin Leys's study *European Politics in Southern Rhodesia* (London: Oxford University Press, 1959), pp. 5–13.

27. Mason, *Year of Decision: Rhodesia and Nyasaland in 1960* (London and New York: Oxford University Press, 1960), p. 5.

28. Leys, *op. cit.,* p. 27.

29. See William Barber's contribution on the economy, in Colin Leys and Cranford Pratt (eds.), *A New Deal in Central Africa* (New York: Frederick A. Praeger, 1960), p. 85.

30. See Leys, *European Politics in Southern Rhodesia,* pp. 28–29. He estimates that slightly less than 30 per cent of the European land is arable.

31. However, officials expect that 85 per cent of the eligible school-children will be in school in 1961. This is considerably higher than in most other African areas.

32. Leys, *European Politics in Southern Rhodesia,* pp. 170–71.

33. *Ibid.,* p. 44.

34. The British-created Monckton Commission in 1960 recommended gradual transition to an African majority in the Federal Assembly and a redistribution of federal powers to the territorial governments, but this report was rejected by the ruling European parties.

35. Leys and Pratt, *op. cit.,* pp. 210–12.

Chapter 5

THE GROWTH OF COMMUNIST INFLUENCE

1. Quoted in P. I. Idenburg, "Soviet Russia's Interest in Africa," *International Spectator*, XIV, No. 1 (January 8, 1960).
2. Victor DuBois, "Guinea Educates a New Generation," *Africa Report*, VI, No. 8 (July, 1961), 8.
3. *The New York Times*, December 12, 1960.
4. Dr. Idenburg estimates that there are 250 African students at the Institute for Economic Studies at Prague alone.
5. I. Potekhin, then Vice-Director of the Institute of Ethnography of of the U.S.S.R. Academy of Sciences and now Director of the Institute of African Studies, wrote an article in 1954 entitled "Peoples of Africa," in which he said, "The Convention Peoples Party, reflecting the interests of powerful bourgeoisie, did not fulfill the expectations of the masses."
6. For most of this information, I am indebted to an article by Christopher Bird, "Soviet Scholars Embark on Major Program of African Research," *Africa Special Report*, III, No. 4 (April, 1958), 12–14.
7. See *West Africa*, November 8, 1958, for Professor Potekhin's reports of his findings. Dr. Idenburg feels that Potekhin, despite his earlier errors, has influenced Soviet policy in Africa toward a realistic appraisal of bourgeois nationalist movements and has stimulated Soviet aid to non-Communist African governments.
8. The Russians felt that Nkrumah and the conference were dominated by American influence. See *West Africa*, March 21 1959.
9. Quoted by Leonard Kenworthy in "Bourguiba, Kingpin in North Africa," *The Progressive*, XXII, No. 9 (September, 1958), 38–41.
10. Robert D. Baum, in his contribution (a commentary) to C. Grove Haines (ed.), *Africa Today* (Baltimore: Johns Hopkins University Press, 1955), p. 284, discusses a center of Communist activity among railway workers in Omdurmand and Khartoum. The Sudanese Democratic Liberation Movement is based on Marxist principles and led by young militants. Along with all other political parties, it has been banned.
11. When Nkrumah was arrested and imprisoned in the Gold Coast in 1950, an unsigned Communist Party card was found in his wallet. He claimed that he had used it to get into Communist meetings in London in order to observe Party tactics.
12. Padmore gave a thorough account of Communist and fellow-traveling influences in his *Pan-Africanism or Communism*, p. 355. He believes that the ANC in South Africa was at one time directed

by fellow travelers like **Dr. P. B. Xuma** of Johannesburg, but passed
into non-Communist leadership.

13. See Helmut Sonnenfelt, "Soviet Strategy in Africa," *Africa Report,*
V, No. 11 (November, 1960). The author maintains that the
U.S.S.R., for ideological reasons, supported a radical though non-
Communist government. He points out that Communist China has
developed different strategies, appealing to the actual Communist
groups within African nationalist movements. It is entirely possible, therefore, that a rivalry between China and Russia is developing in Africa.

14. See Alan P. Merriam, *Congo: Background of Conflict* (Evanston,
Ill.: Northwestern University Press, 1960), pp. 303–5.

15. Walter Laqueur made this point well (although his terminology is
regrettable): "In the transition from the age of proletarian inter-
nationalism to the era of schism, we will do well to encourage independence of mind and to avoid confusing radical nationalism
or Afro-Communism with orthodox Marxism-Leninism." "Communism and Nationalism in Tropical Africa," *Foreign Affairs,*
XXXIX, No. 4 (July, 1961), 621.

Chapter 6

AFRICA AT THE UNITED NATIONS

1. There are substantial limitations to majority voting in the U.N.,
where a consensus is more important than it is in national politics.
For a full discussion of this, see Inis Claude, *Swords into Plowshares*
(New York: Random House, 1956), pp. 126–41. Professor Claude
stresses the importance of using the traditional instruments of
diplomacy, persuasion, compromise, and agreement to achieve a
gradual resolution of conflict.

2. The Afro-Asian bloc has been more successful in the committees,
where only a majority vote is required. Many strongly worded
resolutions from the committees have failed to be adopted by the
General Assembly.

3. General Assembly Resolutions 611 (VII) (December 17, 1952) and
812 (IX) (December 17, 1954).

4. An excellent, detailed discussion of the international implications
of the Algerian war can be found in Herbert Luethy's "The Crisis
of French Colonialism," *The Atlantic Monthly,* May, 1956, pp.
60–65; see also Lorna Hahn, "Algeria, The End of an Era," *Middle Eastern Affairs,* VII.

5. See reports of the United Nations Commission on the Racial Situation in the Union of South Africa (General Assembly, 1953–56).

6. *Issues Before the Tenth General Assembly,* (New York: International Conciliation, No. 504 [1955]), p. 129.

7. For elaboration of the case of South West Africa, see Scott, *The Orphans' Heritage: The Story of the South West African Mandate* (London: Africa Bureau, 1960).

8. "International Status of South West Africa," *International Court of Justice Reports* (1950), pp. 128, 139.

9. General Assembly Resolution No. 21 (1949).

10. Eritrea was allowed to federate with Ethiopia in 1952.

11. See Richard J. Kuzicki's contribution, "The United Nations and Colonialism," in Robert Strausz-Hupé and Harry Hazard (ed.), *The Idea of Colonialism* (New York: Frederick A. Praeger, 1958), pp. 390–406.

12. See Emil Sady, *The United Nations and Dependent Peoples* (Washington, D.C.: Brookings Institution, 1956), pp. 66–77.

13. See Benjamin Rivlin, *Self-Determination and Colonial Areas* (New York: International Conciliation, No. 501 [January, 1955]), pp. 238–43.

Chapter 7

ORIGINS OF AMERICAN POLICY

1. Program of African Studies, Northwestern University, *Africa: A Study Prepared at the Request of the Committee on Foreign Relations, United States Senate* (Washington, D.C.: U.S. Government Printing Office, 1959), p. 1.

2. *Ibid.,* p. 12.

3. De Kiewiet, "African Dilemmas," *Foreign Affairs* (April, 1955), p. 444.

4. Morgenthau, in Calvin Stillman (ed.), *Africa in the Modern World* (Chicago: University of Chicago Press, 1955), p. 321.

5. Bowles, *Africa's Challenge to America* (Berkeley, Calif.: University of California Press, 1957), p. 134.

6. Ross, *African Heritage* (New York: Friendship Press, 1952), p. 138.

7. One of the best collections of American Negro intellectual thought about Africa is *Africa Seen by American Negroes,* prepared by the American Society for African Culture in collaboration with *Présence Africain,* 1956. The Society publishes a number of conference reports and studies.

8. The African Studies Association was founded in the U.S. in 1958, and more than 200 scholars attended its first conference, at Evanston, Illinois.

9. H. B. Cole, "Economic Development in Liberia," *The African World,* November, 1957.

10. See A. M. Kamarck, "The African Economy and International Trade," in Walter Goldschmidt (ed.), *The United States and Africa* (New York: Columbia University Press, 1958), pp. 117–36.
11. *Survey of Current Business* (U.S. Department of Commerce, September, 1958), p. 18. Although Liberia had a greater total ($380 million), most of it was in shipping.
12. Vernon McKay, "Foreign Aid in Africa," *Current History*, August, 1957, p. 91.
13. John D. Montgomery, *Aid to Africa: New Test for U.S. Policy* (Foreign Policy Association Pamphlet No. 149, September-October, 1961), p. 7. In the fiscal year, 1961, American economic aid to Africa amounted to over $500 million—including mutual-assistance programs, but excluding specifically military aid, which remains very limited.
14. James K. Penfield, *The Role of the United States in Africa* (U.S. State Department Bulletin, June 8, 1959), p. 5.
15. See William Hance, *African Economic Development* (New York: Harper & Brothers, 1958), pp. 85–135, for a concise treatment of the communications gap.
16. See Admiral Richard L. Connolly, USN, "Africa's Strategic Significance," in Haines, *op. cit.*, pp. 55–64.
17. Assistant Secretary of State Joseph C. Satterthwaite, testifying before the Senate Foreign Relations Committee in 1960, said that the agreement "does make it clear that we take a great interest in the defense of Liberia, but goes no further, of course, than an agreement to consult in case Liberia's integrity would be endangered." Hearing, U.S. Senate, Eighty-Sixth Congress, Second Session, on "United States Foreign Policy in Africa," p. 141.
18. Typical of this fearful, defensive policy was the statement of Assistant Secretary of State George V. Allen in 1956, in which he elaborated on his fear that a Communist minority might seize the leadership of African nationalism. "United States Policy in Africa," *The Annals*, CCCVI (July, 1956), pp. 118–19.
19. James S. Coleman and Carl G. Rosberg—in their perceptive pamphlet on American policy *New Perspectives on Sub-Sahara Africa* (Washington, D.C.: Union for Democratic Action, 1961), p. 19— date the shift in American policy from 1958.
20. See Elizabeth Landis, "Two Cheers: The U.S. at the U.N.," *Africa Today*, VIII, No. 5 (May, 1961), 5-10. The author observes that the new U.N. delegation sent by the Kennedy Administration had a record in the resumed General Assembly meeting of supporting the African nations in twelve out of eighteen key votes.
21. Ronald Segal, "The Free World's Other Face," in *Africa Speaks*, p. 205.

Chapter 8

NEW POLICY APPROACHES

1. Rostow, "The Idea and Reality," *Confluence*, VI, No. 3 (Fall, 1957), p. 212.
2. Sir Andrew Cohen, former British representative on the Trusteeship Council, makes this point well in *British Policy in Changing Africa* (Evanston, Ill.: Northwestern University Press, 1959), p. 114.
3. Kitchen, "Africa and the Kennedy Era," *The New Republic*, December 12, 1960, p. 18.
4. Coleman and Rosberg, *op. cit.*, pp. 23–24. They approach this matter by discussing whether we should give preferential treatment to pro-Western African states. "The consensus of most sensitive and informed observers is that a policy of differential treatment would be most unwise. It would not only deepen the cleavages among these groups but would inevitably push the more radical states into closer alliance with the Sino-Soviet bloc. Moreover, there is evidence that the radical states represent the 'wave of the future' in Africa and other new states will join their ranks. Thus, rather than censuring or opposing them we should seek to identify ourselves with the dynamism of which they are the principal carriers."
5. See Arnold Rivkin, "Arms for Africa," *Foreign Affairs*, October, 1959, pp. 84–94, for some thoughtful suggestions on arms control in Africa.
6. Gunnar Myrdal, Eugene Staley, and other economists have long argued that such industrialization actually increases trade between developed and underdeveloped regions, rather than diminishing it. See Staley, *The Future of Underdeveloped Countries* (rev. ed.; New York: Harper & Brothers (cloth), Frederick A. Praeger (paperback), 1961), pp. 286–311.
7. K. Panikkar, *The Afro-Asian States and Their Problem* (New York: The John Day Company, 1960), p. 98.

Bibliography

PERIODICALS

Africa. International African Institute, 10–11 Fetter Lane, London, EC 4.

Africa Report. African-American Institute, Dupont Circle Bldg., Washington 6, D.C.

Africa South. Abford House, Wilton Rd., London, SW 1.

Africa Today. American Committee on Africa, 801 Second Ave., New York, N. Y.

African Abstracts. International African Institute, 10–11 Fetter Lane, London, EC 4.

African Affairs. Royal African Society, 18 Northumberland Ave., London, WC 2.

Afrique Action. 198 Avenue de Paris, Tunis, Tunisia.

The Central African Examiner. Salisbury, Southern Rhodesia.

East Africa and Rhodesia. 66 Great Russell St., London, WC 1.

Journal of African Administration. Colonial Office, London.

Journal of African History. Cambridge University Press, 200 Euston Rd., London.

Journal of Racial Affairs. South African Bureau of Racial Affairs, P.O. Box 238, Stallenbosch, Cape Province, South Africa.

Présence Africaine. 16 Rue H. Barbusse, Paris 5e.

Publications of the French Information Service (pertaining to Africa), 972 Fifth Avenue, New York, N.Y.

Publications of the Office de l'Information et des Relations Publiques pour le Congo Belge et le Ruanda-Urundi, Brussels, Belgium.

Race Relations Journal and *Race Relations News.* South African Institute of Race Relations, P.O. Box 97, Johannesburg, South Africa.

Tanganyika Notes and Records. P.O. Box 511, Dar es Salaam.

Uganda Journal. Uganda Society, Kampala, Uganda.

229

230   Bibliography

University Herald. University College, Ibadan, Nigeria.
Venture. Fabian Society, 11 Dartmouth Street, Westminster, London.
West Africa. 7-9 Breems Bldg., Fetter Lane, London, EC 4.
West African Worker. Accra Trade Union Congress, Accra, Ghana.

BOOKS AND ARTICLES
General

ADAM, THOMAS R. *Government and Politics in Africa South of the Sahara.* New York: Random House, 1959.
The African Who's Who. London: London Diplomatic Press, 1960.
ALMOND, GABRIEL, and COLEMAN, JAMES. *Politics of Developing Areas.* Princeton, N.J.: Princeton University Press, 1960.
BASCOM, WILLIAM, and HERSKOVITS, MELVILLE. *Continuity and Change in African Cultures.* Chicago: University of Chicago Press, 1958.
BOWLES, CHESTER. *Africa's Challenge to America.* Berkeley, Calif.: University of California Press, 1957.
CAMERON, JAMES. *The African Revolution.* New York: Random House, 1961.
CARTER, GWENDOLEN. *Independence for Africa.* New York: Frederick A. Praeger, 1960.
COHEN, SIR ANDREW. *British Policy in Changing Africa.* Evanston, Ill.: Northwestern University Press, 1959.
DAVIDSON, BASIL. *The Lost Cities of Africa.* Boston: Little, Brown & Co. (Atlantic Monthly Press Book), 1957.
DAVIS, JOHN A. (ed.). *Africa Seen by American Negroes. Présence Africaine.* Paris: 1958.
DE GRAFT-JOHNSON, JOHN C. *African Glory, the Story of Vanished Negro Civilizations.* New York: Frederick A. Praeger, 1959.
DOOB, L. W. *Becoming More Civilized.* New Haven, Conn.: Yale University Press, 1960.
DUFFY, JAMES, and MANNERS, ROBERT. *Africa Speaks.* New York: D. Van Nostrand Co., 1961.
FAGE, J. D. *An Atlas of African History.* London: Arnold & Son, 1958.
FORTES, M., and EVANS-PRITCHARD, E. E. *African Political Systems.* London: Oxford University Press, 1958.
GOLDSCHMIDT, WALTER (ed.). *The United States and Africa.* New York: Columbia University Press, 1958.
GLUCKMAN, MAX. *Custom and Conflict in Africa.* Oxford: Basil Blackwell, 1955.
HAILEY, LORD. *An African Survey.* London: Oxford University Press, 1956.
HAINES, GROVE C. (ed.). *Africa Today.* Baltimore, Md.: The Johns Hopkins Press, 1955.
HANCE, W. A. *African Economic Development.* New York: Harper & Brothers, 1958.

HATCH, JOHN. *Africa Today and Tomorrow.* Revised ed.; New York: Frederick A. Praeger, 1962.

HODGKIN, THOMAS. *Nationalism in Colonial Africa.* New York: New York University Press, 1957.

JAHN, JANHEINZ. *Muntu: The Outlines of Neo-African Culture.* London: Evergreen Books, 1961.

KIMBLE, GEORGE H. T. *Tropical Africa.* 2 vols. New York: The Twentieth Century Fund, 1960.

KITCHEN, HELEN (ed.). *The Press in Africa.* Washington, D.C.: Ruth Sloan Associates, 1956.

MACKENZIE, W. J. M., and ROBINSON, K. (eds.). *Five Elections in Africa.* New York: Oxford University Press, 1960.

MARCUM, JOHN. "The Challenge of Africa," *The New Leader,* February, 1960.

MARCUS, EDWARD, and MILDRED, R. *Investment and Development Possibilities in Tropical Africa.* New York: Twayne Publishers, 1960.

MURDOCK, GEORGE P. *Africa: Its People and Their Cultural History.* New York: McGraw-Hill Book Co., 1959.

PADMORE, GEORGE. *Pan-Africanism or Communism?* New York: Roy Publishers, 1956.

READ, MARGARET. *Education and Social Change in Tropical Areas.* London: Thomas Nelson & Sons, 1955.

RITNER, PETER V. *The Death of Africa.* New York: The Macmillan Co., 1959.

SEGAL, RONALD. *Political Africa: A Who's Who of Personalities and Parties.* New York: Frederick A. Praeger, 1961.

SENGHOR, LÉOPOLD S. *African Socialism: A Report to the Constitutive Congress of the Party of the African Federation.* New York: American Society for African Culture, 1960.

SITHOLE, N. *African Nationalism.* New York: Oxford University Press, 1959.

STILLMAN, CALVIN (ed.). *Africa in the Modern World.* Chicago: University of Chicago Press, 1955.

UNITED NATIONS. *Economic Survey of Africa Since 1950.* New York: United Nations, 1960.

———. *Report on the World Social Situation.* New York: United Nations, 1957.

———. *Social Implications of Industrialization and Urbanization in Africa South of the Sahara.* New York: United Nations, 1956.

WALLENSTEIN, M.; APTER, D.; ROSBERG, C.; and MARCUS, E. *The Political Economy of Contemporary Africa.* Washington, D.C.: George Washington University Press, 1960.

WODDIS, JACK. *Africa: The Roots of Revolt.* London: Lawrence & Wishart, 1960.

West Africa

CARNEY, DAVID E. *Government and Economy in British West Africa* (Nigeria, Ghana, Sierra Leone, Gambia, 1947-55). New York: Bookman Associates, 1961.

COWAN, L. GRAY. *Local Government in West Africa.* New York: Columbia University Press, 1958.

FAGE, J. D. *An Introduction to the History of West Africa.* London: Cambridge University Press, 1955.

HERSKOVITS, MELVILLE J., and FRANCES S. *Dahomean Narrative: A Cross-Cultural Anaylsis.* Evanston, Ill.: Northwestern University Press, 1958.

PEDLER, F. J. *Economic Geography of West Africa.* London: Longmans, Green & Co., 1955.

WARMINGTON, W. A. *A West African Trade Union: A Case Study of the Cameroons Development Corporation Workers Union.* Nigerian Institute of Social and Economic Research; London: Oxford University Press, 1960.

Nigeria

AWOLOWO, OBAFEMI. *Awo: The Autobiography of Chief Obafemi Awolowo.* New York: Cambridge University Press, 1961.

AZIKIWE, N. (ed.). *Zik: A Selection from Speeches of Nnamdi Azikiwe.* New York: Cambridge University Press, 1961.

BURNS, SIR ALAN. *History of Nigeria.* London: Allen & Unwin, 1955.

COLEMAN, JAMES S. *Nigeria: Background to Nationalism.* Berkeley, Calif.: University of California, 1958.

DICKSON, M. *New Nigerians, Story of the First Training Center in West Africa for the Education of Civil Servants.* London: Dennis Dobson, 1960.

EZERA, KALU. *Constitutional Developments in Nigeria.* London: Cambridge University Press, 1960.

HODGKIN, THOMAS. *Nigerian Perspectives.* London: Oxford University Press, 1960.

LUGARD, SIR F. D. *The Dual Mandate in British Tropical Africa.* London: Blackwood & Sons, 1922.

MELLANBY, K. *The Birth of Nigeria's University.* London: Methuen & Co., 1958.

Nigeria: The Political and Economic Background. Royal Institute of International Affairs. London: Oxford University Press, 1960.

SMYTHE, HUGH and MABEL. *The New Nigerian Elite.* Stanford, Calif.: Stanford University Press, 1960.

French-Speaking Africa

DELAVIGNETTE, ROBERT. *Freedom and Authority in French West Africa.* New York: Oxford University Press, 1950.
———. *Les Paysans Noir.* Paris: Gallimard, 1955.
HODGKIN, THOMAS, and SCHACHTER, RUTH. *French-Speaking West Africa in Transition.* New York: International Conciliation, No. 528 (May, 1960).
THOMPSON, V., and ADOLFF, R. *French West Africa.* Stanford, Calif.: Stanford University Press, 1957.
———. *The Emerging States of French Equatorial Africa.* Stanford, Calif.: Stanford University Press, 1960.

The Congo

LANGENHAVE, FERNAND VAN. *Le Congo et les Problèmes de la Décolonisation.* Brussels: Institute Royal des Relations Internationales, 1961.
LEGUM, COLIN. *Congo Disaster.* Baltimore: Penguin Books, 1961.
MERRIAM, ALAN P. *Congo: Background of Conflict.* Evanston, Ill.: Northwestern University Press, 1960.

Liberia

ANDERSON, ROBERT E. *Liberia, America's Friend.* Chapel Hill, N.C.: University of North Carolina, 1952.
BANTON, MICHAEL. *West African City: A Study of Tribal Life in Freetown.* London: Oxford University Press, 1957.
TAYLOR, W. C. *Liberia: Case Study of the Firestone Operations in Liberia.* Washington: National Planning Association, 1956.
TOWNSEND, REGINALD (ed.). *President Tubman of Liberia Speaks.* London: Allen & Unwin, 1959.
YANCY, E. J. *Republic of Liberia.* London: Allan & Unwin, 1959.

East Africa

APTER, DAVID E. *The Political Kingdom in Uganda.* Princeton, N.J.: Princeton University Press, 1961.
CARFIELD, F. D. *Historical Survey of the Origin and Growth of Mau Mau.* London: Colonial Office, 1961.
CASTAGNO, A. A. *Somalia.* New York: International Conciliation, No. 522 (1959).
CHIDZERO, B. T. G. *Tanganyika and International Trusteeship.* New York: Oxford University Press, 1961.

HICKMAN, G. M., and DICKENS, W. H. G. *The Lands and Peoples of East Africa*. London: Longmans, Green & Co., 1960.

HILL, J. F. R. *Tanganyika Territory*. Dar es Salaam: Government Printer.

INTERNATIONAL BANK FOR RECONSTRUCTION AND DEVELOPMENT. *The Economic Development of Tanganyika*. Baltimore: The Johns Hopkins Press, 1961.

KOENIG, OSKAR. *The Masai Story*. London: M. Joseph, 1956.

RAWCLIFFE, D. H. *The Struggle for Kenya*. London: Victor Gollancz, 1954.

RICHARDS, AUDREY I. (ed.). *East African Chiefs: A Study of Political Development in Some Uganda and Tanganyika Tribes*. New York: Frederick A. Praeger, 1960.

SKEFFINGTON, ARTHUR. *Tanganyika in Transition*. London: Fabian Commonwealth Bureau, 1960.

SLATER, MONTAGU. *The Trial of Jomo Kenyatta*. London: Secker & Warburg, 1955.

YOUNG, ROLAND, and FOSBROOKE, HENRY A. *Smoke in the Hills: Political Tension in the Morogoro District of Tanganyika*. Evanston, Ill.: Northwestern University Press, 1959.

Ghana

APTER, DAVID E. *The Gold Coast in Transition*. Princeton, N.J.: Princeton University Press, 1955.

BOURRET, F. M. *Ghana: The Road to Independence*. Stanford, Calif.: Stanford University Press, 1960.

BUSIA, K. W. *The Position of the Chief in the Modern Political System of Ashanti*. London: Oxford University Press, 1951.

CLARIDGE, W. W. *A History of the Gold Coast and the Ashanti*. 2 vols. London: Murray, 1915.

FAGE, J. D. *Ghana: A Historical Interpretation*. Madison, Wis.: University of Wisconsin Press, 1959.

LYSTAD, ROBERT A. *The Ashanti: A Proud People*. New Brunswick, N.J.: Rutgers University Press, 1958.

NKRUMAH, KWAME. *The Autobiography of Kwame Nkrumah*. New York: Thomas Nelson & Sons, 1957.

ROYAL INSTITUTE OF INTERNATIONAL AFFAIRS. *Ghana: A Brief Political and Economic Survey*. London: Oxford University Press, 1957.

SAUTOY, P. DE. *Community Development in Ghana*. London: Oxford University Press, 1958.

TIMOTHY, BANKOLE. *Kwame Nkrumah, His Rise to Power*. London: Allen & Unwin, 1955.

WARD, W. E. F. *A History of Ghana*. London: Allen & Unwin, 1958.

Guinea

Giant Stride Forward. Republic of Guinea, Information Service of the Embassy of Guinea to the United States, 1960.
GOUILLY, ALPHONSE. *L'Islam dans l'Afrique Occidentale Française.* Paris: Larose, 1952.
PAULEME, DENISE. *Les Civilizations Africaines.* Paris: Presses Universitaires, 1953.
TOURÉ, SÉKOU. *African Independence and Unity.* New York: Embassy of Guinea to the United Nations, 1959.

Morocco

AL FASSI, ALLAL. *The Independence Movements of North Africa.* Washington, D.C.: American Council of Learned Societies, 1954.
ASHFORD, DOUGLAS. *Political Change in Morocco.* Princeton, N.J.: Princeton University Press, 1961.
HAHN, LORNA. *North Africa: Nationalism to Nationhood.* Washington, D.C.: Public Affairs Press, 1960.
JULIEN, CHARLES-ANDRE. *Histoire de l'Afrique du Nord.* 2nd ed. Paris: Payot, 1956.
KNIGHT, M. M. *Morocco as a French Economic Venture.* New York: Appleton-Century-Crofts, 1937.
LANDAU, ROM. *Moroccan Drama, 1900–1955.* San Francisco: American Academy of Asian Studies, 1955.
———. *The Sultan of Morocco.* London: Robert Hale, 1951.
TERRASSE, HENRI. *Histoire du Moroc.* 2 vols. Casablanca: Editions Atlantides, 1950.
WHARTON, EDITH. *In Morocco.* New York: Charles Scribner's Sons, 1920.

Ethiopia

HOWARD, WILLIAM E. H. *Public Administration in Ethiopia: A Study in Retrospect and Prospect.* Groningen, Wolters, 1956.
HYATT, HARRY M. *The Church of Abyssinia.* London: Luzac & Co., 1928.
LEWIS, I. M. *Peoples of the Horn of Africa.* London: International African Institute, 1955.
LUTHER, ERNEST W. *Ethiopia Today.* Stanford: Stanford University Press, 1958.
PERHAM, MARGERY. *The Government of Ethiopia.* London: Faber & Faber, 1948.
TRIMINGHAM, JOHN S. *Islam in Ethiopia.* London: Oxford University Press, 1952.

Southern Rhodesia and Central Africa

BRELSFORD, W. V. *The Tribes of Northern Rhodesia.* Lusaka: Northern Rhodesia, Government Printer, 1956.

COLSON, ELIZABETH. *Social Organization of the Gwembe Tonga.* New York: Humanities Press, 1960.

EVANS, MAURICE S. *Black and White in South East Africa: A Study in Sociology.* New York: Longmans, Green & Co., 1911.

FRANCK, THOMAS M. *Race and Nationalism: The Struggle for Power in Rhodesia-Nyasaland.* New York: Fordham University Press, 1960.

GANN, L. H. *The Birth of a Plural Society: The Development of Northern Rhodesia Under the British South African Company, 1894–1914.* New York: Humanities Press, 1958.

GREEN, JOHN E. S. *Rhodes Goes North.* London: Bell & Sons, 1936.

LEYS, COLIN. *European Politics in Southern Rhodesia.* London: Oxford University Press, 1959.

——, and PRATT CRANFORD (eds.). *A New Deal in Central Africa.* New York: Frederick A. Praeger, 1960.

MASON, PHILIP. *The Birth of a Dilemma: The Conquest and Settlement of Rhodesia.* New York: Oxford University Press, 1958.

——. *Year of Decision: Rhodesia and Nyasaland in 1960.* London and New York: Oxford University Press, 1960.

SANGER, CLYDE. *Central African Emergency.* London: William Heinemann, 1960.

STONEHOUSE, JOHN. *Prohibited Immigrant.* London: Bodley Head, 1960.

VAN DER POST, LAURENS. *Venture to the Interior.* New York: William Morrow & Co., 1951.

WALLIS, J. P. R. *The Matabele Journal of Robert Moffat 1829–1860.* London: Chatto and Windus, 1945.

Portuguese Territories

DAVIDSON, BASIL. *The African Awakening.* London: Jonathan Cape, 1955.

DUFFY, JAMES. *Portuguese Africa.* Cambridge, Mass.: Harvard University Press, 1959.

EGERTON, F., and CLEMENT, C. *Angola in Perspective, Endeavour and Achievement in Portuguese West Africa.* London: Routledge & Kegan Paul, 1957.

HARRIS, MARVIN. *Portugal's African "Wards": A First-Hand Report on Labor and Education in Mozambique.* New York: American Committee on Africa, 1958.

JACK, HOMER A. *Angola: Repression and Revolt in Portuguese Africa.* New York: American Committee on Africa, 1960.

South Africa

ABRAHAMS, PETER. *Tell Freedom: Memories of Africa.* New York: Alfred A. Knopf, 1954.
BROOKES, E. H., and MACAULAY, J. B. *Civil Liberty in South Africa.* Cape Town: Oxford University Press, 1958.
CARTER, GWENDOLEN M. *The Politics of Inequality.* New York: Frederick A. Praeger, 1958.
DE KIEWIET, C. W. *The Anatomy of South African Misery.* New York: Oxford University Press, 1956.
FULLER, BASIL. *South Africa—Not Guilty.* Johannesburg: Mint, 1957.
HOERNLÉ, REINHOLD F. *South African Native Policy and the Liberal Spirit.* Cape Town: Lovedale Press, 1939.
JUNOD, H. A. *The Life of a South African Tribe.* London: Nutt, 1912–13.
KEET, B. B. *Whither South Africa?* Grahamstown: University Publishers, 1956.
KUPER, LEO. *Passive Resistance in South Africa.* New Haven, Conn.: Yale University Press, 1960.
———. *Durban: A Study in Racial Ecology.* London: Jonathan Cape, 1958.
South Africa (Economic, Financial, and Statistical Yearbook for the Union of South Africa). Cape Town: Culemborg.
South Africa and the Rule of Law. Geneva: International Commission of Jurists, 1960.

Index

Index